UNIVERSITY OF NORTH CAROLINA AT CHAPEL HILL

DEPARTMENT OF ROMANCE LANGUAGES

NORTH CAROLINA STUDIES
IN THE ROMANCE LANGUAGES AND LITERATURES

Founder: URBAN TIGNER HOLMES

Distributed by:

UNIVERSITY OF NORTH CAROLINA PRESS

CHAPEL HILL
North Carolina 27514
U.S.A.

NORTH CAROLINA STUDIES IN THE
ROMANCE LANGUAGES AND LITERATURES

Number 197

THE TRAGIC FALL:

DON ÁLVARO DE LUNA AND OTHER FAVORITES IN SPANISH GOLDEN AGE DRAMA

THE TRAGIC FALL:

DON ÁLVARO DE LUNA AND OTHER FAVORITES IN SPANISH GOLDEN AGE DRAMA

BY

RAYMOND R. MACCURDY

CHAPEL HILL

NORTH CAROLINA STUDIES IN THE ROMANCE
LANGUAGES AND LITERATURES
U.N.C. DEPARTMENT OF ROMANCE LANGUAGES

1978

3844607

Library of Congress Cataloging in Publication Data

MacCurdy, Raymond R
   The tragic fall.

   (North Carolina studies in the Romance languages and literature; no. 197)
   Bibliography: p.
   Includes index.
   1. Spanish drama—Classical period, 1500-1700—History and criticism. 2. Spanish drama (Tragedy)—History and criticism. 3. Favorites, Royal, in literature. 4. Luna, Álvaro de, d. 1453, in fiction, drama, poetry, etc. I. Title. II. Series.

PQ6105.M23   862'.3'09   78-5565
ISBN 0-8078-9197-5

I.S.B.N. 0-8078-9197-5

PRINTED IN SPAIN

IMPRESO EN ESPAÑA

DEPÓSITO LEGAL: V. 1.433 - 1978   I.S.B.N. 84-399-8352-2

ARTES GRÁFICAS SOLER, S. A. - JÁVEA, 28 - VALENCIA (8) - 1978

To Becky, *encore*

CONTENTS

PREFACE

The purpose of this book is twofold: (1) to present an historical and critical survey of representative Golden Age *tragedias de privanza*, a small body of plays which dramatize the rise and fall of royal ministers and favorites; and (2) to assess the contributions these plays make toward a clarification of the "problem" of Golden Age tragedy. More will be said about the "problem" in a moment.

Hispanists have long been familiar with some of the fallen-favorite tragedies, especially with the Don Álvaro de Luna plays, but little attention has been given to them as a whole. The first scholar to analyze several of the plays as a type was the late Claude E. Anibal, who, in his edition of Mira de Amescua's *El arpa de David* (Columbus, Ohio, 1925), discussed some of their major structural and thematic elements. Anibal also advanced sound arguments for attributing to Mira de Amescua the authorship of *La próspera fortuna de don Álvaro de Luna y adversa de Ruy López de Ávalos* and *La adversa fortuna de don Álvaro de Luna.*

It will be remembered that the authorship of these two plays has long been shrouded in doubt since they were first printed in the *Segunda parte de las comedias del Maestro Tirso de Molina* (Madrid, 1635), about which the author says in his *Dedicatoria:* ". . . dedico, de estas doce comedias, cuatro que son mías, en mi nombre; y en el de los dueños de las otras ocho (que no sé por qué infortunio suyo, siendo hijas de tan ilustres padres, las echaron a mis puertas), las que restan." The fairly recent discovery of an autograph manuscript of Mira de Amescua of the second play, approved for presentation on October 17, 1624, seems to offer incontrovertible evidence that he was the author, at least a joint author, of the second play, and probably of the first. However, the last word has probably not been said about the authorship of the two Don Álvaro de Luna plays, but it is assumed throughout this book that Mira was the author of both.

The most thorough study of the theme of favoritism in Spanish drama is found in the doctoral dissertation of Sister Mary Austin Cauvin, O. P., "The *comedia de privanza* in the Seventeenth Century" (Diss. Univ. of Pennsylvania, 1957). In this carefully researched thesis, the author treats the political background of the period and considers the sources and literary qualities of fifty plays. Of course the great majority of these plays are not tragedies, nor do they include all the tragedies studied in the present book.

Nellie E. Sánchez-Arce's editions of Mira de Amescua's *Comedia famosa de Ruy López de Ávalos (Primera parte de don Álvaro de Luna)* (Mexico, 1965) and *La segunda de don Álvaro [Adversa fortuna de don Álvaro de Luna]* (Mexico, 1960) contain valuable introductions and notes, including a bibliography of most of the pertinent writings on the authorship of the two plays. Also Luigi de Filippo's edition of *Adversa fortuna de don Álvaro de Luna* (Firenze, 1960) contains much useful information on the theme of favoritism, especially in non-dramatic literature. Unfortunately, another valuable study which bears directly on some of the plays and themes considered in the present book was published long after my manuscript went to the printer but not to press: Jesús Gutiérrez, *La "Fortuna Bifrons" en el teatro del Siglo de Oro* (Santander, 1975). Fortunately (if I may play with Fortuna) I was able to retrieve my Preface in order to acknowledge Gutiérrez's significant book, though I was unable to make use of it.

To the persons named above — Anibal, Sister Mary Austin Cauvin, Sánchez-Arce, Luigi de Filippo — I am indebted for some of my material and ideas.

Now for the "problem" of Golden Age tragedy, a problem that has perplexed many Hispanists and one that continues to occupy students of the Spanish drama. In order to look at it in its simplest terms, the problem can be stated in a few questions:

Did — or did not — Spanish dramatists of the seventeenth century cultivate tragedy? Or, to put it more baldly, did they write any tragedies? If not, why not? If so, which are those tragedies? And, finally, are there any Golden Age tragedies that are not "problematical"?

Chapter I, entitled "The 'Problem' of Golden Age Tragedy," is addressed to answering some of these questions. The chapter represents a synthesis and revision of two articles which I published previously. The first, "Lope de Vega y la pretendida inhabilidad española para la tragedia: resumen crítico" (in *Homenaje a William L. Fichter. Estudios sobre el teatro antiguo hispánico y otros ensayos* [Madrid, 1971], pp. 525-35), examines the various factors which, according to critics from the time of Lope de Vega to the present, have contributed to the alleged paucity of Spanish tragedy.

The second article, "The 'Problem' of Spanish Golden Age Tragedy: A Review and Reconsideration," *South Atlantic Bulletin,* 38 (1973), 3-15, focuses on Spanish tragedy from an entirely different point of view. It examines the positive claims made for Spanish tragedy, claims that are reflected in the revaluations made by modern critics of certain dramatists and plays, including the honor dramas. It also deals with new interpretations of tragic theory as applied to Spanish drama by some of the same critics.

Chapter II, "The Political Scene," is devoted to a brief examination of political events which led to the execution in 1621 of Don Rodrigo Calderón. The same chapter also demonstrates how the execution of Calderón revived memories of the execution of that far greater favorite, Don Álvaro de Luna, nearly two centuries earlier. Both executions — one, the scandal of the moment; the other, long buried in the national conscience — awakened Spaniards to the high risks of favoritism and inspired an abundance of literature: ballads, plays, and political and moral treatises.

Chapter III, "The Doctrinal and Non-Dramatic Literature," is concerned with these treatises and with favoritism as a political institution: its history, its theory, its agents, its pros and cons. It should be said in all candor that this chapter is not essential to the underlying theme of The Tragic Fall. However, I have

decided to retain it for its value as "background," though readers
familiar with the subject may wish to skip over it.

Chapter IV, "Generic Characteristics of the Fallen-Favorite
Tragedies," surveys the plays as a whole and considers their
peculiar literary qualities: their purpose, plots, characters, themes,
and rhetorical elements. Chapter V, "The Don Álvaro de Luna
Plays," examines the Castilian favorite as an historical figure (as
he is revealed in the chronicles), as a "poetic" hero (as he is
"created" by the ballads), and as the tragic hero in various plays.
Among these plays is the anonymous and little known *Morales,
paje de don Álvaro,* which is included to complete the cycle of
the Don Álvaro de Luna tragedies, though the play itself would
normally merit only a footnote. A small amount of material included in this chapter is taken from my earlier article, "Tragic
'Hamartia' in *La próspera y Adversa fortuna de don Álvaro de
Luna,*" *Hispania,* 47 (1964), 82-90.

Subsequent chapters are devoted to other favorites who came
to a tragic end. Although the dozen plays studied in the course
of the book have not purposefully been taken up in chronological
order, in point of fact the chapters devoted to them do follow,
except in a few cases, the order in which the plays were written.
This fact has led to certain disadvantages, the chief of which is
that the later plays, though not necessarily inferior in artistic
quality to the earlier ones, have lost their sense of urgency and
earnestness with regard to *privanza* as a theme. Moreover, the
later plays tend to be derivative and imitative, so that one has
the impression of reading a twice told tale. Inevitably, the repetitiousness of some of the plays has engendered a certain
repetitiousness in the analysis of them.

Since a major purpose of this study is to present a survey of
representative *tragedias de privanza,* something should be said
about some of the plays that have been omitted, even though
a few of them have a strong claim on tragedy. I have not made a
separate analysis of Mira de Amescua's *La próspera* and *Adversa
fortuna de don Bernardo de Cabrera* nor of its *refundición, También tiene el sol menguante* by Luis Vélez de Guevara and Francisco de Rojas Zorrilla, because these plays contribute little not
found in Mira's earlier *privanza* plays. I have also excluded

several plays in which the theme of favoritism is not of major concern or in which the death of the protagonist is motivated by considerations other than his office. Among such plays, to mention a few, are: Lope de Vega's *Lo que hay que confiar del mundo* and *El Duque de Viseo*; Juan de Grajal's two-part play, *La próspera* and *Adversa fortuna del Caballero del Espíritu Santo*, which deal with the rise and fall of the Italian revolutionary, Cola di Rienzi; Juan Ruiz de Alarcón's *El dueño de las estrellas*, on the death of Lycurgus; and Álvaro Cubillo de Aragón's *La tragedia del Duque de Berganza*.

A word should be said about the troublesome matter as to the use of the English and Spanish forms of proper names and titles. In general, I have used the English form in the discussion of characters as historial personages (but I have been unable to bring myself to call Don Álvaro, Alvare). On the other hand, I have generally used the Spanish form of characters' names when they are being treated as characters in a play. I have also used the Spanish form of such titles as Condestable and Maestre, rather than the English Constable and Master. However, I must plead guilty to numerous inconsistencies, because at times I have employed the form that struck me as most appropriate at the moment.

It is my pleasure to express my gratitude to those persons who have read the manuscript and made helpful suggestions: Juan Bautista Avalle-Arce, cherished friend and colleague, and Edwin S. Morby, whose seminal articles laid the groundwork for fruitful discussion of Golden Age tragedy. I owe special thanks to William C. McCrary whose valuable suggestions for improving the book arrived, alas, after the manuscript had gone to the printer.

RAYMOND R. MacCURDY

Albuquerque, New Mexico

I

THE "PROBLEM" OF SPANISH GOLDEN AGE TRAGEDY

> "Ahora se me ha venido al pensamiento; no
> sé si es muy   propósito, cómo en España no se
> representan Tragedias. ¿Es, por ventura, porque
> tratan de cosas tristes, y somos más inclinados a
> cosas alegres?"
>
> (Francisco Cascales, *Tablas poéticas*, 1617)

In his highly acclaimed book *The Vision of Tragedy*, Richard
Sewall asserts that Unamuno's *Del sentimiento trágico de la vida*
represents a landmark in the discussion of tragedy, comparable
in importance to Nietzsche's *The Birth of Tragedy*. [1] Yet, as his
readers know, Unamuno did not concern himself with tragedy
as a literary form; rather, it was his purpose to define and bring
together those attitudes, feelings, and ideas that we commonly
call tragic. In essence, the tragic sense of life as Unamuno saw
it is that man's furious hunger for being "is denied by the ineluctable fact of nonbeing, death." [2] Further, as the full title of
Unamuno's book indicates — *Del sentimiento trágico de la vida
en los hombres y en los pueblos* — not only are some individuals
more prone than others to experience the tragic sense of life,
but some races, some countries, are especially composed and
destined to know its anguish. Spain, argues Unamuno, is such a
country. [3]

---

[1] Richard B. Sewall, *The Vision of Tragedy* (1959; rpt. New Haven,
1962), p. 150, n. 7.

[2] Ibid.

[3] Miguel de Unamuno, *Del sentimiento trágico de la vida en los hombres y en los pueblos* (Buenos Aires, 1937), p. 223.

Yet, students of the drama are not likely to look to the Spanish theater for significant contributions to tragedy, for they have been told by literary historians, both Spanish and foreign alike, that their search would be in vain. To cite only one example, in his dictionary of literature Federico Carlos Sáinz de Robles makes the categorical statement: "En España no hubo tragedia, ni en los tiempos del Renacimiento." [4] Even though more judicious critics would probably challenge the accuracy of this assertion, the fact remains that most historians of the Spanish stage, until fairly recently at least, have skimmed over the subject of Spanish tragedy as if it were a matter of little consequence, or they have omitted talking about it as if it did not exist. In short, if we had to judge by the paucity of critical attention devoted to Spanish tragedy over the years, we would have to conclude that indeed there was a dearth of Golden Age tragedy — and, of course, such may be the case.

And why the dearth, or alleged dearth, of tragedy in a country characterized as having an acute tragic sense of life, a country which, at the same time, is noted for the enormous number of its plays? There are several theories or assumptions which should be mentioned briefly. One assumption — a tacit one — seems to be that Spaniards, always obsessed by death, chose to celebrate it in rituals other than in strict dramatic form: in the bull fight, in the *auto de fe,* in the processions of Holy Week. Another commonly held view is that the hundreds of Spanish dramatists who wrote several thousand plays in the seventeenth century [5] rejected tragedy because of the national character and temperament, and also because a complex of other factors — esthetic, social, philosophical, ethical and religious — induced them to cultivate other forms of drama. These are the factors that I examined in one of the articles cited in the Preface ("Lope de Vega y la pretendida inhabilidad española para la

---

[4] *Ensayo de un diccionario de la literatura,* 2 vols. (Madrid, 1949), I, 1273.

[5] Arnold G. Reichenberger, "La comedia clásica española y el hombre del siglo xx," *Filología Moderna,* 4 (1961), 28, notes that in the appendix of La Barrera's *Catálogo bibliográfico* approximately 4800 titles are listed by author.

tragedia: resumen crítico"), and I shall summarize them briefly here.

The question voiced in Cascales' *Tablas poéticas* as to why tragedies (as he understood tragedy) were not performed in the theater of his day ("¿Es, por ventura, porque tratan de cosas tristes, y somos más inclinados a cosas alegres?") is one that many Spaniards have asked themselves in one form or another over the centuries. It is a question that leads to the more fundamental one: Were — and are — Spaniards incapable of writing tragedy because of their racial character? In the eighteenth century Agustín Montiano pondered this question in his *Discurso sobre las tragedias españolas*, 2 vols. (Madrid, 1750), I, 72, and came up with a direct, if dubious, answer: Spaniards have always had a special inclination for tragedy, but Lope de Vega vitiated their taste — if he did not destroy their talent — by feeding them a dramatic potpourri.

Again, in the nineteenth century Martínez de la Rosa reflected on the same question in his *Apéndice sobre la tragedia,* printed in his *Obras literarias* (Paris, 1827). In his view, Spaniards possess an innate capacity for writing both tragedy and comedy; for that reason he expresses indignation with the observations of two foreigners, observations that strike him as utterly nonsensical: "La verdadera comedia nunca fue conocida de los Españoles (dice Bettinelli, en su *Historia de la restauración de Italia*) porque ni reír quieren sin gravedad"; and "No quieren los Españoles (dice el abate Quadrio en su *Historia poética*) salir del teatro conmovidos por ningún afecto de desprecio, de odio, o de amor: les parecería vergonzoso perder en una representación su natural indiferencia" (pp. 231-32). And once again, Martínez de la Rosa blames the plight of Spanish tragedy on Lope de Vega, not on the national character: "La culpa no ha consistido, pues, en el carácter nacional; sino en el mal sesgo que tomaron nuestros antiguos dramáticos, arrastrados por el ejemplo de Lope; y tan exacta es esta observación, que aun los más ciegos apasionados de aquel ingenio no pudieron ocultar el desdén y desvío con que había tratado a la tragedia" (p. 234).

In our century, a contrary opinion is expressed by Ramón Sender in his essay, "Valle-Inclán y la dificultad de la tragedia,"

Cuadernos Americanos, 11, No. 5 (1952), 241-54. Sender not only finds the Spanish character to be an impediment to both tragedy and comedy, but his observations recall those of the two foreigners cited by Martínez de la Rosa: "Lo que tiene el español es el pudor y la vergüenza de la alegría y de la tristeza naturales. . . . España es un pueblo que trata de superar la risa y el llanto" (p. 242). Finally, in Sender's view, "El español no es inhábil para la tragedia por pudor de su desgracia, sino por el desdén de la piedad y el miedo metafísico o el pudor de los demás" (Ibid.). And so the debate over the compatibility — or incompatibility — of the Spanish character and tragedy goes on.

But what about the alleged "bad example" set by Lope de Vega, whose New Art determined the course of Spanish drama for more than a century? The "charges" against him are twofold: one pertains to *his* character; the other to his faulty conception of dramatic art. The idea that Lope had an aversion to tragedy — and especially to tragic endings — because of his excessively indulgent nature is expressed by Rennert and Castro, among others: "La más notable observación que se ha hecho en este sentido es la repugnancia de Lope por los desenlaces trágicos; y sería de gran interés estudiar hasta qué punto los desenlaces funestos no estaban ya condicionados por las fuentes de que se servía." [6] The result of Lope's aversion to tragedy, so the argument runs, was that his followers were forced to shun tragic endings if they wished to win the approval of theater-goers.

Of greater interest is the charge that Lope de Vega and other Golden Age dramatists were incapable of writing tragedies because they were divorced from the classical tradition and ignorant of neo-classical theory and rules. According to this notion, it was natural that writers like Lope and Calderón should compose — as Duncan Moir puts it — "wild, odd, irregular, 'romantic' things which can best be described as tragicom-

---

[6] Hugo A. Rennert and Américo Castro, *Vida de Lope de Vega (1562-1635)* (Madrid, 1919), p. 424; cited by Edwin S. Morby, "Some Observations on 'tragedia' and 'tragicomedia' in Lope," *Hispanic Review*, 11 (1943), 207. Morby's article is indispensable for its treatment of Lope de Vega and the tragedy.

edies. . . ." [7] Of course the idea that Spanish dramatists were ignorant of classical theory regarding tragedy is not true, as will be made evident later in this chapter. But of greater importance is the fact that Lope de Vega and his followers wilfully disregarded the classical precepts, in spite of the strictures of their contemporary academic critics. And indeed when they wrote plays based on tragic themes, they departed radically from tragic form as it was cultivated by the ancients and their Renaissance imitators. The reason is not hard to find.

Since the publication of Ramón Menéndez Pidal's important study, "Lope de Vega, el arte nuevo y la nueva biografía," [8] the idea that Lope's *Arte nuevo de hacer comedias* contains a complete and thoroughly modern esthetic doctrine has acquired increased acceptance. Thus, when Lope advocated mixing the tragic and the comic ("lo trágico y lo cómico mezclado, / . . . buen exemplo nos da naturaleza, / que por tal variedad tiene belleza"), he was consciously setting forth the principle that art should imitate the *variety* of life and nature. Now, granted that Lope formulated his own dramatic theories and that they should be taken much more seriously than former critics believed, it is clear that tragedy, as a separate and independent form, does not figure among those theories. It is also understandable that Lope's *comedia nueva,* made up of "lo trágico y lo cómico mezclado," should commonly be regarded as tragicomedy.

In an often quoted passage from his *Apologético de las comedias españolas* (1616), Ricardo de Turia (a pseudonym of Pedro Juan de Rejaule y Toledo?) insists that "ninguna comedia de cuantas se representan en España lo es, sino tragicomedia, que es un mixto formado de lo cómico y lo trágico." [9] He then distinguishes between "lo mixto" and "lo compuesto" — that is, between a blend and a compound: "en lo mixto las partes pierden su forma, y hacen una tercer materia muy diferente, y en lo

---

[7] Duncan Moir, "Spanish Dramatic Theory and Practice in the Seventeenth Century," in *Classical Drama and Its Influence. Essays Presented to H. D. F. Kitto,* ed. M. J. Anderson (London, 1965), p. 194. Moir, of course, is summarizing the opinion of neo-classical critics, not his own.

[8] *Revista de Filología Española,* 22 (1935), 337-98.

[9] In *Poetas dramáticos valencianos,* ed. E. Juliá Martínez, 2 vols. (Madrid, 1929), I, 623.

compuesto cada parte se conserva ella misma como antes era, sin alterarse ni mudarse. . . ." [10] According to this argument, the Spanish *comedia* is a blend of the dramatic genres; it is a new dramatic form and, therefore, *sui generis*. For this reason, some modern critics are not satisfied to use any traditional terminology to apply to the *comedia*. Even the term "tragicomedy" is not wholly suitable because it may suggest a compound of separable parts rather than a blend. Sánchez Escribano, for example, thought it necessary to invent his own terminology: "Digo 'comedias serias' porque para el siglo XVII no tenemos otro remedio que aludir a 'comedias serias' y 'comedias farsas.' Los términos 'tragedia,' 'comedia,' 'tragicomedia,' 'de capa y espada' no me satisfacen. La 'comedia seria' puede acercarse a la 'tragedia' greco-romana o puede ser lo que Diderot llamó 'drame.' " [11]

Notwithstanding the scruples expressed by Sánchez Escribano and other critics, most commentators continue to regard the tragicomedy as the most typical genre of Spanish drama. In a recent essay, the contemporary playwright Alfonso Paso stresses how deeply the tragicomedy is rooted in the national tradition and how appropriate it is to the Spanish character and genius:

> Nadie ha querido hasta poco reparar en las vivencias y la personalidad particularísima de la tragicomedia española. De todas las tragicomedias es la nuestra la más nacional, la más concreta, la menos exportable, la menos inteligible para el que no conozca nuestra manera de ser y nuestra especial idiosincrasia. No sé por qué me parece que la tragicomedia española es herencia inmediata de nuestro origen semita. La tragicomedia española tiene mucho de hebreo, muchísimo, y bastante de árabe. . . . La tragicomedia española es sobre todo un género de extremos. Un género de profundos contrastes, feroz, agresivo, burlón, despiadado, donde la fatalidad, la lucha contra el sino invencible, suelen ser tratadas con acre ironía . . . [12]

---

[10] Ibid.

[11] F. Sánchez Escribano, "Cuatro contribuciones españolas a la preceptiva dramática mundial," *Bulletin of the Comediantes*, 13 (Spring, 1961), 3.

[12] Alfonso Paso, "La tragicomedia," *ABC* (Madrid), 30 May 1961, unpaginated.

By way of recapitulation, it should be reiterated that those who hold Lope de Vega responsible for the neglect of tragedy advance two principal arguments: temperamentally, he was incapable of confronting tragic issues; esthetically, his conception of art ruled out tragedy as a dramatic form in favor of the hybrid tragicomedy. But there are those — like Alfonso Paso — who insist that tragicomedy is the most appropriate dramatic form for the Spanish character.

Many critics agree that the social, ethical, and religious conditions which prevailed in seventeenth-century Spain prevented the cultivation of tragedy because those conditions caused Spaniards to take an untragic view of suffering and death. Specifically, according to this line of thought, the main obstacle to tragedy was the Catholic faith, because the truly tragic is incompatible with the essential optimism of Christianity. For this reason, Clifford Leech writes: "... we should not look for tragedy in the drama of seventeenth-century Spain, for always there the spirit of religion burned brightly; Calderón and Lope de Vega might show evil in their plays, but it was an evil which attended on divine forgiveness or on an acceptable retribution; they might show suffering, but with them indeed it was the suffering of purgatorial fire." [13]

Leech's statement agrees with the earlier observation made by Karl Vossler that suffering in Lope's plays is always made to serve, not tragic, but redemptive purposes. [14] And José Bergamín

---

[13] Clifford Leech, *Shakespeare's Tragedies and Other Studies in Seventeenth-Century Drama* (London, 1950), pp. 18-19. Cf. H. J. Muller, *The Spirit of Tragedy* (New York, 1956), p. 149: "For Spain remained orthodox Catholic, hierarchical; and Spain wrote no tragedy. Its greatest dramatist, Calderón, presented some nominally tragic actions but always arrived at a pious or patriotic conclusion, resounding with devotion to God, king or country." And, because of his anti-Spanish and anti-Catholic bias, Jacob Burckhardt, *The Civilization of the Renaissance in Italy* (New York, 1954), asks: "Why did the Italians of the Renaissance do nothing above the second rank in tragedy?" And he answers, "It was the Inquisitors and Spaniards who cowed the Italian spirit, and rendered impossible the representation of the greatest and most sublime themes..." (pp. 233, 235). See also the fundamental article by Arnold G. Reichenberger, "The Uniqueness of the *Comedia*," *Hispanic Review*, 27 (1959), 303-16, in which the incompatibility of Spanish faith and the tragic view of life is emphasized.

[14] Karl Vossler, *Lope de Vega y su tiempo*, trans. Ramón de la Serna (Madrid, 1933), p. 315.

goes even farther: he not only insists that death is not treated tragically, but he speaks of the pleasure of dying — *el placer del morir* — as if it were one of the principal dramatic *devices* employed in Golden Age drama:

> *El placer del morir* es el que le ha dado vida a toda esta poesía de la fe, teatralizada o popularizada, en España, por Lope de Vega y Calderón, por lopistas y calderonianos: porque *el placer del morir* es lo único capaz de calmar, colmándola, esa desesperante impaciencia española de lo eterno.... *La cólera de un español sentado no se templa* más que a ese ritmo palpitante de eternidad en su oído: el que le canta en la *música* de su sangre la comedia lopista y calderoniana ... [15]

And speaking of the many deaths that occur in Spanish drama for reasons of honor or jealousy, Bergamín goes on to say: "Esos enamorados matan o mueren lírica y no trágicamente, porque han idealizado o concebido la muerte como un ideal: y hasta como un ideal del amor, radical y divino." [16]

Finally, in his essay "Shakespeare y Lope de Vega," Esteban Pujals asserts that one of the great differences between the two playwrights — a difference that presumably accounts for their dissimilar commitment to tragedy — is that Lope de Vega accepted all the values and beliefs of his country and age, whereas Shakespeare did not: "El español se mueve en un mundo conceptual inconmovible: religión, patria, monarquía, derecho y deber constituyen para Lope, como para la mayor parte de sus compatriotas contemporáneos, un sistema de valores de indestructible solidez." [17] While this statement is undoubtedly true as far as Lope is concerned, many students of Shakespeare would argue that he also shared the values, beliefs, and prejudices of his countrymen — but, of course, that did not keep him from writing tragedy.

---

[15] José Bergamín, *Mangas y capirotes* (*España en su laberinto teatral del XVVII*) (Madrid 1933) p. 92.

[16] Ibid., p. 100.

[17] Esteban Pujals, "Shakespeare y Lope de Vega," *Revista de Literatura*, 1 (1952), 42.

In recent years a few Hispanists have begun to challenge the *idée reçue* that Spanish dramatists were incapable of writing tragedy — indeed wrote no "real" tragedies — and they have also started to reexamine the theoretical concepts on which that idea is based. In the main these contemporary dissidents find deficient any definition of tragedy that would perforce exclude certain Spanish plays from the realm of tragic drama, because any such definition, they contend, is too narrow, too simplistic, or just too simple-minded. One tendency is to reject any *a priori* definition in favor of seeking a new definition, one which may be said to emerge from an analysis of those plays of a given dramatist in which he communicates his vision of the tragic sense of life. An example of this approach is found in Alexander A. Parker's thoughtful essay, "Towards a Definition of Calderonian Tragedy." [18] Although Parker does not deal with Spanish tragedy as a whole but rather with a single dramatist, it is fitting to quote at length from his essay in order to indicate one kind of critical approach that is gaining acceptance in Hispanic circles.

Calderón's tragic vision is based on his concept of the diffusion of moral responsibility, which Parker explains as follows:

> This linking of dramatic causality with some degree of moral guilt in all the major characters of the play constitutes the centre of Calderón's concept of tragedy. The individual human being must base his judgement and actions on "I and my circumstances"; yet an individual's circumstances are never his own: they are the tangled net of human relationships cast wide in time, a net in which all men are caught up by the inescapable fact that, though individuals, they are cast in a collective mould. The dramatic originality that flows from this sense of human solidarity is to have extended the traditional conception of tragedy as a catastrophe resulting from a flaw in the character of the individual hero or from an error in his judgement. The flaw is not his alone, there is a flaw in each and every character; each single error trickles down and combines with all the others to form the river that floods the tragic stage of

---

[18] *Bulletin of Hispanic Studies*, 39 (1962), 222-37.

life. No single man has the right to protest in indignation against the unjust suffering that is the lot of humanity, since all men in solidarity together make life what it is. [19]

Since others are to a large extent guilty of the errors committed by the individual, they not only feel pity for the wrongdoer but they also participate in his suffering. This "co-suffering," as Parker calls it, represents an expansion of the Aristotelian catharsis. Parker concludes:

> If, as I would contend, this expansion of the Aristotelian catharsis is clearly grounded in the fact of experience, and as such adds to our understanding of life, then the Spanish drama of the Golden Age, through Calderón, has a contribution to make to the theory of tragedy and to tragic drama which should no longer be so consistently ignored. [20]

Parker's definition of Calderonian tragedy is — and was meant to be — a tentative one; therefore, it necessarily does not take into full account various considerations that normally would be dealt with in a more definitive discussion of tragedy. Little is said about the character of the tragic hero, although Parker points out that one will not find in Calderón's plays the glorification of the tragic rebel — the Promethean hero — who can be overthrown but not overcome. Nor will one find a sense of triumph in defeat, because in Spanish drama that kind of exaltation is reserved for Christian martyrs. [21] And again, little or

---

[19] Ibid., p. 233.

[20] Ibid., p. 236.

[21] The question as to whether or not the Christian martyr can be a proper tragic hero is discussed by Arnold G. Reichenberger, "Calderón's *El príncipe constante*, a Tragedy?" in *Critical Essays on the Theatre of Calderón*, ed. Bruce W. Wardropper (New York, 1965), pp. 161-63; this volume is hereafter abbreviated as *Critical Essays*. Reichenberger writes concerning the protagonist: "Fernando is a flawless character who lives unflinchingly by a code of hierarchically arranged values, both secular and religious. His death, chosen by himself in the exercise of his *libre albedrío*, is the logical conclusion of his Christian constancy. His re-appearance as a spirit after death brings on the triumph of right. Fernando is a martyr and a saint, but not a tragic hero" (p. 163). The broader and much debated question as to whether or not there can be any Christian tragedy is brilliantly examined by Roger L. Cox, "Tragedy and the Gospel Narratives," *The Yale Review* (Summer, 1968), 545-70.

nothing is said about such matters as tragic reversal, recognition, and reconciliation — matters that have preoccupied theorists from Aristotle to Arthur Miller.

But quite apart from the formal and substantive considerations that are barely touched on or omitted in Parker's essay, some students of the tragedy will likely reject out of hand the idea that the "linking of dramatic causality with some degree of moral guilt in all the major characters of the play" has anything to do with tragedy, although that idea is said to constitute the "centre of Calderón's concept of tragedy." Moral guilt, many will contend, is not the primary stuff of tragedy but only incidental. Moreover, those have been schooled to believe that in tragedy, if nowhere else, the hero must act in accordance with his own will (no matter how strongly he may be swayed by the curse upon his House), that he must go it alone, and that he must bear the full burden of his acts, will be disconcerted by a concept of tragedy in which these principles are contradicted. In fine, Calderón's view of the human condition is certainly a pessimistic one with regard to man's earthly existence; but many critics will probably continue to regard him as a Christian determinist, not a tragedian.

Another recent essay, Duncan Moir's "The Classical Tradition in Spanish Dramatic Theory and Practice in the Seventeenth Century," [22] approaches Spanish tragedy in a different way. Contrary to previous treatises on the subject, Moir's essay has the merit of showing, not what is anti-classical or non-classical in Spanish dramaturgy, but rather how fundamentally classical much of that dramaturgy is. Moir holds that even the most ardent apologists for the popular national theater were advocates of what might be called "Spanish Aristotelianism, although their ideas were, for the most part, derived from the fusion of Aristotelian and Horatian doctrines." [23]

Moir deals with the question of form and with the affective quality of tragedy, but his most provocative observation concerns the tragic hero: ". . . Spanish drama's greatest original contribu-

---

[22] Op. cit., pp. 193-228.
[23] Ibid., p. 199.

tion to the European tragic tradition is, precisely, its demonstration, in plays such as *Fuenteovejuna, Peribáñez,* and *The Mayor
of Zalamea,* that even the peasant may be a truly tragic hero or
heroine." [24] Admittedly, it is tempting to look upon these peasants
as precursors of the type of common man that Arthur Miller
advocates as an appropriate tragic hero in our time — and in a
certain sense they are. Especially do they possess the kind of
"tragic flaw" that Miller speaks of in "Tragedy and the Common
Man": "The flaw, or crack in the character, is really nothing —
and need be nothing, but his inherent unwillingness to remain
passive in the face of what he considers to be a challenge to his
dignity, his image of his rightful status. Only the passive, only
those who accept their lot without active retaliation, are
'flawless.' " [25]

It will be objected by many, however, that the Spanish
peasant heroes cannot be tragic heroes for the simple reason that
the plays in which they appear are not tragedies; that is, these
plays cannot be tragedies because they end happily with the
death of the vicious nobleman and the vindication of the noble
peasant. To such an objection Moir has a ready answer: tragedy
does not have to end in deep misfortune as the "Sophocles or
nothing" school would demand. What is important is that "fear
and pity can be produced, with lasting effects, during the course
of the action of a tragedy, whatever the ending of this action
may be." [26] Upon the theoretical base which these words imply,

---

[24] Ibid., p. 225.

[25] Arthur Miller, "Tragedy and the Common Man," in *Tragedy: Vision
and Form,* ed. Robert W. Corrigan (San Francisco, 1965), p. 149.

[26] Of course, Moir's contention that tragedy does not have to end in
misfortune but may have a happy ending has the support of numerous
"authorities." Aristotle, *On the Art of Poetry,* trans. S. H. Butcher (New
York, 1948), p. 17, specifies that there is a kind of tragedy, although of
the "second rank," in which the wicked are punished and the virtuous are
rewarded with a happy ending, but: "The pleasure, however, thence
derived is not the true tragic pleasure. It is proper rather to Comedy..."
In his perceptive commentary on Aristotle, Alonso López Pinciano, *Philosophía antigua poética,* ed. Alfredo Carballo Picazo, 3 vols. (first edition,
1596; Madrid, 1953), II, 319, refers to this kind of tragedy as *tragedia
morata,* about which he says: "La segunda especie, dicha morata o bien
acostumbrada, aunque es de más vtilidad, no de tanto deleyte trágico,
porque la persona que tiene la acción en las partes principales, o es buena,

Moir cites a number of titles to prove that Spain produced "many tragedies." He then concludes: "The Spanish drama of the seventeenth century was by far the most prolific of the three great national dramas of the classical tradition in that time. And it was by no means the least fertile, moving and subtle in the tragic genre." [27]

In spite of Moir's demonstration of the fundamental classicism of much of Spanish drama and his arguments for a broader concept of tragedy, it is unlikely that his essay will cause many readers to change their minds concerning the dearth of Spanish tragedies. Granted that most of the plays cited by Moir — and especially *Fuenteovejuna, Peribáñez,* and *El alcalde de Zalamea* — are powerful dramas filled with intense tragic moments, I do not think that they are informed with a tragic vision of life. Nor do I think, to use Moir's own gauge, that the pity and fear aroused during the course of their actions can have "lasting effects." These plays are excellent examples of the Spanish *comedia,* in which the action moves, as stated by Arnold Reichenberger, "from order disturbed to order restored." [28] They say in effect — but not in the crude terms of melodrama — that this is a well-ordered universe in which the good and the just, although made to suffer temporarily, are ultimately rewarded and

---

o mala; si es buena la persona, para ser morata la acción y que enseñe buenas costumbres, ha de passar de infelicidad a felicidad, y passando assí, carece la acción del fin espantoso y misericordioso; carece, al fin, de la compassión, la qual es tan importante a la tragedia como vemos en su definición . . ."

Antonio Buero Vallejo presents an eloquent refutation of narrow theories regarding tragedy in "La tragedia," in *El teatro. Enciclopedia del arte escénico,* ed. Guillermo Díaz-Plaja (Barcelona, 1958), pp. 61-87. With regard to certain classical tragedies and one of his own plays, Buero argues that the happy ending does not detract from their tragic nature (*La señal que se espera,* in *Colección Teatro,* No. 21 [Madrid, 1953], pp. 66-67; cited by Kessel Schwartz, "Buero Vallejo and the Concept of Tragedy," *Hispania,* 51 (1968), 818). Although it may be quibbling over terms, I personally prefer to look upon Lope's and Calderón's peasant-hero plays as that rare kind of tragicomedy described by Eric Bentley, *The Life of the Drama* (New York, 1964), p. 319, as "a kind of 'tragedy with a happy ending' which is not 'tragedy averted' but 'tragedy transcended.'"

[27] Op. cit., p. 226.
[28] "The Uniqueness of the *Comedia,*" p. 307.

the wicked are punished. Moreover, God's own agent — the king — is always there to see that this is so.

But there is a type of Spanish drama whose somber mood is not only sustained but characteristically developed to provide the appropriate dramatic and affective atmosphere for a rousing conclusion: the honor play. Because of the fact that Lope de Vega referred to his own honor drama *El castigo sin venganza* as a tragedy "written in Spanish style," critics have long argued as to whether the honor plays should be included in, or excluded from, tragedy's domain. More than a century ago the French critic Louis de Viel Castel made an analogy between the function of the honor code in the Spanish honor dramas and fate in Greek tragedy because, as he saw it, both the honor code and fate are inexorable forces that the individual cannot evade or escape. [29] But it has been within the last two decades, when the whole question of Spanish tragedy has been undergoing reexamination, that the honor plays have come in for closer scrutiny.

Bruce Wardropper holds in his article "Poetry and Drama in Calderón's *El médico de su honra*" that the honor play is the typical tragedy of the Spanish Baroque, "one not quite like that of Sophocles, Shakespeare, or Racine, but with some points of contact." [30] Although Wardropper is not primarily concerned with examining Calderón's play in the light of tragic theory, he notes several distinctive tragic qualities of the play, including its catharsis of *admiración*, that is, the wonder or astonishment resulting from the startling dénouement. It will be remembered that the startling dénouement is owed largely to the manner in which the husband sacrifices his innocent wife on the altar of honor: he has a bloodletter bleed her to death in a setting which

---

[29] Cited by Ramón Menéndez Pidal "Del honor en el teatro español," in *De Cervantes y Lope de Vega* (Buenos Aires, 1940), p. 160. Menéndez Pelayo did not think that Viel Castel's point was well taken, as he made clear in his preface to Antonio Rubió y Lluch, *El sentido del honor en el teatro de Calderón* (Barcelona, 1882). Cf. Clifford Leech, *Shakespeare's Tragedies*, p. 216: "It [honour] led to plays with violent endings, but these are rarely tragedies proper, because they are concerned more frequently with pointing a moral, the moral that at all costs honour is sacred, than with showing the individual at odds with fate." See also Reichenberger, "The Uniqueness of the *Comedia*," pp. 308-11.

[30] *Romanic Review*, 49 (1958), 7-8.

literally resembles an altar — a bed flanked with candles on either side and a crucifix hanging over the head of the sacrificial victim.

There is no doubt that Calderón's play succeeds in arousing *admiratio*, which Renaissance commentators on Aristotle associated with his theory of the marvelous and which they believed could best be achieved by unexpected turns in the plot, highlighted by spectacular scenic representation. [31] Nor is there any doubt that the play produces *perturbation* (that is, a sense of disquietude or confusion) which some theorists believed to be as appropriate as pity and fear as an emotional response to tragedy. [32] Calderón's bloody catastrophe takes care of that. But largely because of its emphasis on *admiratio* and *perturbation*, *El médico de su honra* leaves no one with a sense of reconciliation. Rather, when the king sanctions the husband's act, when the prospect of a happy ending is held out for the wife-killer through a second marriage, the tragic focus goes askew. Spectator and reader are left with a sense of outrage. It is understandable why several British Hispanists have seen in Calderón's play an eloquent condemnation of the barbarity of the code of conjugal honor. [33]

Another approach to a Calderonian honor play is taken by A. Irvine Watson in his article "*El pintor de su deshonra* and the Neo-Aristotelian Theory of Tragedy." [34] Watson sets forth the theories of three leading Spanish commentators on Aristotle — López Pinciano, Francisco Cascales, and González de Salas — and shows that whether Calderón knew their works or not, he followed substantially their theories regarding the nature of the tragic plot

[31] For more on the "catharsis of *admiración*," see J. E. Gillet, "A Note on the Tragic *Admiratio*," *Modern Language Review*, 13 (1918), 233-38; and Edward C. Riley, "Aspectos del concepto 'admiratio' en la teoría literaria del siglo de oro," in *Studia Philologica: Homenaje ofrecido a Dámaso Alonso* ... (Madrid, 1963), III, 173-83.

[32] Cf. Jusepe Antonio González de Salas, *Nveva idea de de la tragedia antigua, o ilvstración última al libro singvlar "De Poética." De Aristóteles Stagirita* (1633; rpt. Madrid, 1778), I, 70-72.

[33] Edward H. Wilson, "Gerald Brenan's Calderón," *Bulletin of the Comediantes*, 4 (1952), 1, was probably the first modern scholar to demonstrate that Calderón "took the laws of honour and shewed their virtues and their cruelty."

[34] In *Critical Essays*, pp. 203-23.

and the character of the tragic hero. In fact, Watson concludes, so closely does Calderón follow these neo-Aristotelians that they themselves could only approve of his play, except for one objection: the mixture of tragic and comic elements. We are back on familiar ground.

I should like to add a word about *El pintor de su deshonra* and its hero because they — both the play and the protagonist — occupy a special place among the honor dramas. What is noteworthy in this play is not just the fact that the hero complains bitterly that the honor code infringes upon his autonomy or that it prescribes a law of vengeance that is, as he says, an "infamous ritual"; rather, it is exceptional in that when Don Juan Roca discovers his wife in the arms of her former lover (although in fact, if not in appearance, she is innocent of wrongdoing), he is incited by jealousy and rage to act spontaneously in accordance with the honor code that he intellectually condemns. Or, to put it another way, honor code or no honor code, Don Juan, believing that his wife is guilty of adultery, does what *he* feels he should under the circumstances. This — the spontaneous act of the protagonist produced by his afflicted will — is what distinguishes *El pintor de su deshonra* from the other honor plays and brings it within an ambience of tragedy that can be universally understood. [35]

From what I have been saying, it is probably obvious that I am not disposed to accept most honor dramas as tragedies. This is so, not because of prejudice against the genre, but because of the peculiar focus of these plays. By focus, I mean the relationship or interplay among incidents of plot, the motivation of the characters, their acts, and their reaction to their acts. If in most honor plays the protagonist is not responsible for creating his dilemma, if he acts involuntarily in taking blood revenge on his wife but yet feels vindicated, although certainly saddened, I do not believe these plays have the proper focus to be true tragedies.

---

[35] I agree with Parker, who says (p. 237): "What, one may ask, would any man do if, like Don Juan Roca, he were to find his abducted wife in the arms of another? It would need no acquaintance with or training in Spanish seventeenth-century *pundonor* to feel, under the stress of emotion, the instinctive urge to violence."

For this reason, several years ago I wrote that the hero must be fully autonomous and that his actions must spring from personal conviction and inner compulsion; therefore — and I am quoting myself here — "When the individual does not create or even contribute to his own tragic situation, when his 'tragic act' — committed in response to external imperatives — results in the death of others than himself, his experience may be painful, it may be lamentable, but it is not truly tragic." [36]

Not surprisingly, the ideas expressed above have provoked considerable disagreement. [37] But it seems to me that those who insist that the general run of honor dramas are other than "Spanish tragedies" do a disservice to a highly distinctive art form that developed its own canon and esthetics — an art form whose originality consists largely in its refusal to adhere to the stereotyped patterns of the neo-Senecan revenge tragedy cultivated at that time in the rest of Europe. [38] *El médico de su honra* and the other good honor dramas lose nothing when they are judged within the dramatic conventions of the honor code.

---

[36] Raymond R. MacCurdy, *Francisco de Rojas Zorrilla and the Tragedy* (1958; rpt. Albuquerque, 1966), p. 21. It should be mentioned, however, that during the last two decades several articles have been devoted to demonstrating that in some honor plays the husband-protagonist is not only responsible for creating his plight (and acting unwisely in the face of it) but occasionally the tragic victim, the murdered wife, may also be partly responsible, through imprudence or an unconscious desire for wrongdoing, for bringing about her death. See Edward M. Wilson, "La discreción de don Lope de Almeida," *Clavileño,* Año II, No. 9 (1951), 1-10 (on Calderón's *A secreto agravio secreta venganza*); Bruce W. Wardropper, "The Unconscious Mind in Calderón's *El pintor de su deshonra," Hispanic Review,* 18 (1950), 285-301; and Albert E. Sloman, "*El médico de su honra,*" in *The Dramatic Craftsmanship of Calderón* (Oxford, 1958), pp. 38, 40-41.

[37] See, for example, Parker, p. 237, and Watson, pp. 204 ff.

[38] The relationship between the Spanish honor dramas and the neo-Senecan revenge tragedies, in which honor almost always has considerable motivational and rhetorical importance, has not been thoroughly explored in print; but I have not seen the unpublished Ph. D. dissertation of Bruce Golden, "Elizabethan Revenge and Spanish Honor: Analogues of Action in the Popular Drama of the Renaissance" (Columbia University, 1969). Daniel Clive Stuart, "Honor in the Spanish Drama," *Romanic Review,* 1 (1910), 247-58, 357-66, makes a start on the subject by pointing out some verbal and conceptual similarities in the treatment of honor between a few Spanish plays and certain sixteenth-century Italian neo-Senecan revenge tragedies (Rucellai's *Rosmunda,* Dolce's *Marianna,* Giraldi's *Orbecche* and *Arrenopia,* etc.).

They only lose when they are compared with tragedies like Shakespeare's *Othello,* with which they should never be compared.

To sum up recent criticism and theory on Golden Age tragedy, two different approaches can be discerned. On the one hand, there is a tendency to seek a new and broader concept of tragedy than the prescriptive traditional ones, in order to discover and elucidate a hitherto undefined sense of tragic experience. Such a tendency is represented principally by Alexander Parker. On the other hand, there has been an effort (represented by Moir and Watson) to prove that seventeenth-century Spanish drama is characterized, in both theory and practice, by a greater degree of classicism than was formerly believed to be the case. The honor plays have been subjected to both approaches. Because of the tendency to broaden the concept of tragedy, they have been qualified as tragedies. Because of the tendency to seek out the classical aspects of Spanish drama, some of the honor plays, after careful analysis, have been found to be *quasi*-Aristotelian tragedies.

To return to the "problem" of Spanish tragedy, part of the problem, it should be obvious by now, is one of definition; but part of it also stems, I think, from an attitude of defensiveness held by some Hispanists, an attitude which has led them to make excessive claims — or counterclaims — in order to refute the scoffers who have demeaned Golden Age drama. I shall deal first with the claims.

Tragedy, of course, has long been held in high esteem by students of literature, and it is only natural that specialists in any one national theater should like to claim for its products the prestigious caste of tragedy. But in my opinion students of Spanish drama should content themselves with the knowledge that the Spanish *comedia* is unique and its contributions to the theatrical arts have been rich and varied. To go back to Lope de Vega's and Calderón's peasant-hero plays — *Fuenteovejuna, Peribáñez,* and *El alcalde de Zalamea* — I am quite happy to accept them as tragicomedies, tragicomedies which remain unsurpassed in their expression of the dignity and personal worth of the common man. I am also happy to accept the honor plays for what they are — "Spanish tragedies," if you like [39] — knowing full well that Aristotle probably would not approve of them. But we know that the best among them make exciting theater.

In his article, "Tragedy in the Spanish Golden Age," C. A. Jones covers much of the same material that we have been considering here. [40] He cites or quotes a few of the same critics; he refers to some of the same plays. Elaborating on earlier observations on tragedy made by Aldous Huxley and Edwin Morby, Jones comes to the conclusion that for Spanish dramatists of the Golden Age, tragedy was not enough. They felt compelled to capture the complexity of life, with all its comic and tragic dimensions, within a single play. They tried to communicate the "whole truth." I agree. And I can think of no better statement concerning the *comedia* as a vehicle for expressing the whole truth — the whole poetic truth — than that contained in a passage of Francisco de Barreda, *Invectiva a las comedias que prohibió Trajano y apología por las nuestras* (Madrid, 1622):

> Advirtiendo primero que las comedias que hoy gozamos dichosamente, son un orbe perfecto de la Poesía, que encierra y ciñe en sí toda la diferencia de poemas cuyas especies, aun repartidas, dieron lustre a los antiguos. Hay en las comedias nuestras la majestad, el esplendor y grandeza del poema épico. Tienen sus fábulas, sus episodios, y tal vez su verdad de historia, como el épico. Hay también las flores y dulzuras sonoras del lírico, las veras y severidad del trágico, las burlas y risas del cómico, los sainetes y sales del mímico, la gravedad y libertad de la sátira. *De manera que en nuestros tiempos no puede ser perfeta la comedia que no coronare toda la poesía* [my italics]. [41]

---

[39] Although "Spanish tragedy" is a convenient term for the honor play, it is probable that when Lope de Vega referred to *El castigo sin venganza* as a tragedy "escrita al estilo español," he did so, not because it employs the honor theme, but because it dispenses with certain paraphernalia of classical tragedy ("huyendo de las sombras, Nuncios, y coros").

[40] In *The Drama of the Renaissance: Essays for Leicester Bradner* (Providence, 1970), pp. 100-07.

[41] Quoted in Federico Sánchez Escribano y Alberto Porqueras Mayo, *Preceptiva dramática española del Renacimiento y el Barroco*, segunda edición muy ampliada (Madrid, 1972), pp. 217-18.

Now, the problem of definition will not take us long. Since it is incumbent upon critics to reexamine old definitions and throw out those that are no longer valid or useful, it is no wonder that many contemporary students of the drama feel that Aristotle's definition of tragedy will no longer do — not just because few people can agree on what Aristotle meant but because his observations were based on Greek tragedy of 2400 years ago. But I must confess that I am uneasy when some of my colleagues ask students of other literatures to accept new concepts of tragedy — with their implied definitions — that may well lead to greater confusion or to outright skepticism regarding the merits of Spanish drama. One example: Duncan Moir calls Tirso de Molina's *El burlador de Sevilla* a "great social tragedy." English scholars might well call it a "punitive comedy." It will not help matters to say, the "whole truth" is that it is both. [42]

Notwithstanding the concern expressed above over the excessive claims made for certain Spanish plays as tragedies, it is a major thesis of this book that the *tragedias de privanza* or fallen-favorite plays do not require new definitions of tragedy and must occupy a central position in any discussion of "Spanish Aristotelianism." The theme of the downfall of the great *(casus Fortunae)* had long provided writers of tragic or moralistic bent with material for their reflections. It is a theme which bemused the chroniclers of the Old Testament; it absorbed dramatists, historians, and biographers of antiquity; it obsessed medieval

---

[42] I share Moir's view that *El burlador de Sevilla* may be regarded as a tragedy, but only, I think, in a modern, "absurd" sense. In the Introduction to my edition of *El burlador* (New York, 1965), after comparing Don Quijote and Don Juan as baroque heroes (and as *engagés,* in different ways of course, as any modern existentialist could wish), I concluded: "In his final moments Don Quijote, recognizing the folly of his single-handed efforts to reform the world, reclaims the name of Alonso Quijano, confesses, and dies a Christian death. In a sense his return to sanity comes as the tragic conclusion to his 'comical' adventures. Don Quijote stands as Spain's greatest tragic hero, a type of tragic hero unknown in earlier literature.

"In his final moments Don Juan, recognizing that the game of *burlas* is up, calls for confession. It is denied him, and he is sent to hell. His damnation comes as a fitting — hence, 'comical' — conclusion to his adventures that left tragedy in their wake. The *burlador* stands as Spain's most absurd hero, absurd because he invites destruction by willful capriciousness" (pp. 12-14).

moralists; and it furnished the base of one of the most influential books of the early Renaissance, Boccaccio's *De casibus virorum illustrium.*

During the first quarter of the seventeenth century, as favorites' heads fell throughout much of Europe (in England, Essex and Raleigh; in France, the Duke of Biron; in Spain, Don Rodrigo Calderón), political writers were moved to compose manuals designed to instruct ministers and favorites in the arts of their office and to warn them against personal ambition, greed, and Machiavellian treachery. And, inevitably, since favoritism became a matter of general concern in England, France, and Spain, it also became a prime subject for the national theaters of those countries.

In Spain, where the court of Philip III was kept in constant turmoil because of the feuds and machinations of favorites or would-be favorites, dramatists wrote more than fifty plays in which favoritism is a major theme. Of course, not all these plays — not even the majority — are tragedies. Some are dramas of intrigue in which the rivalry of favorites serves only to complicate the plot (Jacinto Cordero, *De lo que es privar*). Some are historical dramas in which the theme of favoritism is incidental to the representation of historical events (Tirso de Molina, *La prudencia en la mujer*). A very few are doctrinal pieces whose purpose is to expound on the qualities of the perfect favorite and to show how he should conduct himself in relation to the king and vassals (Quevedo, *Cómo ha de ser el privado*). Indeed, no more than a dozen and a half of the plays on favoritism may properly be termed fallen-favorite tragedies.

But let me express a caveat once again, because I do not want to leave the impression that all the *tragedias de privanza* are worthwhile tragedies. Obviously the demise of a favorite, no matter how awesome his fall or how moving the circumstances of his death, does not guarantee the quality of a tragedy. But by and large, these plays are deeply rooted in the realities and tensions of the Spanish experience, and the best of them reveal a tragic sense of life as it was felt by a generation of concerned artists.

II

THE POLITICAL SCENE

> "He took the axe in his hand, kissed the
> blade, and said to the sheriff, *'Tis a sharp med-
> icine, but a sound cure for all diseases.'*"
>
> (Sir Walter Raleigh, executed on October
> 29, 1618)

On October 21, 1621, Don Rodrigo Calderón, the Marquis of
Siete Iglesias and former secretary of the chamber of Philip III,
was beheaded in the main square of Madrid. The charges against
him, 244 in number, included malfeasance in office, simony,
witchcraft, murder, and complicity in the poisoning of Queen
Marguerite (who died in 1614 of complications resulting from
childbirth). The last two charges were dropped during the course
of the trial. [1] We shall never know how many of the remaining

---

[1] Ángel Ossorio, *Los hombres de toga en el proceso de D. Rodrigo
Calderón* (Madrid, n. d.) gives a detailed account of the charges against
the accused and an extensive bibliography of the material, both printed and
unprinted, concerning his trial. Although the charge of witchcraft was
dropped, Calderón was accused of having among his possessions in Valladolid a pouch of verbena with which was found a written conjuration. The
conjuration is quoted in part because of the light it sheds on the superstitious
nature of the period: "... conjúrote verbena por el cielo y la tierra y por
el mar y por todos los lugares y por Dios vivo y vero que de cualquiera
Rey o Reina, o Conde o Barón o Caballero o Doctor o Papa o Emperador, o
Cardenal o Obispo o Arzobispo tanto de las personas temporales como de
las espirituales que cada uno haga mi voluntad y nada me puedan negar y
siempre me puedan amar. Y a ti verbena digo, me hayas de hacer victo-
rioso sobre todos mis enemigos como fue Daniel sobre los suyos. Conjúrote
verbena por la cabeza de San Juan Bautista y por todos los Santos de Dios.

charges he was guilty of — he confessed only to participation in one assassination — but the circumstances of his trial and execution touched off a political crisis and brought on a national *crise de conscience*.

Calderón was the victim of a drama of intrigue that had long enthralled the country, although he played only a secondary part — except for his role of scapegoat in the final scene. When Philip III, who inherited his father's piety but not his disposition to rule, ascended to the throne in 1598, he turned over the reins of government to his tutor, the Duke of Lerma. For twenty years Lerma and his henchmen, of whom Rodrigo Calderón was one, presided over the affairs of a nation sinking rapidly into bankruptcy and military impotence. Not the least of Lerma's problems was to deal with the machinations of his political rivals, among whom his own son, the Duke of Uceda, and the king's confessor, Fray Luis de Aliaga, were the most vicious. In 1618, realizing that his days of favor were numbered, Lerma requested, and received, permission to retire to his estates far from the court. He also received, as compensation for his long years of service, a cardinal's hat. His friends were not so lucky. When Uceda and Aliaga became entrenched in power, they initiated a general purge leading to the exile or imprisonment of several former magnates. Calderón's arrest in 1619 and his execution two years later concluded only one act of the political drama.

When Philip III died, also in 1621, he was succeeded by his son Philip IV, who like his father relinquished many of his royal responsibilities to his own tutor and favorite, the Count-Duke Olivares. Both Aliaga, the conniving confessor, and Uceda, Lerma's ungracious son, were promptly exiled. Uceda later died in prison. Much of the doctrinal literature and some of the plays composed at this time on the subject of favoritism were informed with the hope that the new king and the new *privado* would prove more worthy than their predecessors.[2] But more worthy or not, Olivares lasted until 1643 when he also fell from grace.

Amén" (p. 70). The defense successfully maintained that the verbena and the conjuration belonged not to Calderón but to his father-in-law.

[2] See Ruth Lee Kennedy, "*La prudencia en la mujer* and the Ambient That Brought It Forth," *PMLA*, 43 (1948), 1133 ff.

As the most striking spectacle in this political drama, Don Rodrigo Calderón's public execution was an awesome event indeed. His conduct on the scaffold was exemplary. His dignity and composure in the face of death aroused the admiration of the multitude and — as most Spanish schoolboys know — gave rise to a new saying in the language: *tener más orgullo que don Rodrigo en la horca.* Ballad-mongers and poets of renown, former friends and foes alike, sought to capture the beauty and pathos of his death. [3] The more pious among them pointed to his good luck in knowing the precise day he would die, because his soul would be in readiness. Some pondered the ways of fortune [4] and decried the vanity of human glory. Others refurbished old platitudes on the suddenness of the tragic fall. Even the Count of Villamediana, whose mordant muse seldom moved him to compassion (he mocked Calderón ferociously on the occasion of his imprisonment), dedicated a sonnet to his "glorious" death:

> Éste que en la fortuna más subida
> No cupo en sí, ni cupo en él su suerte,
> Viviendo pareció digno de muerte,
> Muriendo pareció digno de vida.
> ¡Oh providencia no comprehendida!
> ¡Auxilio superior, aviso fuerte!
> ¡El humo en que el aplauso se convierte
> Hace la misma afrenta esclarecida!
> Purificó el cuchillo los perfetos
> Modos que religión celante ordena,
> Para ascender a la mayor vitoria;

---

[3] See the *Introducción bibliográfica* to Antonio Pérez Gómez, ed. *Romancero de don Rodrigo Calderón (1621-1800)* (Valencia, 1955), pp. 9-35. Among those who paid warm tribute to the deceased was Francisco López de Zárate, who owed his position in the Secretariat of State to Calderón's intercession in his behalf. López de Zárate, who lost his job when his patron lost his head, dedicated to him a moving sonnet, "Al Marqués de Siete Iglesias Don Rodrigo Calderón en su sepulcro," printed in *Obras varias de . . .*, ed. José Simón Díaz (Madrid, 1947), II, 124.

[4] For the sake of uniformity, throughout the text I have written "fortune" with a small *f* to apply both to the abstract idea of fortune and to the goddess Fortuna; however, in quotations I have respected the spelling of the original authors.

Y trocando las causas sus efetos,
Si glorias le conducen a la pena,
Penas le restituyen a la gloria.

(BAE, XLII, 155-56) [5]

One of Calderón's most implacable enemies was the great satirist Francisco de Quevedo, who also wrote a sonnet on his death and a mock-epitaph ("A don Rodrigo Calderón, Marqués de Siete Iglesias, que murió degollado en pública plaza"), in which he comments wryly on the quantity of poetry inspired by the favorite's execution. Four *redondillas* of the "Epitafio" follow:

Yo soy aquel delincuente,
porque a llorar te acomodes,
que vivió como un Herodes,
murió como un inocente.
... ...

Cocodrilos descubiertos
son poetas vengativos;
que a los que se comen vivos
los lloran después de muertos.

Nadie con ellos se meta
mientras tuviese sentido;
que, al fin, a cada valido
se le llega su poeta.

Mi sentencia me azuzaron
con décimas que escribieron;
ellos la copla me hicieron,
y muerto me epitafiaron.... [6]

And again, in his *Anales de quince días,* Quevedo mused on the irony that the same poets — the "cocodrilos" — who vilified Calderón during his life praised him after his death: "Siguieron a la muerte de D. Rodrigo elogios muy encarecidos; y los poetas que fulminaron el primero proceso en consonantes, le hicieron

---

[5] Here — and throughout the text — BAE is employed as an abbreviation for the Biblioteca de Autores Españoles. Only the volume and page numbers will be cited, since other bibliographical data have been rendered inconsequential because of the frequent reprintings of the collection. Similarly, the Nueva Biblioteca de Autores Españoles is abbreviated NBAE.
[6] Francisco de Quevedo, *Obra poética,* ed. José Manuel Blecua, 3 vols. (Madrid, 1971), III, 218.

otros tantos epitafios, como decimos, llorando como cocodrilos al que se habían comido." [7] Irony attends the death of every fallen favorite.

From a literary point of view the most important result of Rodrigo Calderón's execution was that it hurried the spate of writings, both doctrinal and literary, on the subject of favoritism; and, equally important, it also recalled the rise and fall of a much greater favorite, Don Álvaro de Luna, almost two centuries earlier. One of the greatest men of Spanish history, Don Álvaro de Luna served John II of Castile for more than forty years, first as a page, then as a soldier and statesman. It was he who kept rebellious feudal lords at bay and defended the kingdom against the encroachments of other Spanish princes; it was he who carried the war to the Moors. But Don Álvaro had powerful enemies in Castile, and on more than one occasion they persuaded the king to banish him from the court. On each occasion, however, John, whose dependence on Luna bordered on the pathological, recalled him to his side. Finally, jealous of Don Álvaro's power and wealth, and urged on by his Portuguese wife (whose marriage to John was arranged personally by Luna without the king's knowledge), John allowed his favorite to be brought to trial. The charges against him included treason, murder, and bewitching the king. Legend has it that the queen helped guide John's trembling hand to sign the death warrant. Don Álvaro de Luna was beheaded in the main square of Valladolid on June 2, 1453. John could no longer call him back.

Even during his lifetime Don Álvaro's splendor was dear to Spanish poets, for he seemed to be living proof that man can be immune to "the slings and arrows of outrageous fortune." And after his demise his tragic fall served many a writer of moralistic bent, for he was dead proof of the fragility of human life. Three of the greatest poets of the fifteenth century — Juan de Mena, the Marquis of Santillana, and Jorge Manrique — looked upon the rise and fall of the Constable of Castile from different personal perspectives. In *El laberinto de fortuna,* finished and dedicated to John II in 1444, nine years before the execution of

---

[7] *BAE,* XXIII, 210.

Don Álvaro de Luna, Mena portrays the favorite at the height of his power, riding rough-herd on fortune:

> Éste cavalga sobre la Fortuna
> e doma su cuello con ásperas riendas;
> y aunque dél tenga tan muchas prendas,
> ella no le osa tocar a ninguna. . . . [8]

But later the poet, although no enemy of Don Álvaro, predicts, through a resuscitated corpse, the favorite's downfall:

> E del condestable judgando su fecho
> assí determino su fado e pregono:
> será retraído del sublime trono
> e aun a la fin del todo desfecho. . . . [9]

It is no wonder that Juan de Mena, like Enrique de Villena, was thought by some of his contemporaries to be able to divine the future.

The Marquis of Santillana, an unrelenting foe of Don Álvaro whom he regarded as an insufferable *parvenu*, took advantage of the favorite's death not only to advance his own political fortunes but also to admonish other *privados*. Santillana's *Doctrinal de privados*, together with other didactic works on the dangers of favoritism, will be examined in the following chapter; but suffice it to say now that Santillana took a much more charitable view toward his deceased enemy than Quevedo took toward Don Rodrigo Calderón.

Santillana's young kinsman Jorge Manrique, who was too young to experience personally the brunt of Don Álvaro's alleged political tyranny, found no cause to exult over the favorite's death. In his *Coplas por la muerte de su padre* the poet recalls the Constable's tragic end in order to remind the reader that the acquisition of worldly goods leads only to grief when they have to be abandoned:

---

[8] *El laberinto de fortuna o Las trescientas*, ed. José Manuel Blecua, *Clásicos Castellanos*, vol. 11 (Madrid, 1943), p. 122.

[9] Ibid., p. 132.

> Pues aquel gran Condestable,
> maestre que conocimos
>   tan privado,
> non cumple que de él se hable,
> sino sólo que lo vimos
>   degollado.
> Sus infinitos tesoros,
> sus villas y sus lugares,
>   su mandar,
> ¿qué le fueron sino lloros?
> ¿Qué fueron sino pesares
>   al dejar? [10]

Notwithstanding the great differences between Don Álvaro de Luna and Don Rodrigo Calderón, especially the difference in their stature as political leaders, the parallel between their rise and fall was apparent to many perceptive Spaniards. Both came from rather obscure origins, both were the objects of unrelenting envy and scurrilous attack, and only they, of all those who were privy to the king, were executed during two centuries of Spanish history. Even before Calderón was sentenced to death, the two favorites were linked in common disaster by the fertile mind of the Count of Villamediana. During Calderón's imprisonment Villamediana wrote:

> Golpes de fortuna son
> Vueltos ya contra su dueño,
> Pues un *Calderón* pequeño
> Se hace de un gran *Calderón.*
> Mil causas de esta prisión
> Cuenta el vulgo novelero,
> Y dice que el Rey severo
> Lo mandó mil siglos ha;
> Tanto que teme que irá
> La soga tras el *caldero....*
>   Privado, que serlo esperas,
> Tu conciencia no se tizne
> Porque cantes como un cisne,
> No cual cuervo cuando mueras.
> Tiznáronse tus *calderas*

---

[10] In *Antología general de la literatura española,* eds. Ángel y Amelia del Río, 2 vols. (New York, 1960), I, 133.

Al fuego de la ambición,
Y aunque ha puesto admiración,
No es nunca vista fortuna:
Que do se tiznó una *luna*
Tiznaráse un *calderón*. [11]

While Villamediana jibed at Rodrigo Calderón's predicament, more compassionate writers, so it is conjectured, composed works dramatizing the tragic end of Don Álvaro de Luna as a means of urging the king to extend clemency to Calderón. For example, Cotarelo y Mori (who attributed *La adversa fortuna de don Álvaro de Luna* to Tirso de Molina, not to Mira de Amescua) speculated that the play was written in 1621, while Calderón was awaiting execution, in order to influence the newly crowned Philip IV to intercede in the condemned man's behalf: "Esta segunda de D. Álvaro parece haber sido escrita en los terribles momentos que precedieron al suplicio de D. Rodrigo Calderón. Y ¿quién sabe si eran un memorial en pro de la salvación de aquel infeliz privado estos versos que se ponen en boca del arrepentido D. Juan II?:

Reyes deste siglo, nunca
deshagáis vuestras mercedes,
ni borréis vuestras hechuras.
¡Oh, quién a mis descendientes
avisara que no huyan
de los que bien eligieron
para la mudanza suya!" [12]

Although the careers and destiny of Don Álvaro de Luna and Don Rodrigo Calderón were bound together in the minds of some seventeenth-century writers before Calderón's death, it was

[11] Emilio Cotarelo y Mori, *El Conde de Villamediana, estudio biográfico-crítico, con varias poesías inéditas del mismo* (Madrid, 1886), pp. 86-87. The italics in the poem quoted are Cotarelo's.

[12] Emilio Cotarelo y Mori, ed. *Comedias de Tirso de Molina*, in *NBAE*, IV (Madrid, 1906), I, lxiv. Because of the discovery of Mira de Amescua's autograph of *La adversa fortuna de don Álvaro de Luna*, it now appears that the final version of the play was not written — or approved for representation — until 1624, after Calderón's death. But in view of Calderón's imprisonment, Cotarelo had good reason to postulate the earlier date.

not until after his execution that the two men became fully
identified in the national consciousness. Probably the best measure of that identification is provided by the ballads on the two
fallen favorites. As observed by Antonio Pérez Gómez, the ballads
devoted to Calderón were, in the main, only "unfortunate" imitations of those composed earlier on the rise and fall of Don
Álvaro. [13] One ballad, in particular, has Calderón himself point
to the parallel between the two men:

> A don Álvaro de Luna
> representa hoy mi tragedia,
> que él fue page y yo lo fui,
> mirad qué dicha la nuestra. [14]

In spite of the fact that the ballads on the two favorites are
similar in themes, imagery, and sentiment, their deaths did not
provoke similar responses in other forms of literature. While
almost all the ballads on Don Álvaro de Luna are sympathetic
to him (those ballads will be treated in a later chapter), the earliest
ones were not composed until almost a century after his death. [15]
The ballads on Don Rodrigo Calderón were written during his
imprisonment or shortly after his execution. Apart from Santillana's *Doctrinal de privados*, the death of Don Álvaro occasioned
no significant literature on favoritism; it inspired little immediate
poetry. However, it is more than a coincidence that a large body
of literature on the theme of fortune was written shortly before
and after Don Álvaro's demise, since the times witnessed so many

---

[13] *Romancero de don Rodrigo Calderón*, p. 14.

[14] Ibid., p. 58. Cited by Nellie E. Sánchez-Arce, ed. *La segunda de
don Álvaro*, p. 7.

[15] Antonio Pérez Gómez, ed. *Romancero de don Álvaro de Luna (1540-
(1800)* (Valencia, 1953), p. 16, observes that of all the extant ballads on
Don Álvaro, only one (No. 17 in his edition) is strongly unfavorable to the
favorite. That ballad, contained in *El cancionero manuscrito de Pedro del
Pozo (1547)*, ed. Antonio Rodríguez-Moñino (Madrid, 1950), is believed to
be the earliest one on Don Álvaro. In it he is accused, among other things,
of having caused the poisoning of Queen María of Castile and Queen
Leonor of Portugal. The same charge is also made in the *Crónica de
Juan II (BAE, LXVIII, 65)*, but it was not brought up during his trial. The
ballads on Don Álvaro are discussed more fully in chapter V.

inexplicable reverses.[16] And finally — and not surprisingly — the favorite's death led to many biased accounts of his career, the majority of which were unfavorable to him. Certainly Don Álvaro had his apologists even after his death (notably, the author of the *Crónica de don Álvaro de Luna,* which will be considered later, together with the other chronicles), but for the most part, the chief chroniclers of the fifteenth century, including Fernán Pérez de Guzmán and Alfonso Fernández de Palencia, were too partisan to be other than vindictive. Palencia, in particular, brutally excoriated the fallen favorite.

Perhaps because he was a lesser figure who did not control the destiny of Castile and its subjects, Don Rodrigo Calderón inspired momentary pity but little wrath after his death. But coming when it did, his execution aroused the anxiety of political writers, moralists, and poets. The burgeoning doctrinal literature on favoritism (whose motivation corresponds to that of the literature on fortune in the fifteenth century) is one measure of that anxiety.

---

[16] The theme of fortune was popular throughout Europe, including Spain, in the fifteenth century, with Boethius, Seneca, and Petrarch being favorite authors. See P. Fernando Rubio, "El tema de la fortuna en la literatura castellana del siglo xv," *BAE,* CLXXI, xv-xxiv, and Otis H. Green, Chapter VII, "Fortune and Fate," *Spain and the Western Tradition,* 4 vols. (Madison, Wis., 1964), II, 279-337. In addition to Juan de Mena's *El laberinto de fortuna,* a few of the more important works on fortune written shortly before or after the death of Don Álvaro are: Fray Lope Barrientos, *Tratado de caso e fortuna,* c. 1450; Fray Martín de Córdoba, *Compendio de la fortuna,* written between 1440 and 1453 and dedicated to Don Álvaro; and Mosén Diego de Valera, *Tratado de Providencia contra Fortuna,* composed between 1458 and 1467.

III

DOCTRINAL AND NON-DRAMATIC LITERATURE

In my palace of Castile,
I, a king, for kings can feel.
There my thoughts the matter roll,
And solve and oft resolve the whole.
And, for I'm styled Alphonse the Wise,
Ye shall not fail for sound advice.
                    (Ralph Waldo Emerson, "Alphonso of
                    Castile")

"Otrosí, debe haber homes sabidores, é en-
tendidos, é leales, que le sirvan de fecho en
aquellas cosas que son menester para su consejo,
é para facer justicia, é derecho a la gente; ca él
solo no podría ver nin librar todas las cosas,
porque ha menester por fuerza ser ayudado de
otros de quien se fíe."
                    (Alfonso X, *Las siete partidas*, Partida II,
                    Título I, Ley III)

In spite of the prophetic vision attributed to Alfonso X by
Emerson, Lord Byron, and other poets who saw the learned king
as a fellow seer, it is improbable that he foresaw the day when
future Spanish kings, inept like himself to cope with the problems
of practical politics, would entrust the affairs of state to a single
favorite. Alfonso never learned to solve his own problems, much
less the "whole." However, his advice that kings should surround
themselves with presumably learned, intelligent, and loyal men
to counsel them was duly carried out by his successors.

Although several Castilian kings before and after Alfonso had
their favorites, it was not until the reign of the later Trastamara

kings in the fifteenth century that the royal authority was sur-
rogated to favorites. And even though John II and Henry IV
defaulted on the obligations of the crown by investing their *privados* with unprecedented authority, the rule by favorites was
a bitterly contested political issue and, at best, a matter of temporary expedience. The fact that the "temporary" expedience
lasted more than half a century during the seemingly interminable
reigns of John and Henry only made the sufferance more in-
tolerable. But by and large, until the seventeenth century Spanish
kings functioned as kings, and most of them saw fit to follow the
advice of Alfonso X, surrounding themselves with ministers and
counselors in whom they thought they could trust. [1]

Not until midway through the reign of Philip III were Spaniards forced to recognize favoritism as a *de facto* political institution — as an inescapable fact of the national life. The emergence

---

[1] During the reign of Ferdinand and Isabel the old *Consejo Real,*
which had long been in existence and which had undergone certain reforms
during the reigns of Sancho IV and John I, was thoroughly overhauled.
Further conciliar reforms were carried out during the reign of Charles V.
Under the leadership of the Grand Chancellor Gattinatta, the *Consejo de
Castilla* was developed from the old *Consejo Real;* and about the same time
(1522) the *Consejo de Estado* was formed, which became the best known
of all the advisory councils during the later years of the Hapsburg kings.
For the development of the conciliar system, see J. H. Elliot, *Imperial Spain,
1469-1716* (New York, 1966), pp. 167-78.

Perhaps the two men who came closest in the sixteenth century to
fitting the image of a royal favorite were Francisco de los Cobos, secretary
to Charles V and secretary of several councils, who died a wealthy man in
1547, and Antonio Pérez, secretary to Philip II and secretary of the *Consejo
de Estado,* whose favoritism was cut short by his arrest in 1578 for the
murder of Juan de Escobedo and his subsequent escape and flight to
France. For the careers of Cobos and Antonio Pérez, see Hayward Keniston,
Francisco de los Cobos. Secretary of the Emperor Charles V (Pittsburgh,
1960), and Gregorio Marañón, *Antonio Pérez, el hombre, el drama, la época,*
séptima edición (Madrid, 1963). Antonio Pérez's own writings — *Las obras
y relaciones, Memorial del hecho de su causa, Aforismos,* and *Cartas* —
contain many observations on the politics and perils of *privanza.* Both
Antonio Pérez and Baltasar Álamos de Barrientos have been credited with
the authorship of a *Norte de príncipes* (not to be confused with the book
of the same title by Juan Pablo Mártir Rizo, discussed later in this chapter)
which has been recently reprinted under Pérez's name: *Norte de príncipes,
virreyes, presidentes, consejeros, y governadores, y advertencias políticas
sobre lo publico y particular de una monarquia importantisimas a los tales:
fundadas en materia y razon de estado, y govierno. Escritas por Antonio
Perez* ... Nota preliminar de Martín de Riquer (Madrid, 1969).

in the first half of the seventeenth century of a single dominant royal minister — *the* favorite — was, of course, a European phenomenon, not one peculiar to Spain. Julián Juderías has called attention to the fact that the same pattern developed in the major European powers and, more or less, for the same reasons: forceful kings — Philip II in Spain, Henry IV in France, Elizabeth in England — were followed by weak, abulic successors who were only too happy to surrender the affairs of state into the hands of ambitious, albeit patriotic, ministers who were eager to improve their own lot as well as the common weal. [2] If Philip III had his Lerma, Louis XIII had his Richelieu, and James I his Somerset, Buckingham, and Bacon. If Philip, Louis, and James had been stronger men and more skillful executives, perhaps the rise of favoritism could have been abated, but admittedly the art of kingship was becoming more complex. The king could no longer regard himself as primarily a military leader because domestic political and economic problems absorbed his time. Territorial expansion brought with it many new and unforeseen difficulties. The disappearance of the feudal system led to the greater centralization of government, adding to the burden of the crown. Confronted with a burgeoning bureaucracy, it is no wonder that the otherworldly Philip and his foreign counterparts felt that governance by counsel and councils, requiring their personal attention, was a bore. Why not a first minister, a trusted confidant, to run the show?

The quantity and character of the literature on favoritism were conditioned, understandably, by the development of favoritism as a political institution and its recognition as a reality of the national life. During the Middle Ages didactic literature on the art of statecraft was addressed largely to the sovereign, and its principal concern was to remind the ruler, as the appointed of God, of his Christian obligations. Saint Augustine's *De civitate Dei* continued to serve as the vademecum of all political writers of the period, including Saint Thomas Aquinas, whose *De regimine principum* focused directly on the king's seeking and

---

[2] Julián Juderías, *Don Francisco de Quevedo y Villegas. La época, el hombre, las doctrinas* (Madrid, 1922), pp. 25-26.

taking counsel. [3] Not only is taking counsel useful in a pragmatic way, says Saint Thomas (like his younger contemporary, Alfonso X), but it is a divinely sanctioned practice. [4] It follows that the counselors themselves must be men of probity and deeply committed to the preservation of the faith, as evidenced by their personal lives.

Representative of the medieval works addressed specifically to the role of counselors is the *Libro del consejo e de los consejeros* by the enigmatic Maestre Pedro, whose elusive identity makes impossible the positive dating of the book, although it appears to belong to the early fourteenth century. [5] Based largely on the Scriptures and the writings of Seneca, Saint Augustine, and especially Albertanus Brixiensis, the book includes a chapter entitled "De quantas cosas les conviene a los consejeros que ayan en sí." Six requisites are considered essential for counselors: (1) that they be men of virtue; (2) they must be prudent and wise; (3) they should be diligent and elderly, so that they will be more experienced; (4) they should be firm and constant, so that they will not be influenced by fear, love, or greed in carrying out what they must do, especially in regard to God's justice; (5) they should be genuine friends who will give honest counsel to those whom they are to advise; (6) they must be tried and true. [6] It did not occur to Maestre Pedro to speak of the attributes of a single royal favorite (who, ideally, would not exist), but most of the qualities that he prescribes for counselors are echoed in the seventeenth-century manuals on the selection of favorites.

When John II persistently chose to ignore the opinion of his other counselors in order to follow the advice — or behest — of Don Álvaro de Luna, among the disgruntled nobility stood Don Íñigo López de Mendoza, the Marquis of Santillana. Although Santillana furiously resented the usurper, he bided his time. His hour came when, in 1453, Don Álvaro was led to the execution

---

[3] José A. Maravall, *La teoría española del estado en el siglo XVII* (Madrid, 1944), pp. 309 ff.

[4] Ibid., pp. 313-16.

[5] Agapito Rey, ed. Maestre Pedro, *Libro del consejo e de los consejeros,* in *Biblioteca del Hispanista,* vol. V (Zaragoza, 1962), p. 12.

[6] Ibid., pp. 34-37.

block. Santillana responded by writing the *Doctrinal de privados, fecho a la muerte del Maestre de Santiago, don Álvaro de Luna; donde se introduce el autor, fablando en nombre del Maestre.* Called Santillana's masterpiece by Menéndez Pidal — and praised by him for its moral and artistic qualities — the *Doctrinal de privados* is more than a venomous diatribe (as some critics have viewed it) against a fallen foe. [7] Santillana makes little attempt to conceal his joy that a formidable — and to him, a vicious — political enemy had been removed, but the poet senses that Don Álvaro was not simply the victim of his own ambition and avarice but that he, as a fallible human being, was corrupted by his awesome power. Presumably, however, Don Álvaro escaped absolute corruption because the circumstances of his demise stand as proof that he never had absolute power.

Although Santillana speaks for Don Álvaro in the first person (a transparent device for having the Maestre incriminate himself), the use of the first person plural, especially in the repetition of the possessive *nuestros,* implicates all mankind in a common destiny of sin and death:

> Vi thesoros ayuntados
> por grand daño de su dueño:
> asy como sombra o sueño
> son nuestros días contados.
> E si fueron prorrogados
> por sus lágrimas a algunos,
> déstos non vemos ningunos
> por nuestros negros pecados. [8]

---

[7] Ramón Menéndez Pidal, *Poesía árabe y poesía europea* (Buenos Aires, 1943), p. 90. Cf. Agustín Millares Carlo, *Literatura española hasta fines del siglo XV* (México, 1950), p. 204, and Fernando Gutiérrez, ed. Marqués de Santillana, *Páginas escogidas* (Barcelona, 1939), pp. 173-74. See also the excellent analysis of the poem contained in David W. Foster, *The Marqués de Santillana* (New York, 1971), pp. 39-47. Foster also discusses briefly Santillana's little known *Coplas del dicho señor marqués* on the fall of Don Álvaro de Luna, and he mentions the *Favor de Hércules contra fortuna,* inspired by Santillana's hatred of Don Álvaro.

[8] R. Foulché-Delbosc, ed. *Cancionero castellano del siglo XV,* in *NBAE,* XIX, 2 vols. (Madrid, 1922), I, 503.

As the title suggests, the *Doctrinal de privados* was intended to communicate a body of useful doctrine to all actual and would-be favorites. Its teachings are projected on Don Álvaro's failings:

> Lo que no fize, fazed,
> favoridos e privados:
> si queredes ser amados,
> non vos teman, mas temed.
> Templad la cupida sed;
> aconsejad retos juyçios;
> esquivad los perjudiçios,
> la razón obedeced. [9]

As a didactic poem inspired by the death of Don Álvaro de Luna, the *Doctrinal de privados* sounds a warning to all *privados* to follow a path of moral rectitude and to avoid the errors which led John II's favorite to his execution; but in a more universal sense it also underscores the theme of the vanity of human glory, a theme characteristic of so much Spanish medieval and baroque literature. It is the same theme which inspired the verses that Jorge Manrique devoted to Don Álvaro in the *Coplas* (previously quoted), the same theme which Boccaccio voices repeatedly in his *De casibus virorum illustrium*.

Nothing of much importance on the subject of favoritism appeared for more than a century and half after Santillana's *Doctrinal,* probably because no favorite was allowed to occupy center-stage during the long reigns of Charles V and Philip II. To be sure, throughout the sixteenth century references to the perils of *privanza* — perils affecting both the *privado* and the state — occur sporadically in various kinds of literature, but in the main such references lack urgency, if not sincerity. The grand old poet Cristóbal de Castillejo, writing during the reign of Charles V, added the ephemeral nature of *privanza* to the long list of his disillusionments contained in his *Diálogo y discurso de la vida de corte:*

---

[9] Ibid., p. 504.

La privanza...
Cuanto más está encumbrada,
Encarecida y honrada,
Hasta el fin de la jornada
Siempre vive peligrosa
De caída,
Por holgar y estar tenida
A voluntad que no dura
Del hombre; que en esta vida
No hay prenda menos segura
Ni durable,
Más incierta y variable...

(*BAE*, XXXII, 224)

Antonio de Guevara's *Aviso de privados o despertador de cortesanos* (Valladolid, 1539), modelled after Castiglione's *Cortegiano*, is a practical guide designed to instruct its readers on how to succeed at court. Although chapters XIII and XIV are devoted largely to the subject of *Privanza*, Guevara's urbanity never permits him to come to grips with the complexities of the favorite's role. So you want to be a successful, durable favorite? Then, above all, rid yourself of arrogance and avarice:

Guárdense, guárdense, guárdense los privados de los príncipes de ser elatos superbos y mal acondicionados, porque en el corazón do reina soberbia allí arma fortuna su zancadilla.... Todos los hombres viciosos tienen excusas para sus vicios, excepto los hombres soberbios, porque si caemos en algún vicio es de flacos, mas si somos soberbios es de locos.... [10]

Noten bien los familiares de los reyes esta palabra, y es que sobrada privanza, juntamente con mucha avaricia, es imposible que se sustenten mucho tiempo en una persona, porque si quieren sustentar la privanza han de dejar la codicia, y si quisieren seguir la codicia es forzoso que han de perder la privanza. [11]

Not only is the *Aviso de privados* platitudinous, but it is also excessively cautious, since Guevara, a prototype of the prudent

---

[10] Antonio de Guevara, *Aviso de privados o despertador de cortesanos* (Paris, n. d.), pp. 172-73.

[11] Ibid., p. 180.

man nurtured by the sixteenth century, avoids concrete reference to Spanish historical figures and events.

Not so cautious nor so genteel was Juan de Horozco y Covarrubias, the Bishop of Guadix and brother of the lexicographer Sebastián de Covarrubias (who switched his surnames). In his *Emblemas morales* (first edition, Segovia, 1589) the bishop inveighs against the same vices decried by Antonio de Guevara — arrogance, ambition, and avarice — and he also offers a neat inquisitorial solution to get rid of a hypothetical "guilty" favorite: he has him burned at the stake. His castigation of the vicious *privado* (which seems to carry within it an implicit condemnation of all favorites) may be interpreted as a protest against the possible institutionalization of favoritism. Curiously, however, the "system" never really got started until a dozen or more years after the dire warning sounded in the *Emblemas morales;* and it was another dozen years — about midway through the reign of Philip III — before the literature on *privanza* began to acquire momentum.

As noted by José Maravall, the didactic writings on the art of statecraft underwent a gradual evolution. [12] During the early years of Philip III political writers continued to turn out works on the education of the prince, works still grounded on Saint Augustine's *De civitate Dei* and Saint Thomas Aquinas' *De regimine principum,* and informed with the hope that something could be done to mold the king into a paragon of civic responsibility and righteousness. No one doubted Philip's moral righteousness, but as the years wore on, it became apparent that not much could be done to change the sovereign's abulic nature. Consequently, the writers' concern began to center more and more on the ministers and counselors that the king kept about him. By 1620, near the end of Philip's reign, the emphasis had definitely changed: the futile efforts to form — or reform — the king had given way to a broad, albeit uncoordinated, campaign directed toward the proper selection and education of ministers, including the royal favorite.

---

[12] Maravall, pp. 310 ff.

Much of the doctrinal literature on *privanza* touches on one or more of the following questions: (1) Should there be a favorite — or favorites? (2) If so, how many? (3) How should the *privado* be selected and educated? (4) What are the essential qualities that the *privado* should possess? (5) Should the relationship between the king and favorite extend to personal friendship? (6) Underlying the previous questions, there existed another basic concern expressed by several writers: How to avoid an insidious Machiavellian trend in Spain? Finally, most authors — historians, essayists, and poets — admonish would-be favorites to beware the risks of *privanza,* and they set forth precepts intended to minimize those risks.

Soon after Philip IV ascended to the throne in 1621, it became apparent to many observers that the new king, like his father, would delegate much of the royal authority to his first-minister and favorite, the Count-Duke Olivares. The realization of this fact put political writers in an embarrassing position: they could not afford to provoke the ire of the all-powerful minister; they could only urge that the royal favorite, under the watchful eye of a just king, be temperate in his actions and attentive to the common good — no matter, of course, "who" the favorite and the king might be. Faced with a *de facto* situation, the great majority of commentators conceded that there should be one or more *privados,* but their opinions were often colored by theological considerations on the one hand and by personal bias on the other.

As was to be expected, there were a few writers who, as Olivares' tenure dragged on, changed their tune. Although written as a play, Francisco de Quevedo's *Cómo ha de ser el privado* (dated variously between 1624 and 1628) [13] is a heavily didactic work designed more to indoctrinate than to entertain. As the title indicates, the play presents a model favorite, one who is

---

[13] Miguel Artigas, ed. *Teatro inédito de* ... *Quevedo* (Madrid, 1927), pp. XVII-XXI, concludes that *Cómo ha de ser el privado* was written near the end of 1627 or at the beginning of 1628. For studies of the play, see Melvina Somers, "Quevedo's Ideology in *Cómo ha de ser el privado,*" *Hispania,* 39 (1956), 261-68, and Raimundo Lida, "*Cómo ha de ser el privado*: de la comedia de Quevedo a su *Política de Dios,*" in *Letras hispánicas* (México-Buenos Aires, 1958), pp. 149-56, 332-33.

loyal, prudent, selfless, industrious, incorruptible, and eminently just. This ideal minister is none other than the Count-Duke Olivares, who appears in the play under the anagram of the Marqués de Valisero.

It is obvious that when Quevedo wrote this play, he was willing to accept favoritism as a political system — provided, of course, that the favorite should continue to live up to Quevedo's high expectations. But let the corrupt *privado* beware, because:

> Si algún Ministro o Privado
> justamente está culpado,
> le cortarán la cabeza
> en la plaza mayor.
>
> (Act I, pp. 5-6)

Similarly, in the first part of his *Política de Dios,* dedicated to the Count-Duke Olivares and published in 1626, Quevedo was still willing to admit the necessity of favoritism, but he remained adamant that bad ministers should not go unpunished. Rather, public example should be made of them, as stated in the heading of Chapter IX, "Castigar a los ministros malos públicamente es dar exemplo, a imitación de Christo, y consentirlos es dar escándalo, a imitación de Satanás...." [14]

But by the time Quevedo had finished the second part of the *Política de Dios* (completed by 1635, not published until 1655), he had already begun to take an unfavorable view of *privanza,* probably because he had become increasingly disillusioned with Olivares, with whom his relations had sharply deteriorated. Quevedo now prescribed for the favorite an impossible role: just as the perfect prince should imitate Christ, so the model favorite should be cast in the mold of Saint John the Baptist. Addressing the king, Quevedo exclaims:

> Sacra, Católica, Real Magestad, dé Dios a V. M. ministros imitadores del Bautista; que sean medios iluminados, y voz del que clama en desierto; que vistan pieles de Camellos, y no de Leones, y Lobos; que coman lan-

---

[14] Francisco de Quevedo, *Política de Dios. Govierno de Christo,* ed. James O. Crosby (Madrid, 1966), p. 72.

gostas, y no sean langostas que coman los pueblos; que
contradigan las grandes mercedes, antes que solicitarlas:
que digan lo que no han de callar, y no callen lo que
deben dezir. [15]

As noted by Raimundo Lida, following the fall of Olivares in
1643, Quevedo made it clear in the *Panegírico a la Majestad
del Rey nuestro Señor don Felipe IV* that he had arrived at the
conclusion toward which his gnawing disillusionment had long
been leading him: the delegation of royal authority to ministers
should cease once and for all. Lida summarizes Quevedo's thought
in the following words:

En su comedia, veinte años antes, Quevedo había que-
rido pintar las calidades del perfecto privado. En su
pensamiento político final, ya no hay para qué distinguir
calidades. El destino de España está sellado; todo se ha
simplificado trágicamente. ¿Para qué sutilizar? A la pre-
gunta de 'cómo ha de ser el privado', Quevedo responde
ahora simple y amargamente: Lo mejor es que el privado no sea. [16]

Although Quevedo was not alone in opposing the delegation of
royal authority to favorites, the majority of his contemporaries
reconciled themselves to the situation at hand and moved on to
other considerations, including the question: How many ministers
or favorites should a king have? Most writers, again mindful
of the actual relationship of their immediate kings and chief
ministers — first, Philip III and Lerma, then Philip IV and Olivares — conceded that a single minister or favorite was preferable,
provided that he was selected with extreme care. Other commentators qualify their concession by stipulating that the favorite's prerogatives should be limited to administrative matters but
that decisions on policy must be left to the monarch. The favorite

---

[15] Ibid., p. 207.

[16] Lida, p. 156. Cf. Peter Frank de Andrea, "El 'Ars Gubernandi' de
Quevedo," *Cuadernos Americanos,* 24 (Nov.-Dic., 1945), 181: "Para Quevedo, los favoritos eran su verdadera 'bête noire' .... En efecto, gran parte
de la *Política de Dios* es una virulenta diatriba contra los ministros ruines.
Con particular goce, los coloca en el infierno. Lo peor que puede suceder
a un príncipe es dejarse gobernar por un ministro."

could execute but only the king should legislate. There was, however, at least one voice that protested strongly against the single favorite: Fray Juan de Santa María, author of the *Tratado de república y politicia christiana. Para reyes y príncipes y para los que en el gobierno tienen sus veces* (Valencia, 1619). Santa María, who was not enthusiastic over favoritism in any form, held that there should be several royal ministers in order to avoid any possibility that the king might come under the domination of a single favorite.

How should the favorite be selected and educated? Influenced by Saint Thomas Aquinas' notion that the monarch's solicitation of advice from trusted counselors was a practice sanctioned by God, a few theorists argued that it followed that the selection of the royal favorite, as of the king, was the result of the operation of the Divine Will; consequently, the favorite's authority came from God. [17] The proof was to be found in the many biblical case histories in which an unlikely subject was miraculously elevated to the position of royal favorite of his king — Joseph and Pharaoh, Daniel and Nebuchadnezzar, etc. Not many writers, however, seem to have been persuaded by the extension of Saint Augustine's doctrine to include the divine right of ministers. By and large they accepted the fact that the favorite was selected by more human processes, and they concerned themselves with educating the favorite for his office.

When the theorists became convinced that it would be easier to mold the favorite than the king, works *de regimine principum,* cultivated vigorously in Spain as in the rest of Europe since the late Middle Ages, gave way to didactic manuals addressed specifically to the education of royal ministers. Accordingly, many of the precepts formerly aimed at educating the prince were refurbished and restated to apply directly to the favorite, although most writers were too circumspect toward the royal authority to lose sight of the enormous difference between king and vassal.

---

[17] As evidence of the "divine right" of favorites, Maravall, pp. 309-12, cites the arguments of Fray José Laynez, *El privado christiano, deducido de las vidas de Joseph y Daniel* . . . (Madrid, 1641), and Jerónimo Ortega y Robles, *El despertador que avisa a un príncipe católico* . . . (Madrid, 1647).

One of the most detailed preceptive treatises is Pedro Fernández Navarrete's *Carta de Lelio Peregrino a Estanislao Borbio, privado del rey de Polonia,* which bears the date of May 30, 1612, although the *Carta* was first (?) printed in the same author's *Conservación de monarquías y discursos políticos sobre la gran consulta que el consejo hizo al señor rey don Felipe Tercero* (first edition, Madrid, 1621?). [18] More practical than theoretical, Fernández Navarrete's *Carta* sets forth nineteen precepts for the conduct of the favorite, including admonitions against ambition, arrogance, and avarice, the three vices most frequently attacked by the theorists.

Fernández Navarrete's most arresting bit of advice — and certainly a practical consideration — is that the favorite should do everything in his power to win the good will of the queen: "... es cosa cierta para las tormentas de los privados no hay puerto más seguro que el amparo de las Reynas, como al contrario su disfavor es el escollo más peligroso, en que vienen a naufragar los que no las veneran y sirven." [19] In support of his contention, the author recalls the role of Queen Isabel in the fall of Don Álvaro de Luna: "Y si la [Reyna] de Castilla no hubiera fomentado la indignación del Rey don Juan el Segundo, fuera posible le hubiera faltado brío para dar la sentencia contra don Álvaro de Luna, a quien tiernamente había amado." [20] Again, with the exception of the mention of Don Álvaro de Luna, Fernández Navarrete limits himself to pointing out only Roman and biblical favorites as praiseworthy or blameworthy. And once more the perfect favorite is to be found among biblical models: Joshua, Joseph, and Daniel. But at least Fernández Navarrete, unlike Que-

---

[18] There is some confusion about the date of both the *Carta* and the *Conservación de monarquías.* In his bibliography in *La teoría española del estado en el siglo XVII,* Maravall gives the year of the first edition of the *Conservación* as 1626; he does not give a date for the *Carta.* James Lyman Whitney, *Catalogue of the Spanish Library and of the Portuguese Books Bequeathed by George Ticknor to the Boston Public Library* ... (Boston, 1879), p. 247, gives 1621 for the first edition of the *Conservación,* and May 30, 1612, as the date of the *Carta.* Citations here are to the fourth edition of the *Conservación* (Madrid, 1792), which is followed by the *Carta.*

[19] Edition cited, pp. 454-55.

[20] Ibid., p. 455.

vedo, did not make impossible demands on the favorite by insisting that he be another John the Baptist.

The busy biographer and translator, Juan Pablo Mártir Rizo, author of the *Norte de Príncipes* (Madrid, 1626), stresses three qualities as essential for the successful favorite: he must be rich, noble, and prudent — rich, because the man who needs nothing will not be moved by any price to act unjustly; noble, because the nobly born have a greater obligation to be virtuous and because they can more easily gain the respect and avoid the scorn of other nobles; prudent, because prudence is the North Star to guide all good actions. [21] But Mártir Rizo takes pains to remind the prince that the favorite, notwithstanding his rank and wealth, should continually be honored and rewarded lest he succumb to personal ambition and self-interest.

In addition to the *Norte de Príncipes*, with its general reflections on the art of statecraft, Mártir Rizo also wrote or translated a series of biographies of historical favorites (Maecenas, Seneca, Sejanus, Philippa of Catania, the Duke of Biron), biographies which later served as the primary sources of a number of fallen-favorite tragedies. The biographies will be considered when the plays themselves are examined.

A question that concerned most political theorists was whether or not the king and the favorite should be friends, and if so, what should be the nature of their friendship? Most writers agree that the king, as a human being whose position isolates him from normal social intercourse, should cherish the friendship of his favorite minister. Moreover, by definition a *privado* is one who is bound in perfect friendship to another, or, as Fray José Laynez puts it in *El privado cristiano* (Madrid, 1641), "Privado llamamos a aquél con quien a solas y singularmente se comunica, a quien no hay cosa secreta, escogido entre los demás para una cierta manera de igualdad fundada en amor y perfecta amistad." [22] It follows that the friendship between monarch and minister may even extend to intimacy, provided that their familiarity be kept within the bounds of privacy.

---

[21] Juan Pablo Mártir Rizo, *Norte de Príncipes y Vida de Rómulo*, ed. José A. Maravall (Madrid, 1945), pp. 79-81.

[22] Quoted by Maravall, p. 309.

Both king and favorite, however, must be constantly on guard to remember their different responsibilities and prerogatives. The sovereign must never permit the favorite to intrude on the exercise of his royal authority; he must never subject himself to his vassal's will. Conversely, the *privado* must never be tempted to rule his master; he should advise but not legislate. Above all, he should never overshadow the king. Perhaps the best expression of the delicate balance that should obtain in the relationship between the king and his favorite is found in Quevedo's *Cómo ha de ser el privado*. Here, reflecting on the relationship of John II and Don Álvaro de Luna, the Marqués de Valisero blames the king for upsetting the balance between friendship and fealty:

MARQUÉS
Fue gran Rey
el rey don Juan; mas le dan
culpa todas sus historias.

REY
¿Cuál?

MARQUÉS
Haberse sujetado
con extremo a su Privado. . . .

REY
¿Cómo, Marqués, siendo vos
mi Privado, estáis opuesto
a que se haga un compuesto
de la amistad de los dos,
y con estrecha amistad
estén el Rey y el Valido,
y en dos pechos repartido
un ser y una voluntad?

MARQUÉS
Sí, Señor, porque un Privado,
que es un átomo pequeño
junto al Rey, no ha de ser dueño
de la luz que el sol le ha dado.
Es un ministro de ley,
es un brazo, un instrumento
por donde pasa el aliento
a la voluntad del Rey.

(Act I, pp. 10-11)

The fear that the favorite might exert undue influence over the king led some essayists to warn against the insidious tactics of Machiavelli, although references to the Florentine are not abundant in the manuals concerning the education of the royal favorite. [23] A few writers, however, did evince an ambivalent attitude towards Machiavelli — ambivalent enough to suggest that they perceived some merit in his philosophy if one would pick and choose judiciously among his doctrines. In chapters XVI and XVII of his *Norte de Príncipes* Juan Pablo Mártir Rizo attacks the "false doctrine" of Machiavelli, but in his *Vida de Rómulo* he does not conceal his admiration for Romulus's Machiavellian *virtù* — his resourcefulness, courage, and strength. [24]

Another writer, Lorenzo Ramírez de Prado, does not mention Machiavelli by name, but he points out how useful some of the doctrines usually associated with the Italian can be to the royal minister. Chapter II, "Ha de ser el ingenio dócil y acomodado para encubrirse a sí mismo," of Ramírez de Prado's *Consejo y consejero de príncipes* (Madrid, 1617), [25] treats, among other things, the necessity of the minister's knowing how and when to dissemble — but the author first expresses a mild caveat: "Los políticos de nuestra edad distinguen, fundándose más en conveniencias humanas, que en respetos divinos, permitiendo para atajar venganzas, perdonar culpas y salvar la inocencia, el fingir y engañar oficiosamente." [26] Then speaking editorially, the author

---

[23] This is not to say that anti-Machiavellian literature was not extensive in seventeenth-century Spain; it was. The campaign against Machiavelli's doctrines was launched by Padre Pedro de Rivadeneira, *Tratado de la religión y virtudes que debe tener el príncipe cristiano para gobernar y conservar sus estados, contra lo que Nicolás Maquiavelo y los políticos de este tiempo enseñan* (Madrid, 1595); reprinted in *BAE*, LX, 449-587. See also Gonzalo Fernández de la Mora, "Maquiavelo visto por los tratadistas españoles de la contrarreforma," *Arbor*, 13 (1949), 417-49, and Donald W. Bleznick, "Spanish Reaction to Machiavelli in the Sixteenth and Seventeenth Centuries," *Journal of the History of Ideas*, 19 (1958), 542-50.

[24] Ed. Maravall, p. L.

[25] Ramírez de Prado's *Consejo* is a translation of the first twelve chapters of Book III of Jean Surlet de Chokier, *Thesaurus politicorum aphorismorum* (Rome, 1610), followed by the translator's *Notas y discursos*, which often exceed in length the original chapters on which they are based. Citations here are to Juan Beneyto's edition of *Consejo y consejero de príncipes* (Madrid, 1958).

[26] Edition cited, pp. 74-75.

justifies the use of dissimulation to achieve virtuous ends, supporting his stand by citing the biblical David as an advocate of "altruistic expedience." [27] But most Spaniards would argue that Machiavelli, as the devil's advocate, was not concerned with altruistic expedience but only with his own self-interest.

Although many Spaniards were reluctant to discuss Machiavelli's ideas in relation to the role of the favorite, some satirists were not hesitant in identifying *privados* as disciples of the perverse secretary. Probably the strongest indictment of the favorite as a Machiavellian monster is found in Antonio Enríquez Gómez, *El siglo pitagórico, y vida de don Gregorio Guadaña* (first edition, Rouen, 1644), in which the protagonist, by means of the transmigration of the soul, occupies the bodies of several individuals who represent various professions and social positions. In *Transmigración IV* the protagonist speaks of the *valido* whose body he now inhabits:

> Luego que supo fulminar las leyes
> (Descanso de los Reyes)
> Se armó de un Machiavelo,
> Libro que fue de su señor Abuelo.
>
> Fue entrando en el gobierno
> Rezando en estas horas del Infierno,
> Y quanto más sus Reglas observaba,
> Tanto más de virtud se desnudaba.... [28]

The soul then reproaches the *valido:*

---

[27] Ibid. Bleznick, p. 550, points out that several "Spaniards recommended the use of fraud, cunning, deceit, and dissimulation 'when necessary' to preserve the reputation of the ruler, to wage a successful war, or to preserve the strength of the state. In this way, they justified the alteration of absolute Christian ethics to meet the demand of practical politics. Yet the permission of immoral acts 'when necessary' could easily lead to the rise of many evils which Spaniards attributed to Machiavellian politics." Bleznick also points out that even Padre Rivadeneira, staunch moralist that he was, recommended that the prince use dissimulation to protect himself and his subjects, "but he stipulated that this had to be done in such a manner that the prince did not make himself a disciple of Machiavelli nor lose sight of Christian simplicity" (p. 549).

[28] *El siglo pitagórico,* second edition (Rouen, 1682), pp. 36-37.

Rezando en Machiavelo
¿Te quieres ir al Cielo?
Alborotando Pueblos y Naciones,
¿Quieres ganar perdones?
Con una y otra (al parecer victoria)
¿Piensas ganar la Gloria?
¡Qué lindo disparate! [29]

Not only does Enríquez Gómez despise the Machiavellian minister but he also condemns any favoritism in government, pointing out (as several dramatists also do) that the first favorite was Lucifer, who betrayed God:

Esto de gobernar es un abysmo,
Solo Dios es Valido de sí mismo,
Uno tuvo, si acaso no me olvido,
Este fue Lucifer primer Valido,
Adán entre los hombres, fue el segundo,
Uno arruinaba el Cielo, y otro el Mundo. [30]

Whereas Enríquez Gómez and Quevedo (in his later years) scorned all favorites, most of their contemporaries were sympathetic with the royal favorite because, if for no other reason, he occupied a highly vulnerable and often untenable position. The object of unrelenting envy and unconscionable criticism, the *privado* was regarded as a ready-made victim deserving of compassion. In general, the most eloquent portrayals of the perils suffered by the *privado* were inspired by the fall or disgrace of a favorite to whom the writer owed personal allegiance. In his *Historia de Felipe IV*, for example, Gonzalo de Céspedes y Meneses, reflecting on the dismissal of the Duke of Lerma, uses clichés lavishly to moralize on the hazards that threaten the favorite:

... privança es humo, y polvo, que le esparce qualquiera viento; sueño, y sombra con apariencia de verdad; rosa a la vista deleytable, pero tocada con espinas; trajedia que siempre acaba en mal; mar ancho lleno de vagíos, nauío sin velas, ni timón que está amagando igual peli-

[29] Ibid., p. 43.
[30] Ibid., p. 40.

gro, y que les deue antes servir de auiso de su perdición, que no de puerto en que saluarse, pues hasta aora no hemos visto alguno que llegase a él, ni que saliesse de su golfo, menos que muerto, o destroçado, porque el fauor de la privança es inconstante, y siempre el fin de su subir, es descender. [31]

Although the favorite may be defenseless against the ravages of bad fortune and human deceit, if he is a man of character, he has two resources with which to mitigate his cruel fate: the exercise of virtue and the stoical acceptance of misfortune. In the *Carta de Lelio Peregrino* Fernández Navarrete speaks of two kinds of virtue with which the favorite should be armed: interior, comprising the usual Christian virtues; and exterior, consisting of political sagacity (somewhat similar to Machiavelli's *virtù*). If sagacity fails, the favorite can always depend on his own rugged faith.

More explicitly, in his poem "A un privado" (perhaps addressed to his patron, Don Rodrigo Calderón), Francisco López de Zárate strikes a strong stoic note in urging a vigorous scorn of both good and bad fortune as the most efficacious remedy in combatting the vicissitudes of *privanza*. It is the same remedy expressed in the Stoics' motto *In utrumque paratus,* the same remedy prescribed in Petrarch's *De remediis utriusque fortunae.* [32] The last three stanzas of López de Zárate's poem follow:

> Llámase aquel varón prudente, y fuerte,
> Que sigue su fortuna con desprecio;
> Pues viuirá más siglos, que la muerte.
>
> ¿Qué imperio, qué victoria tuvo precio?
> Y ¿quál se iguala a aquella, que se alcança
> De propia estimación, con menosprecio?

---

[31] Gonzalo de Céspedes y Meneses, *Primera parte de la Historia de D. Felippe el IIII. Rey de las Españas* (Lisboa, 1631), p. 16.

[32] Margaret Wilson, *Spanish Drama of the Golden Age* (Oxford, 1969), p. 145, observes that both the Stoic motto and Petrarch's book provide the basic thought underlying the duality of "próspera y adversa fortuna" in Mira de Amescua's Don Álvaro de Luna plays.

No pueda tu poder, ni tu privança
Prive contigo; viuirás essento
De la injuria del tiempo, y su mudança:
A todos sirve, a nadie de escarmiento. [33]

As a brief compendium of counsel directed to the heads of
state, perhaps no more representative passage can be found than
the final paragraph of Boccaccio's *De casibus virorum illustrium,*
whose homilies and exemplary case histories influenced so many
writers on *privanza,* both essayists and dramatists alike:

> So that you may have something to rejoice about in
> success, and something to alleviate your sadness in ad-
> versity, remember to give God the greatest veneration,
> and honor Him with all your emotions. Follow after
> wisdom and embrace the virtues. Honor those who are
> worthy of honor, and serve your friends with great
> loyalty. Take advice from those who have shown wis-
> dom, and show kindness to those who are beneath you.
> Search for honors, praise, glory, and reputation, and show
> yourself worthy of the majesty you have acquired. And
> if it happens that you are overthrown, then know it oc-
> curred not because of your gift, but rather by the ini-
> quity of changing Fortune. [34]

Boccaccio's concluding remarks are addressed to rulers, not
to their lieutenants; but Spanish authors, in writing to and about
the royal favorite, often repeat his message but with an added
admonition: let the *privado* beware that his search for "honors,
praise, glory, and reputation" be motivated not by personal
ambition but only for the greater glory of his earthly and
heavenly kings.

Both the doctrinal literature on favoritism and the tragedies
of *privanza* are manifestations of the concern with which sensitive
Spaniards viewed the political scene in their country in the first
half of the seventeenth century. That the two genres influenced
one another there can be little doubt; but by necessity the

---

[33] *Obras varias de Francisco López de Zárate. Dedicadas a diferentes
personas* ... (Alcalá, 1651), pp. 112-13.
[34] Giovanni Boccaccio, *The Fates of Illustrious Men,* trans. and abridged
by Louis B. Hall (New York, 1965), pp. 242-43.

dramatists could not spend much time speculating on such questions as to whether or not there should be one or more favorites, how they should be chosen, etc. They were urgently concerned with the issues centering on the question: How does a human being respond to the forces that weigh upon his destiny? [35]

[35] Leicester Bradner, "The Theme of *Privanza* in Spanish and English Drama 1590-1625," *Homenaje a William L. Fichter. Estudios sobre el teatro antiguo español y otros ensayos* (Madrid, 1971), p. 106, observes, correctly I think, that "Spanish dramatists usually exploited the personal and emotional aspects of their tragedies of rise and fall instead of stressing the issues of good and bad government as the English usually do."

IV

GENERIC CHARACTERISTICS OF THE
FALLEN-FAVORITE TRAGEDIES

Tragedie is to seyn a certen storie
As olde bookes maken us memorie,
Of hym that stood in greet prosperitee,
And is yfallen out of heigh degree
Into myserie, and endeth wrecchedly.

(Chaucer, Prologue to the *Monk's Tale*)

I. PURPOSE

Don Álvaro de Luna's great adversary, the Marquis of Santillana, never tried his hand at drama, but as a son of the Renaissance his restless mind led him to inquire into the nature of
tragedy and comedy. Santillana's brief remarks on the tragedy
are not original, but they are illuminating for the reason that
they indicate clearly the concept of tragedy prevalent throughout
Europe during the later Middle Ages and the early Renaissance:

Tragedia es aquella que contiene en sí caídas de
grandes reyes ó príncipes, así como de Hércules, de Pría-
mo, de Agamenón, é de otros atales, cuyos nascimientos
é vidas alegremente se comenzaron é gran tiempo se con-
tinuaron, é después tristemente cayeron; é de fablar de
éstos usó Séneca el mancebo, sobrino de otro Séneca, en
las sus tragedias, é Juan Boccaccio en el libro de *Casibus virorum illustrium*. [1]

---

[1] In the *Prohemio* to Santillana's *Comedieta de Ponza*, in *Epistolario
español*, ed. Eugenio de Ochoa, BAE, LXII, 11. The Spanish translation of

Santillana's definition of tragedy, written in 1444, does not differ essentially from that given by Chaucer about a half century earlier in the *Monk's Tale*. The definitions given by both the English and the Spanish poets are worthy of note for two reasons: (1) there is no implication that tragedy must necessarily be composed in dramatic form; [2] (2) tragedy was conceived of, in terms of content, as belonging to the *de casibus* tradition (of which Boccaccio's book offered the most immediate example). The purpose of tragedy, as understood by Chaucer and Santillana, is also clear: to provide moral *exempla* showing the fall of man from prosperity to disaster, for even the mighty, through their own misdeeds or the malice of others, or simply through mischance, cannot avoid the suffering and death which have been the common lot of mankind since the Fall.

Although the ideas on tragedy as a discrete dramatic form were refined during the century and a half separating Santillana's definition from the earliest fallen-favorite plays, the concept of tragedy as moral *exempla*, linked with the *de casibus* tradition, remained virtually unchanged. The purpose of the tragedies of *privanza* is well expressed in the admonition contained in the *Crónica del rey Juan II* regarding the fall of Don Álvaro de Luna: "Pues los que con tanto estudio trabajáis por haber estados,

---

Boccaccio's *De casibus virorum illustrium* was begun before 1407 by Pero López de Ayala and finished in 1422 by Alonso de Cartagena. It was first printed in Seville in 1495 with the following title: *Aqui comiença vn libro: que presento vn doctor famoso de la cibdad de Florencia llamado Juan bocacio de cercaldo a vn cauallero su amigo: que auia nombre Maginardo mariscal de la reyna de Sicilia: en el qual se cuentan las caydas et los abaxamientos que ouieron de sus estados en este mundo muchos nobles et grandes caualleros: por que los omes no se ensoberuezcan con los abonda-mientos de la fortuna.* For additional bibliographical information on Spanish translations of Boccaccio's book, see Marcelino Menéndez Pelayo, *Orígenes de la novela* (Santander, 1948), II, 350-51.

[2] It is also clear that Santillana did not think of comedy as an exclusively dramatic form. Arnold G. Reichenberger, "The Marqués de Santillana and the Classical Tradition," *Iberoromania*, 1 (1969), 14, quotes Santillana's definition of comedy ("comedia es dicha aquella [manera de fablar], cuyos comienzos son trabajosos, e despues el medio e fin de sus dias alegre, goçoso, e bien aventurado; de esta uso Terencio peno [púnico, africano], e Dante en el su libro"), and concludes that, "It is obvious that Santillana had no idea that *comedia* is a term belonging to the drama."

riquezas, dignidades, mirad qué fin ovo toda la gloria, todo el tesoro, todo el mando, todo el poder deste Maestre e Condestable. . . ." [3]

II. PLOT

In the dedication of his play *Los muertos vivos* to his fellow dramatist Damián Salucio del Poyo, Lope de Vega wrote:

> Lo que la antigüedad llamaba *llevar vasos a Samoa,* dice el adagio vulgar, *hierro a Vizcaya.* Esto es dirigir a V. m. una comedia, habiendo las muchas que ha escrito adquirido tanto nombre, particularmente *La próspera y adversa fortuna del Condestable Ruy López de Avalos,* que ni antes tuvieron ejemplo, ni después imitación. [4]

Lope's reference to Poyo's two plays (written as early as 1604, if not earlier) [5] is significant, for presumably he meant that they were unique in their time because of their subject matter, that is, the rise and fall of a royal favorite. However, if Lope was correct in saying, at the time he wrote the dedication, that Poyo's plays on Ruy López de Ávalos had not been imitated, that situation was not long to continue.

Poyo's two plays on Ruy López de Ávalos are not tragedies because the favorite, exiled in disgrace from Castile, is vindicated before his natural death. However, Poyo himself wrote the first full-fledged tragedy on the fall of a royal favorite, *La privanza y caída de don Álvaro de Luna,* which differs dramatically — and

---

[3] *BAE,* LXVIII, 691.

[4] *Obras de Lope de Vega, publicadas por la Real Academia Española (nueva edición),* VII (Madrid, 1930), 639. The date of composition of Lope's dedication is uncertain. *Los muertos vivos,* first printed in Lope's *Parte XVII* (1621), is believed by Morley and Bruerton to have been written between 1599 and 1602 (*The Chronology of Lope de Vega's "Comedias"* [New York, 1940], pp. 35, 361). Salucio del Poyo died in 1614; hence, the dedication was written before that time.

[5] Poyo's *La próspera fortuna* was performed in Madrid in May, 1604 (H. A. Rennert, "Notes on the Chronology of the Spanish Drama," *Modern Language Review,* 2 [1906-07], 332). Both *La próspera fortuna* and *La adversa fortuna* were performed in Barco de Ávila in 1605 (Rennert, *The Spanish Stage in the Time of Lope de Vega* [New York, 1909], p. 196).

historically — from the López de Ávalos plays in that the hero suffers an ignominious death. [6] But taken together, *La privanza y caída de don Álvaro de Luna* and the two-part *Próspera* and *Adversa fortuna de Ruy López de Ávalos* provide the structural model and the thematic and dramatic properties of several "imitations" that followed one another in rapid succession after the reign of Philip III. Moreover, *la próspera y adversa fortuna* became standard words in the titles of both single and two-part plays to indicate the rise and fall of an ill-starred favorite.

La privanza y caída de don Álvaro de Luna is typical of one group of fallen-favorite tragedies: those which concern the fall from prosperity to adversity of a single protagonist — or, in Aristotelian terms, its plot is single in its issue in that there is but a single change of fortune and that is from good to bad. Apparently Aristotle was disturbed by tragedies with a "double thread of plot" because he viewed them as necessarily involving good and bad characters, with "an opposite catastrophe for the good and for the bad"; [7] however, what he did not foresee — or what he neglected to comment on — was a type of tragedy involving the double change of fortune of two "good" characters. Later dramatists, unmindful of Aristotle's strictures and ignoring the example of Poyo's *La privanza y caída de don Álvaro de Luna* with its plot of single issue, did not hesitate to construct plots involving the change of fortune of two or more characters. [8]

---

[6] The exact date of composition of *La privanza y caída de don Álvaro de Luna* is not known, but it may have been written in 1601 or earlier. On April 17, 1601, a play entitled *Don Álvaro de Luna* was performed in Getafe by the company of Alonso de Morales (Noël Salomon, "Sur les représentations théâtrales dans les 'pueblos' des Madrid et Tolède [1589-1640]," *Bulletin Hispanique*, 62 [1960], 417). The *comedia* in question could be Poyo's.

[7] Aristotle's *Poetics* is too well known for it to be necessary to give page references for the quotations cited. I have used S. H. Butcher's translation, edited by Milton C. Nahm (New York, 1948). Sections VI-XVI are most pertinent to the discussion that follows.

[8] One of Aristotle's Spanish disciples, Jusepe Antonio González de Salas, defended the tragedy of *doblada constitución*, "donde con grande claridad se ven introducidos dos distinctos i lastimosos successos, que discurriendo por todo el cuerpo de la Tragedia, juntos la forman i componen"; and he goes on to say that the plot of *doblada constitución* involves two changes of fortune (*dos mudanzas*), but that they do not necessarily violate the unity of action (*Nveva idea de la tragedia antigva*, II, 35).

In his studies of Mira de Amescua's plays, Claude Anibal called attention to a frequent structural principle of their plot construction: the "simultaneous balanced and graduated rise and fall of two characters." [9] No better example of this principle can be found than that offered by Mira's *La próspera fortuna de don Álvaro de Luna y adversa de Ruy López de Ávalos,* whose title indicates its double thread of plot and the simultaneous rise of the new favorite and the fall of the old. Of course, Don Álvaro's fall provides the subject of Mira's second play, *La adversa fortuna de don Álvaro de Luna.* What distinguishes Mira de Amescua's plays from Poyo's *La próspera fortuna de Ruy López de Ávalos* and *La adversa fortuna de Ruy López de Ávalos* (other than the fact, as previously mentioned, that the latter do not have a tragic conclusion) is simply that Mira's plays dramatize the change of fortune of two characters, whereas Poyo only hints that Don Álvaro de Luna will replace Ruy López as the royal favorite. Don Álvaro does not appear as a character in Poyo's plays on Ruy López de Ávalos.

In sum, with regard to plot construction, the tragedies of *privanza* fall into one of two categories: (1) those like Poyo's *La privanza y caída de don Álvaro de Luna* in which the fall from prosperity to adversity of a single hero is dramatized; (2) those like Mira de Amescua's Ruy López de Ávalos — Don Álvaro de Luna plays in which the simultaneous fall of one favorite and the rise of another are shown. The history of favoritism offered abundant examples of both kinds; it was up to the dramatist to choose.

The plots of most tragedies of *privanza* are, of course, made up of incidents other than those which deal directly with the fall of the royal favorite. Many of the plays, like the Spanish *comedia* in general, contain comic elements; a few have fully developed comic subplots. Others have romantic subplots, relying on love, jealousy, and honor — the staples of cape-and-sword drama — to sustain interest in the dramatic action. Antonio Coello's *El Conde*

---

[9] Claude E. Anibal, ed. Mira de Amescua, *El arpa de David* (Columbus, Ohio, 1925), p. 154. Not surprisingly, Lope de Vega may have been the first Spanish dramatist to employ the "simultaneous balanced and graduated rise and fall" of two favorites, but his *Mudanzas de fortuna* (dated 1604-07 by Morley-Bruerton, p. 223) does not end tragically.

de Sex, for example, is so freighted with intrigue surrounding the love triangle of the Earl of Essex, his sweetheart Blanca, and Queen Elizabeth that the major political issues of the play are all but obscured. In Juan Pérez de Montalbán's *El Mariscal de Birón* the first conflict between Henry IV and his favorite arises over their rivalry for a woman's love. In Juan Ruiz de Alarcón's *El dueño de las estrellas* Lycurgus commits suicide, partly because the king has designs on his wife. The Empress Teodora in Mira de Amescua's *El ejemplo mayor de la desdicha* conspires to bring about the fall of Belisarius because he jilted her. And even in so powerful a tragedy as Mira's *La adversa fortuna de don Álvaro de Luna* the events leading up to the hero's demise are suspended when Doña Juana, Don Álvaro's wife-to-be, erupts into a jealous rage when she discovers the portrait of a foreign princess in his possession.

It matters not that the sources of the fallen-favorite tragedies are largely historical or semi-historical: Spanish audiences never seemed to tire of amorous kings and princesses, and the dramatists were seldom remiss in supplying gratuitous romantic fictions. Calderón sums up the hackneyed amorous conflicts involving king, favorite, and lady in Part I of *La hija del aire* (which is not a tragedy of *privanza,* although favoritism is an important element in the play). Here, Menón tells the king why he has kept his sweetheart Semíramis hidden:

> No, señor, cansado está
> el mundo de ver en farsas
> la competencia de un Rey,
> de un valido y de una dama....
> Saquemos hoy del antiguo
> estilo aquesta ignorancia,
> y en el empeño primero
> a luz los efectos salgan.
> El fin de esto siempre ha sido,
> después de enredos, marañas,
> sospechas, amores, celos,
> gustos, glorias, quejas, ansias,
> generosamente noble
> vencerse el que hace el monarca. [10]

---

[10] A. Valbuena Briones, ed. Calderón, *Obras completas*; Tomo I, *Dramas* (Madrid, 1966), p. 736. Sister Mary Austin Cauvin, "The *comedia de*

Notwithstanding Calderón's words, the authors of the fallen-favorite plays felt that their audiences demanded, not only in "farces" but also in tragedies, "la competencia de un Rey, de un valido y de una dama."

III. The Tragic Hero

There is little evidence that Spanish dramatists of the Golden Age — or, for that matter, other contemporary European dramatists — ever defined for themselves the qualities that a tragic hero should or should not possess. [11] In his *Arte nuevo de hacer comedias en este tiempo* (1609), Lope de Vega says nothing about the tragic hero, nor does Tirso de Molina in his defense of Lopean drama included in *Los cigarrales de Toledo*, although both Lope and Tirso, as well as other Spanish dramatists, were much concerned about the decorum of their characters. [12] In the dedication to Guillén de Castro of *Las almenas de Toro*, Lope speaks briefly of tragedy, mentioning that Sancho II and other characters in the play "son *dignas* de la tragedia." [13] Worthy because of their rank, worthy because of their personal qualities,

---

privanza in the Seventeenth Century," p. 460, refers to the variations of the love triangle as the "*rey enamorado, infanta-privado, reina-privado* themes."

[11] Cf. Hardin Craig, *The Complete Works of Shakespeare* (Glenview, Illinois, 1961), p. 501: "At that time no writer knew theoretically much about the depiction of character. The doctrines of this form of art did not take shape for a long time after the year 1600. But Shakespeare, if he did not know theory, was a great and natural practicioner and filled his canvas with so many varied portraits that the art of character drawing was implicit in his work." It is curious that even French dramatists, in spite of their talent for formulating their perceptions, were so long in qualifying the tragic hero as an "admirable" person. J. E. Gillet, "A Note on the Tragic *Admiratio*," op. cit., pp. 233-38, observes that in the *Examen* (1651) of his *Nicomède* Pierre Corneille seems to have been the first one in his century to identify Aristotle's *admiratio* with the admiration aroused by a virtuous character.

[12] Duncan Moir, p. 209, notes that of all the doctrines subscribed to by Golden Age dramatists, decorum "would seem to be, in many ways, the most important principle of all."

[13] *Obras de Lope de Vega, publicadas por la Real Academia Española,* VIII, 79.

or worthy because of the tragic events in which they become enmeshed? Lope does not say. [14]

The academic critics of the period do not provide much help in defining the tragic hero. Confronted by Aristotle's observation that the tragic hero should not be "eminently good and just" but should be "better than worse," Spanish theorists generally spoke about the hero in terms as imprecise as those of the Master. And often they temporarized by characterizing the hero as being *medio* or *indiferente*. In his *Nueva idea de la tragedia antigua* (1633), González de Salas attempts to explain why the *medios* or *indiferentes* are the most appropriate tragic heroes (accents added):

> Esta doctrina de Aristóteles de los Indifferentes entre Maldad i Virtud se confirma más, considerando, que la maior parte de los hombres son de este género, pues es cierto son muchos menos los extremadamente Virtuosos i perfectos; como también los rematadamente de perdidas costumbres: i assí de essotra Medianía es el maior número; i por esta razón los exemplos de los semejantes tienen respecto a la maior parte de el Auditorio, para poder excitar con su semejanza más comúnmente los affectos repetidos (I, 63-64).

Faced by the dramatists' silence and the theorists' rehash of Aristotle, modern critics (who have always shown a propensity to redefine the tragic hero) can only deduce any special qualities that the hero should possess from the examples that emerge from the mass of Spanish drama. In the case of the heroes of the fallen-favorite plays, the task is not difficult.

On the whole, the authors of the tragedies of *privanza* were not satisfied to present a tragic protagonist who was merely *indiferente*. They tended to populate their plays with exemplary heroes ("los extremadamente virtuosos y perfectos") or with exemplary villains ("los rematadamente de perdidas costumbres"),

---

[14] It is probable, I think, that Lope was referring to the Horatian doctrine of the dignity of the characters because of their rank, a doctrine which became firmly established in the Renaissance canon of tragedy. See J. E. Spingarn, *A History of Literary Criticism in the Renaissance*, 2nd ed. (New York, 1930), pp. 60-65.

depending upon how they viewed the institution of favoritism and how they responded to its agents. Moreover, the all-virtuous hero or the consummate villain would serve equally well to carry out the purpose of the plays: to provide moral *exempla* showing the fall of man as an ineluctable fact of human experience. After all, did not Boccaccio include in his *De casibus virorum illustrium* figures as disparate as the noble-hearted Marcus Atilius Regulus and the infamous Nero for the purpose of showing that fortune knows no favorites?

Golden Age dramatists ranged far beyond Spanish national history in search of exemplary heroes or villains, but it is worthy of note that the favorites in the plays based on Spanish history are, with few exceptions, admirable men whose downfall is brought about, not by their own misdeeds, but by misfortune or the treachery of others who conspire against them. Most dramatists, in addition to being committed to exploring the risks of favoritism, were also interested in examining the character of the favorite in relation to the character of the king under whom he served. To this end, they brought together kings and favorites in all possible combinations, as observed by José Maravall in speaking of the several biographies composed or translated by Juan Pablo Mártir Rizo:

> ... Mecenas será para Mártir Rizo el buen Privado con un buen Rey; Séneca, el buen Privado con un mal Rey; Birón, el mal Privado con buen Rey. Y en las traducciones recogerá otra vez esta grave cuestión, y Seyano le dará ocasión de presentarnos el mal Privado con mal Rey, y Felipa Catanea el mal Privado que domina e inclina malamente a un Rey, relación que en este caso se da entre mujeres. Todo el cuadro de combinaciones posibles está agotado en el conjunto de estas obras. [15]

By and large, all favorites — the good and the bad — are ambitious and vainglorious, although their ambition and vainglory are inspired by different motives. The bad ones (Sejanus, Biron, Philippa of Catania) offer little complexity. Their sole

---

[15] José A. Maravall, ed. Juan Pablo Mártir Rizo, *Norte de Príncipes* (Madrid, 1945), p. LI.

preoccupation is personal aggrandizement; their lust for power is seldom adulterated by concern for the welfare of others. They — and especially Sejanus and Philippa of Catania — are Machiavellian villains in action. And since they were intended to serve as reprehensible examples, it is no wonder that the playwrights who dramatized their careers chose as sources those works in which their subjects are most thoroughly vilified. A case in point is Juan Pérez de Montalbán's *Amor, privanza y castigo,* which borrows details of plot from Tacitus's *Annales* but whose portrait of Sejanus as an unrelieved monster was inspired by a Spanish translation of Pierre Matthieu's biography of the Roman tyrant. Vicencio Squarçafigo's translation, *La vida de Elio Seyano,* ends with the following paragraph: "El [Seyano] quedará para siempre por exemplo prodigioso de suma maldad y ambición; y su trágico fin nos muestra que nunca paró bien el poder mal adquirido; que no se ha de juzgar la felicidad hasta la muerte, el día hasta la noche, el edificio hasta que esté acabado." [16]

No historian has ever presented Sejanus as a lovable character, but for the purpose of depicting him as an "exemplo prodigioso de suma maldad y ambición," Montalbán chose to follow Squarçafigo's translation which gives a relatively favorable portrait of the ruthless Tiberius in order to denigrate by comparison the latter's one-time favorite. Such is the literary fate of the bad *privados*: their villainy must be magnified so that their ambition may be further reviled.

In contrast to the villains stand the faultless favorites. There are not many of them — notably, Belisarius in Mira de Amescua's *El ejemplo mayor de la desdicha* and Duarte Pacheco in Jacinto Cordero's two-part play, *La próspera* and *Adversa fortuna de Duarte Pacheco* — but with their massive virtue they compensate for the wickedness of their lesser fellows. They seek the welfare of others, they remain incredulous when others do harm to them, they return good for evil. Belisarius and Duarte Pacheco are not tainted by personal ambition and vainglory, except insofar as they want to be remembered for their good works; but, because

---

[16] *Vida de Elio Seyano. Compuesto en Frances por Pedro Matheo, Coronista del Christianissimo Luys XIII. Rey de Francia. Traduzida en Castellano por Vicencio Squarçafigo ... En Barcelona ... Año 1621.*

of their goodness and lack of perception, they become victims of other men's treachery. Their tragic fall underscores the fact that even the virtuous are not exempt from the perils of *privanza*.

The most convincing tragic heroes among the fallen-favorites are the *medios* or *indiferentes* because they respond more humanly and unpredictably to the impulses of ambition and vanity. They hunger after power, but at the same time they gratify themselves by distributing largesse and creating beneficiaries, heedless of the fact that they often usurp the king's prerogatives. They are highly theatrical and constantly overplay their roles, but they demand immediate and continuous applause. Conscious or not of their "role-playing," they often delude themselves by mistaking self-righteousness for righteousness. Don Álvaro de Luna is their prototype.

As Salucio del Poyo and especially Mira de Amescua reviewed the chronicles on Don Álvaro's life, one thing above all struck them about his grandiose humanity: his ambition and vanity were motivated by "immortal longings" that could never be satisfied with merely heroic accomplishments. He must emulate God Himself. Several favorites enjoy playing God, but only Don Álvaro, always larger than life, can convince himself that his death is a reenactment of the Passion of Christ. [17]

But whether they are admirably or vilely flawed, all favorites — the good and the bad — have certain traits in common. All are intrepid men, all are over-zealous, all tend to theatricalize their lives and demand center-stage. And, in different ways, all are arrogant: the wicked, in their smug cleverness and insolence; the good, in their presumptuousness and self-righteousness. It is their arrogance, of course, that so often leads to their downfall; it is the nature of their arrogance that determines the emotional response to their demise.

---

[17] In recent years several Spanish secular plays have been interpreted as allegories of the Passion of Christ. This matter is discussed briefly in the following chapter on the Don Álvaro de Luna plays.

IV. Themes

In his edition of Lope de Vega's *La Dorotea,* Edwin Morby
makes the following generalization concerning the "only source"
of tragedy:

> La fuerza inconstrastable que se alza ante el individuo
> —sea del hado, de los planetas, de la predestinación, del
> pundonor o del determinismo psicológico— se impone
> estéticamente en toda época, como fuente única de la
> verdadera tragedia. Puede reflejar las más íntimas con-
> vicciones del artista, o tener muy poca o ninguna rela-
> ción con ellas. [18]

As indicated by the titles of several plays — *próspera* and
adversa fortuna — the mutability of fortune is an abiding theme
in the tragedies of *privanza.* Fortune is the irresistible force
against which the hero is pitted. Fortune provides, as it were, the
mythical context in which the action is set. It accounts for the
rise and fall of the favorite. It yields, if not a moral justification,
an explanation for everything that happens. In short, the mutability of fortune is to the tragedy of *privanza* what fate is to
Greek tragedy.

Spanish moralists and poets from the fifteenth through the
seventeenth centuries never tired of writing about the influence
— or lack of influence — of fortune, fate, and astrology on the
lives of men — just as twentieth-century Hispanists never seem
to tire of writing about the attitude of classical Spanish authors
toward fortune, fate, and astrology. The literature from both
camps — the early writers and the later scholars — is abundant. [19]
The prevalent popular notion in the Middle Ages regarding
fortune, as opposed to the authoritative orthodox view held by
most churchmen and writers, is well summed up in A. Graf's
statement: "The populace ... never abandoned faith in one or
more powers, occult and irresistible, distinct and separated from

---

[18] Edwin S. Morby, ed. Lope de Vega, *La Dorotea* (Berkeley, 1958),
p. 398, n.
[19] See n. 16 of chapter II.

the divine will, and variously designated, as the case might be, by the name of destiny, fortuna, or astrological influence." [20]

The orthodox view is well expressed by the seventeenth-century essayist-novelist Baltasar Mateo Velázquez, who, in *El filósofo del aldea,* rejects fate and fortune as empty superstitions but admits astrological influence, although the stars can never overcome man's free will (accents added):

> *Conuersación quarta,* "De la buena, y mala fortuna." Ellos [los gentiles] entendían, que el Hado era cosa inhabitable, y nosotros sabemos, que no ay Hado ni Fortuna, antes es cosa de juego, y burla; porque los sucessos que vemos en el mundo, vnos en fauor de los hombres, y otros en disfauor suyo, todos son ocultos, y secretos caminos de los juizios de Dios, que en esta vida mortal no alcançamos: assí vn grande Doctor dixo: Que estos nombres, Hado, y Fortuna, son hablillas de viejas, y inuenciones de necios, que lo que se perdió, o por su pereça, o poco saber, lo atribuyen a la fuerça del Hado, a su mala Estrella, y a su corta Fortuna. No os niego yo la verdad Filosófica, y Astrológica, de que los Sinos, y Planetas influyen en estos inferiores; pero no por esso hemos de confessar, que tan necessario que no se ponga encima de la inclinación natural, el uso de la buena razón, y la libertad del libre albedrío, de que Dios dotó a la criatura hombre. [21]

---

[20] A. Graf, *Miti, leggende e superstizioni del Medio Evo;* cited by Howard R. Patch, *The Goddess Fortuna in Medieval Literature* (Cambridge, Mass., 1927), p. 208.

[21] *El filosofo del aldea, y sus conversaciones familiares, y exemplares, por casos, y sucessos casuales, y prodigiosos. Su Avtor. El Alferez Don Baltasar Mateo Velazquez* (Zaragoza, s. a.), fols. 49v.-50r. A more pointed statement to the effect that fortune is always subject to God's will is found in an eighteenth-century *comedia de privanza,* Joseph Julián de Castro's *Más vale nunca que tarde* (Valencia, 1763). Federico, a loyal favorite unjustly imprisoned and condemned to death, muses on the cause of his plight:

> Esta [causa] es Dios, único móvil
> de la humana variación,
> que eso de que la fortuna
> tenga tal jurisdicción
> el Gentil puede creerlo,
> pero el Católico no.   (p. 25)

The opinion on fortune expressed by most Spanish writers is summed up by Otis Green, who distinguishes between what he calls *Fortuna de tejas arriba* and *Fortuna de tejas abajo*: "The first is in the final analysis equated with God's will: *No hay más Fortuna que Dios,* wrote Calderón. The second is a personification of the disorder, the vicissitudes, the ups and downs of human life, equated with human prudence during the up periods and with human stupidity or passionate willfulness during the down periods." [22] Although the authors of the fallen-favorite tragedies often point to God's will as the ultimate cause to which man must reconcile his fate, it is in the arena of *Fortuna de tejas abajo* where he must work out his destiny. As Howard Patch puts it, "Fortune's powers have to do with more secular matters, and we find her particularly associated with the world (which, adopting her qualities, becomes more than ever 'mundane') and the court. Both the world and the court are fickle." [23] It is, of course, in the world and the court where the resourcefulness of the favorite is matched against the caprices of fortune.

The theme of fortune is rendered in various ways in the tragedies of *privanza*: dramatically, in the inevitable and sudden turns of plot brought about by political intrigue; analytically, in the explicit expressions made by the characters as they reflect on the nature of the fickle goddess; poetically, in the metaphors and imagery with which fortune's influence is verbalized. By coincidence the family name of Don Álvaro de Luna, the hero of the first of the tragedies, lends itself strikingly to imagery denoting man's changing fortunes through the varying phases of the moon — now waxing, now full, now waning, eventually eclipsed. The lunar imagery will be discussed in greater detail in the analysis of the ballads and plays on Don Álvaro de Luna, but suffice it to say now that many Spanish poets and dramatists clothe the theme of the inconstancy of fortune with the imagery of the ever-changing moon, no matter whose decline is being treated. For example, in Lope de Vega's *La hermosa Ester* (in which favoritism is of major importance) the treacherous Amán, realizing that his days of power are up, laments:

---

[22] Otis Green, *Spain and the Western Tradition*, II, 280.
[23] Patch, pp. 58-59.

Acabó ya la fortuna
de mostrarme su inconstancia,
que una misma consonancia
hace con la varia luna.
En llegando a desear,
la llena se ha de temer;
que el estado de crecer
es principio del menguar.

(*BAE*, CLIX, 171)

If the theme of the mutability of fortune is the *sine qua non* of the fallen-favorite plays, closely linked with it — or subsumed into it — are the themes of the inexorable onrush of time and the vanity of human ambition and glory. Time is fortune's greatest ally, the favorite's greatest foe. Again and again as he rides the crest of prosperity the favorite cries out to Fortuna to stop her wheel but relentlessly it turns on. Metaphorically, time is turned into rivers, into seas that wash away the sand from the favorite's feet, leaving him no footing. At the beginning of Mira de Amescua's (?) *La adversa fortuna de don Bernardo de Cabrera* [24] when all bodes well for the favorite, the musicians sing joyously:

Ebro, corre apriesa
por llegar al mar,
porque el bien y el agua
no saben parar.
Que alegres cosas
trocadas están
en la noche alegre
del señor San Juan. [25]

But the favorite, still at the height of prosperity, sees no cause for joy:

---

[24] This play was first published under the name of Lope de Vega in *Doce comedias de Lope de Vega Carpio. Parte veinte y nueve. En Huesca... Año 1634.* However, Morley-Bruerton do not think that Lope wrote the play as it now stands: "If he originally wrote the play, it has been very radically recast" (p. 251). Anibal, p. 189, makes a strong case for attributing the play to Mira de Amescua.

[25] *Obras de Lope de Vega, publicadas por la Real Academia Española (nueva edición)*, III, 63.

Roberto, dos versos
de aqueste cantar:
"Porque el bien y el agua
no saben parar",
me han dado gran pena. [26]

The authors of the tragedies of *privanza* dramatize the va-
garies of fortune and the ravages of time as resulting from
supernal forces beyond the control of man. They also show the
pernicious effects of two human impulses: the drive of personal
ambition and the lust for glory. Ironically, so the plays repeatedly
demonstrate, those human motivations over which the individual
should have control are the very agents that promote the destructive work of time and fortune, for it is ambition and vainglory that cause the favorite to expose himself in situations that
make make him vulnerable to fortune's reverses.

As is the case with much of the doctrinal literature on
favoritism, most of the fallen-favorite plays inveigh in one way
or another — often in moralizing speeches, almost always in the
example that emerges from the resolution of the plot — against
the folly of ambition and the vanity of human glory. And again,
almost always, the dramatists suggest a remedy to counteract the
ravages of time and fortune, the same remedy advocated by
the didactic writers: strive for virtue, seek simplicity and tem-
perance, ignore fortune's whims, and keep faith in God's providence.

Unfortunately, such good advice is seldom timely: it either
comes too soon, when the favorite is on the ascent and will not
listen; or it comes too late, when the favorite can no longer
impede the rush of events by turning back. Occasionally, when
there is a pause in the action, the harried favorite will take the
time to engage in nostalgic recollection of his untroubled life
before he was caught up in the turmoil of the court; occasionally
he will add a gloss to the *beatus ille* theme as he yearns to get
away from it all. But such moments are fleeting. His nostalgia
and longing are dispelled when once again he must confront the
problems brought on by his own ambition. Although the favorite

---

[26] Ibid.

seldom profits from the homilies that the writers would have him heed, those homilies are not, or should not be, lost on the spectator and the reader, for they are underscored dramatically with the favorite's blood.

The theme of friendship is an important one in several tragedies of *privanza* because it brings into conflict two orders of reality, personal relations and public politics. As in much of the doctrinal literature, the dramatists defend favoritism as a pragmatic necessity, and, at the same time, they indicate that friendship between king and favorite is both inevitable and desirable — up to a point. Because of the unusual attachment of John II to Don Álvaro de Luna, the theme of friendship is especially prominent in the Don Álvaro plays in which the king's excessive fondness only intensifies the opposition to his favorite. Don Álvaro, aware of the danger of being crushed between the conflicting realities of friendship and politics, tries on more than one occasion to temper his sovereign's generosity toward him, but the doting king is unmindful of the issues. It is tempting to look upon Don Álvaro as the hapless victim of his king's immoderation, but, as will be seen later, this is only partly the case.

In other plays the theme of friendship is sometimes employed to make more dramatic the earlier mentioned "simultaneous balanced and graduated rise and fall of two characters." In Mira de Amescua's (?) *La adversa fortuna de don Bernardo de Cabrera* and its recast by Vélez de Guevara and Rojas Zorrilla, *También tiene el sol menguante,* Don Bernardo, the king's favorite, intercedes time and again in behalf of his luckless friend Don Lope de Luna, but the latter continues to be hounded by misfortune. By the end of the play, however, Don Lope has become the king's favorite, and Don Bernardo is executed in disgrace. The friendship between the two men serves principally to point up the tremendous irony in their changed positions brought about by fortune's caprices.

Envy, called by Unamuno a "genuinely Spanish capital sin," [27] is a major theme in almost all tragedies of *privanza.* The dramatic

---

[27] Miguel de Unamuno, "El individualismo español," in *El concepto contemporáneo de España, antología de ensayos [1895-1931],* eds. Ángel del Río y M. J. Benardete (Buenos Aires, 1946), p. 105.

uses of envy are clear: it accounts for the broadening and in-
tensification of the conflict between the favorite and his enemies;
it leads to the deterioration of relations between the favorite and
the king; it often begets the revenge to which the favorite falls
victim. In Mira de Amescua's *La adversa fortuna de don Álvaro
de Luna* the protagonist's wife stresses the fact that favoritism,
although necessary for the solace and guidance of the king, leads
inevitably to the favorite's destruction, "que siempre las envidias
son fatales / al que el Rey quiere bien." [28]

In some plays envy not only spurs the favorite's rivals to
vindictive action but the nature of envy itself is analyzed at
length in the dramatic dialogue. In Salucio del Poyo's *La privanza y caída de don Álvaro de Luna* the protagonist and Don Juan
Pacheco devote some two hundred verses in a single sequence
of dialogue to probing this "cáncer del alma sangriento," verses
which include a brief catalogue of biblical and historical figures
who have been afflicted with envy — Cain, Saul — and those who
have suffered from the envy of others — Narses, Belisarius, Scipio
Africanus. But Don Álvaro de Luna, after lapsing momentarily
into his God-complex and remembering that Christ Himself was
crucified because of envy ("por ella fue en la cruz puesto"), takes
comfort in the thought that his loyalty to the king will spare him
from his enemies.

In the same play Salucio del Poyo introduces one of the most
common thematic and poetic properties of the tragedies of
privanza: the theme of envy rendered poetically by a series
of images associated with Lucifer's fall and the destruction of
innocence: Lucifer's envy of God, his revolt, his fall into hell
(where envy is engendered and continuously replenishes itself),
his corruption of man, and, finally, the atonement through the
crucifixion of Christ. Several favorites feel that they are also
sacrificial victims, but they do not wear the crown of thorns
convincingly.

Another constant of the fallen-favorite plays is ingratitude.
The theme of ingratitude is generally treated in two different
ways: from an ethical point of view, according to which ingrat-

---

[28] *NBAE,* IV, 279.

itude destroys the harmony and trust among men needed for the preservation of the social order; from a theological point of view, according to which ingratitude is an offense against God. In order to stress the ethical and social implications of ingratitude, some dramatists are fond of incorporating fables into their plays, fables that illustrate the foul consequences resulting from ungrateful conduct and which, not infrequently, contrast the ingratitude of human beings with the loyalty of animals. [29] On the theological level, the dramatists often echo Don Quijote's admonition to the galley slaves who refuse to do his biding after he has freed them: "uno de los pecados que más a Dios ofende es la ingratitud" (Part I, Chapter 22). And again, ingratitude is associated with the Lucifer motif, for just as God's brightest angel turned against Him, so the favorite's creatures *(hechuras)* turn against their earthly creator. Ironically, it is often those who owe the favorite the most who become the chief instruments in bringing about his downfall.

Victimized by fate and foe, betrayed by many of his former friends, and abandoned by his king, the doomed favorite spends his final hours in utter desolation. It is time for the theme of *desengaño,* that favored theme of the Spanish Baroque which is introduced explicitly or which insinuates itself ineluctably into so many serious works of the period. [30] The theme of *desengaño*

---

[29] Mira de Amescua was particularly fond of incorporating fables in his plays in order to emphasize a moral. See Vern G. Williamsen, "The Dramatic Function of 'Cuentecillos' in Some Plays by Mira de Amescua," *Hispania,* 54 (1971), 62-67.

[30] In order to indicate how closely the royal favorite and the theme of *desengaño* were associated in the minds of sixteenth- and seventeenth-century essayists, I quote two paragraphs from Otis Green's excellent chapter on *"Desengaño"* in *Spain and the Western Tradition,* IV, 46-47. The two paragraphs refer to a manuscript (whose title Green gives only in English translation) written by Dr. Francisco de Abila in 1576: *"Dialogues in Which an Effort Is Made to Remove the Presumption and Pride of the Man Whom the Favor and Prosperity of the World Have Rendered Proud and Vainglorius; and to Instill Courage and Spirit into the Man Who Is Weary and Bowed Down by Hardship and Adversity.* This book, obviously a reincarnation of old works of Stoic consolation such as Petrarch's *Remedies for Good and Evil Fortune,* is described by Gallardo in his bibliographical *Ensayo* [in volume I, cols. 3-4]. It is unavailable to me, but Gallardo's account of its 'Argument' is highly suggestive. The author explains that there is one reappearing personage in every one of his dialogues — the allegorical

in Spanish drama corresponds, partly at least, to the hero's recognition (anagnorisis) in classical tragedy. For that reason we should expect the condemned favorite, now thoroughly disillusioned, to turn inward upon himself and to pour out in introspective soliloquies his newly acquired self-knowledge, his new insights and awareness. This, however, is seldom the case.

The absence of probing recognition scenes may be explained in some plays in terms of the character of the protagonist. The villainous favorites are too hardened in their evil ways to learn anything about themselves or the scheme of things. Or they simply do not care. Like Tirso de Molina's Don Juan Tenorio, faced by death, they have a moment of regret that their time has run out, but they seldom experience any repentance or even remorse. And like the *burlador,* they are dispatched without much ado (although scenically, of course, the *burlador* is dispatched with much ado). On the other hand, the faultless heroes can find no grounds for self-recrimination; they can only plead their innocence and let the spectator or the reader deplore the injustice of it all.

In a few plays, however, there is an earnest attempt to make capital out of the theme of *desengaño.* Typically, after he has been sentenced to death, the favorite reflects on the course of his life, underscoring the same themes that have been considered earlier: the inconstancy of fortune, the fugacity of time and the brevity of human life (with the *topos* of the ephemeral beauty of flowers being especially common), the emptiness of human ambition and glory, and the ugliness of envy and ingratitude. And in keeping with the moral purpose of the fallen-favorite plays, the condemned hero's *desengaño* — his new awareness — leads him

---

figure of *Desengaño* — according to the following plan: in the 'Dialogue of the King's Favorite,' we have the Favorite plus *Desengaño;* in the 'Dialogue of the Man with No Friend at Court' *(desfavorecido),* we have the Unfavored One plus *Desengaño;* and so on for each of the twenty-six divisions of the volume.

All of this is instructive. *Desengaño* is here the voice of wisdom, presumably of Stoic wisdom. One is to be neither elated when he becomes the king's favorite (*Desengaño* will undeceive him) nor downcast when he has no friend at court (*Desengaño* will show him the blessedness of more humble callings than that of royal favorite)."

to realize that his greatest error lay in serving earthly kings too well, the King of Heaven not well enough.

So it is that most favorites become reconciled to their fate only because they believe it is divinely ordained; they do not express any reconciliation with the world in which they have lived. Nor do they often look upon death as a release. Although elsewhere in the plays they often confront adversity with stoical equanimity, in their final moments they tend to cling tenaciously to life. And, surprisingly, in view of the general Spanish concern with a "good" death, few favorites — even the most morally just among them — accept death with the same measure of Christian resignation and composure as, say, Don Quijote displays on his deathbed or that Don Rodrigo Calderón is said to have displayed on the scaffold.

By and large (and especially in comparison with the ballads and certain foreign plays), the authors of the tragedies of *privanza* fail to exploit fully the philosophical and esthetic potential of the hero's *desengaño* and final reckoning. Perhaps because Spanish playwrights were committed to the principle that showing is more effective than telling, they preferred to end their plays with a rousing spectacle. However that might be, no Spanish tragedy of *privanza* ends with a really great speech; there is only the eloquent swish of the executioner's blade. [31]

V. Conclusion

It is fitting to conclude the consideration of the generic characteristics of the fallen-favorite plays with a selection that combines some of their major themes and images. Several of the ballads on Don Álvaro de Luna would be suitable for the pur-

---

[31] Occasionally (and for obvious dramatic purposes) an additional scene involving the king may be included. Remorseful after he has signed the death warrant of his favorite, the king rushes to halt the execution but arrives too late (for example, in Mira's *La adversa fortuna de don Álvaro de Luna*, in Antonio Coello's *El Conde de Sex*, and in *El monstruo de la fortuna* by Calderón, Montalbán, and Rojas Zorrilla). Here, recognition on the part of the hero is subordinated to the tragic wonder (*admiratio*) of the plot, as the sight of the decapitated corpse greets the monarch.

pose, but I can think of no better coda than a speech included in Luis Vélez de Guevara's *El espejo del mundo* (which is an excellent drama of *privanza* but not a tragedy because the protagonist escapes death and his reputation is restored). Vélez fashions a scene between Don Álvaro de Luna and Don Basco de Portugal, a former favorite who has been banished and imprisoned for giving the Portuguese king displeasing advice. Don Basco urges the Spanish favorite, who is at the summit of prosperity, to learn from his disgrace:

> Puedo, amigo Condestable,
> aconsejarte, no seas
> exemplo que me acompañes
> en exemplares miserias.
> Ten la rienda al pensamiento,
> mira no te desuanescan
> altas torres, donde viuen
> la privança, y la soberuia.
> Que en sus chapiteles altos
> siruen con gloria y penas
> a los bienes de fortuna
> los priuados de veletas.
> Témela más que a ti mismo,
> y al Rey, que es muger y ciega,
> y como loca y mudable
> en dar y quitar acierta.
> Es pedir firmeza al mar
> pedirle que ella la tenga,
> porque solamente tiene
> en la mudança firmeza.
> Todas las dichas humanas
> son sombras, que quando llegan
> a estar mayores, están
> de ponerse el Sol más cerca.
> Son como Lunas también,
> porque en llegando a estar,
> en esse punto a menguar
> al mismo passo comiençan.
> Son nubes que contra el Sol
> tienen loca competencia,
> que suben a penas, quando
> baxan en agua a la tierra.
> Son Efímeras, que en Libia
> en otras sierpes se engendran,
> que nacen naciendo el Sol,

y mueren quando él se ausenta.
Es un sueño la fortuna,
que al viuo nos representa
lo que duran sus engaños,
y imaginadas quimeras.
Quien sueña que es Rey, y es Rey
aquel espacio que sueña,
que sólo tiene el dudar
algo más de diferencia.
Y es vna modorra al fin
que los sentidos sujeta,
y con la gran calentura
habla sin ellos la lengua.
Es vna casa de locos
el mundo, y ella es la Reyna,
donde cada qual al fin
tiene diferente tema.
Perdóname, Condestable,
tomarme tanta licencia
pues que sin hablar en mí
mi desdicha te aconseja.
Los que te doy son de amigo,
de vn tahur ya sin prendas
que jugó con la fortuna
y te mira a ti que juegas. . . .
Aquesto dize vn caído
que te mira en las Estrellas
por quien passó tu ventura
sólo a enseñarte paciencia. [32]

(Act III)

It remains to be seen how Don Álvaro de Luna responds to
the advice urged upon him by Don Basco.

---

[32] *El espejo del mundo* was first printed in the *Tercera parte de las comedias de Lope de Vega, y otros autores* (Barcelona, 1612). I have used the
Madrid edition of 1613.

V

THE DON ÁLVARO DE LUNA PLAYS

Los que privais con los reyes,
mirad bien la historia mía;
catad que a la fin se engaña
el hombre que en hombres fía.

(Agustín Durán, *Romancero general*,
No. 1001)

I. THE SOURCES—CHRONICLES AND BALLADS

Few figures of Spanish history have engaged the emotions of
their countrymen, past and present, as has Don Álvaro de Luna;
few have had such ardent defenders or impassioned detractors.
Some measure of Don Álvaro's hold over the Spanish imagination
may be seen in the fact that of all Castilian heroes only the Cid
has been the subject of a greater number of ballads; moreover,
of the fifty-eight ballads written about Don Álvaro before 1800,
all but one are favorable or sympathetic to him, but perhaps this
is because the earliest ballad concerning him was composed
nearly a century after his death. [1] Spaniards of the sixteenth

---

[1] Antonio Pérez Gómez, ed. *Romancero de don Álvaro de Luna (1540-
1800)*, p. 12, says of the fifty-eight ballads on Don Álvaro which have been
preserved: "Esta cifra elevada de romances coloca la desventura de Don
Álvaro en el segundo lugar, como tema histórico inspirador de la popular
musa en nuestra poesía. Corresponde al Cid el primero, y siguen, en orden
descendente, Bernardo del Carpio, el Rey Don Rodrigo, los Infantes de
Lara, Fernán González, Don Pedro el Cruel, y el Marqués de Siete Iglesias . . ." As noted earlier (in chapter II, n. 15) the earliest known ballad

century, including the balladeers, could more easily afford to take a sentimental view of the fallen favorite, since he, as the uncrowned king of Castile, no longer dominated their lives; nor did they have to contend with the antagonism of his powerful enemies. Such was not the case, of course, with Don Álvaro's contemporaries.

Most of the writers of Don Álvaro's day waited judiciously until after his execution to assail him with the pen, but his death triggered the release of a torrent of literature, much of it abusive. As remarked earlier, the Marquis of Santillana wrote his *Doctrinal de privados* in 1453, immediately following his enemy's demise. It is to Santillana's credit as a poet and as a man that his *Doctrinal* is as "philosophical" as it is vindictive in its reflections on the favorite's rise and fall. More objective than most of Don Álvaro's enemies in his appraisal of the favorite's character is Santillana's kinsman, Fernán Pérez de Guzmán, who completed most of the manuscript of his *Generaciones y semblanzas* in 1450 (first printed, together with the *Mar de historias*, in Valladolid in 1512), but he did not see fit to add the chapter on Don Álvaro de Luna until 1455, two years after the Condestable's death. Pérez de Guzmán admired him for many of his personal qualities, but reproached him for his ambition and insatiable greed:

> Fue cobdiçioso, en un grande estremo, de uasallos e de tesoros, tanto que asi como los idropigos nunca pierden la sed, ansi el nunca perdia la gana de ganar e auer, nunca recibiendo fartura su insanciable cobdiçia, ca en el dia que el rey le daua o, mejor diria, el le tomaua una grant villa, aquel mismo dia tomaria una lança del rey si vacase: ansi que deseando lo mucho non [desdeñaba] lo poco.... Pues si tanto fue cobdiçioso de villas e vasallos e riquezas, no fue menor su anbiçion de onores e premi-

on Don Álvaro was contained in the manuscript *Cancionero* of Pedro del Pozo (1547), but it is not known when the ballad was written. The first printed on the favorite (the first four lines of which appear at the beginning of this chapter) is found in the 1566 Antwerp edition of Lorenzo de Sepúlveda's *Romances nuevamente sacados de historias antiguas de la crónica de España*. Pérez Gómez observes (p. 33) that it is characteristic of Spaniards to attack viciously their contemporaries who occupy prominent positions for long periods but to take a sentimental attitude toward them after their deaths.

nencias; ca un punto non dexo de cuanto auer pudo, como el escriuio una vez a un su amigo, que en una letra le escriuio que de deuia se tenplar en el ganar, e respondiole con aquella abtoridad evangelical: *Qui venerit ad me non ejiciam foras,* que dize: "Lo que viniere a mi non lançare fuera." [2]

Notwithstanding his strong condemnation of Don Álvaro's official conduct, Pérez de Guzmán acknowleges that the Condestable helped many people, only to be repaid with the ingratitude of his beneficiaries: "ansi que en esto solo e en los fijos le fue muy contraria la fortuna, fallando en algunos poco agradecimiento de grandes bienes que les fizo." [3] Ingratitude, as indicated earlier, is a constant of the fallen-favorite tragedies. It is a major theme in the Don Álvaro de Luna plays.

Although he probably did not originate the rumors, the vitriolic historian Alonso de Palencia is primarily responsible for having propagated some of the ugliest scandals concerning Don Álvaro de Luna. Palencia's *Décadas,* written in Latin and translated into Spanish with the title of *Crónica de Enrique IV,* [4] cover only the last dozen years of the reign of John II, but neither king nor favorite escape Palencia's acid pen. All historians have been struck by John's unusual attachment to Don Álvaro, but Palencia goes so far as to suggest that one of the reasons that John had no children other than the future Henry IV (whose legitimacy he also questions) [5] was that the king was involved in homosexual relations with his favorite:

> Variaban, pues, los juicios y afirmaciones a medida del favor que sus autores disfrutaban, como quiera que el Rey ya desde su más tierna edad se había entregado en manos de D. Álvaro de Luna, no sin sospecha de algún trato indecoroso y de lascivas complacencias por parte del Privado en su familiaridad con el Rey. [6]

---

[2] Fernán Pérez de Guzmán, *Generaciones y semblanzas,* ed. J. Domínguez Bordona, in *Clásicos Castellanos,* vol. 61 (Madrid, 1941), pp. 133, 135.

[3] Ibid., p. 135.

[4] Alonso de Palencia, *Crónica de Enrique IV,* trans. A. Paz y Melia, 4 vols. (Madrid, 1904-08).

[5] Ibid., I, 5.

[6] Ibid., I, p. 6.

Palencia also repeats the rumor that Don Álvaro, fearing that they would endanger his hold over the king, ordered the poisoning in 1445 of John's first queen, María of Castile, and of her sister, Queen Isabel of Portugal, who was living in exile in Toledo:

> Dícese que, deseando librarse [Don Álvaro] de una vez de aquellos dos temores, para que la muerte de la una no fuese aviso para la otra, y contando, según se asegura, con la ausencia del Rey, había puesto mujeres de su confianza en la cámara de cada Reina, encargadas a administrar el tósigo que había de consumir sus vidas con lenta fiebre... Así pereció la esposa infeliz de un rey y madre de un príncipe aún más desdichado... Igual muerte sufrió la Reina, su hermana, víctima en el destierro del mismo crimen por la misma mano perpetrado... [7]

Later historians either ignored or refuted Palencia's insinuations; [8] and, of course, the playwrights who dramatized the career of Don Álvaro avoided making reference to the sordid rumors. However, John's deep affection for, and his utter dependence on, his favorite preoccupied future historians and dramatists who dwelled on the unusual relationship of king and vassal. Even so sober a historian as Juan de Mariana, for example, could find no better explanation for their strong attachment than a "secret cause" which could be attributed only to astral influence. After

---

[7] Ibid., I, p. 70.

[8] A. Paz y Melia, *El cronista Alonso de Palencia* (Madrid, 1914), pp. LV-LVI, makes the following comment on Palencia's insinuation of homosexual relations between Don Álvaro and John II: "Otra acusación grave que ha valido a Palencia fuertes censuras son las criminosas sospechas acerca del fundamento de la privanza de don Álvaro de Luna, 'en cuyo tiempo — dice — tuvieron origen en Castilla los infames tratos obscenos que tan vergonzoso incremento tomaron después.' Estos indignos hábitos, siempre existentes, tienen épocas de recrudecimiento, como la del siglo xv, por el trato con los moros, que hizo necesaria la Cédula de la Reina Católica, con el terrible castigo de la hoguera; en el siglo xvii, por la influencia italiana, y en nuestros días, por cínicas y extranjerizas doctrinas." Juan Rizzo y Ramírez, *Juicio crítico y significación política de Don Álvaro de Luna* (Madrid, 1865), says of Palencia's charge: "Acusación infame, hecha por los enemigos del de Luna, y que la historia debe rechazar y rechaza" (p. 43, n. 2).

stressing the absurdity of the Stoics' concept of fate, Mariana writes:

> Pero necesario es confesar hobo alguna causa secreta que de tal suerte trabó entre sí al rey de Castilla y a don Álvaro de Luna, así aficionó sus corazones y ató sus voluntades, que apenas se podían apartar.... Sin duda tienen algún poder las estrellas, y es de algún momento al nacimiento de cada uno; de allí resultan muchas veces las aficiones de los príncipes y sus aversiones. [9]

But if the mutual affection of king and favorite was ordained by the stars, it was a human act based on political motives that led to their estrangement. After the death of his wife María, John began negotiations to marry a French princess whose heralded beauty had caught his fancy. In the meantime, Don Álvaro, wishing to secure additional allies in his continuing struggles with the royal houses of Navarre and Aragon, arranged without his master's knowledge for him to marry Doña Isabel of Portugal. In his *Crónica abreviada de España* (Seville, 1482), dedicated to Isabel the Catholic, Mosén Diego de Valera (one of Don Álvaro's bitterest enemies who often acted as a messenger for the anti-Luna factions) gives the following account of the affair:

> ... desde Palencia me enbió Su Alteza a llamar a Cuenca, y venido, determinó que secretamente yo fuesse al rey de Francia, y touiese manera cómo de allá se mouiese casamiento suyo con madama Regunda, fija suya. E teniendo ya las letras del rey que menester auía, y mandamiento secreto para Pero Fernández de Lorca, que me diese lo necesario para el viage, él lo reueló al condestable, el qual tenía secretamente tratado casamiento del rey con la señora doña Isabel, madre vuestra, pensando por allí asegurar su estado, y traxo el cuchillo con que se cortó la cabeça, según se dirá donde conuiene.
>
> Deste trato con que el rey me enbiaua el condestable ouo muy grande enojo, y pasaron tales cosas entre el rey y él, de que el condestable quedó muy sentido, y el rey no poco enojado. E dende adelante sienpre lo desamó, aunque lo disimulaua con gran sagacidad. [10]

---

[9] Padre Juan de Mariana, *Historia general de España*, BAE, XXXI, 85.

[10] Mosén Diego de Valera, *Crónica abreviada de España*, chapter 124, included as a supplement in the same author's *Memorial de diversas hazañas*, ed. Juan de Mata Carriazo (Madrid, 1941), pp. 314-15.

On this occasion, which marked their first overt contest of wills, the king agreed — reluctantly — to marry the Portuguese princess, but Don Álvaro's victory cost him dearly. The *Crónica de Juan II* confirms that "después de esto [el Rey] lo desamó much más enteramente."[11] Moreover, in bringing Isabel to Spain, Don Álvaro, instead of securing an ally, brought about his doom — or, as Valera so laconically puts it, *traxo el cuchillo con que se cortó la cabeça*. Not only did Isabel prove to be a delightful partner in the conjugal bed, but taking advantage of the growing disaffection between king and favorite, she was soon plotting with her husband to engineer Don Álvaro's downfall. Mariana states it bluntly: "La suma es que entre el Rey y la Reina sin dilación se trató de la manera que podrían destruir a don Álvaro de Luna."[12] Isabel also made common cause with the Condestable's other enemies and became one of the chief instigators in bringing him to trial. It is for this reason that a century and a half later Pedro Fernández Navarrete cautioned all favorites to do their utmost to keep in the good graces of the queen.[13]

No playwright would be insensitive to the dramatic possibilities suggested by Isabel's role in precipitating Don Álvaro de Luna's fall, for here is a role involving the many faces of woman engaged in a struggle to assert her personal and royal prerogatives: the jealous wife, the ambitious queen, the conspiring adversary, the adamant prosecutor. Isabel was more than a catalyst in bringing about Don Álvaro's disgrace; she was an active agent in promoting his destruction. Understandably, the conflict between Queen Isabel of Castile and the Condestable became an integral part of all the Don Álvaro de Luna tragedies; occasionally the same conflict occurs in plays in which the two have only secondary roles.

Although the later dramatists may or may not have known the foregoing chronicles, they certainly knew and used the following three chronicles or histories which must be regarded as the primary sources for the historical facts contained in the Don Álvaro de Luna tragedies: (1) the *Crónica de Juan II*, edited by

---

[11] *BAE,* LXVIII, 63.
[12] Mariana, *BAE,* XXXI, 127.
[13] See chapter III, p. 60.

Lorenzo Galíndez de Carvajal and printed in Logroño in 1517; (2) the *Crónica de don Álvaro de Luna,* now believed to have been written by Don Álvaro's follower, Gonzalo Chacón, and first printed in Milan in 1546; [14] (3) Juan de Mariana, *Historia general de España,* first Latin edition, 1592; first Spanish edition, 1601. It will be useful to indicate in general terms the types of material, in addition to historical facts, that the dramatists borrowed from these chronicles. The influence of the sixteenth-century ballads on the plays will be considered later.

More or less the official history of the reign of John II, the *Crónica de Juan II* is a long, rambling work that documents the political, military, and ecclesiastical affairs of Castile and the public and personal lives of its leaders. As the man upon whom most of the political conflicts centered, Don Álvaro de Luna necessarily occupies much of the chronicler's attention, as, in lesser degree, do his cohorts and enemies.

Although the *Crónica de Juan II* is not always uncritical of the king, it was written from a partisan point of view that tends to favor the anti-Luna factions and to denigrate the Condestable. As a consequence, the biography of Don Álvaro de Luna that emerges from the chronicle is, on the whole, an unfavorable one, especially beginning with the year 1447 — the year of John's marriage to Isabel — when the relations between the king and his favorite deteriorated sharply. Moreover, the chronicle has about it an air of official sanction (owed to its reproduction of royal edicts, decrees, and letters) that tends to influence its reader's judgment. Especially persuasive is a long letter sent by the king to the cities and towns of Castile on June 20, 1453, to explain the causes of the imprisonment and execution of Don Álvaro. In effect, the letter, with its many detailed accusations, presents under the aegis of royal authority all the evidence accumulated against the favorite. There is, of course, no rebuttal.

Immediately following the letter, whose contents he does not discuss, the chronicler addresses Boccaccio, to whose gallery of fallen greats he would add the name of Don Álvaro de Luna:

---

[14] For a study of the authorship and bibliographical matters relating to the chronicle, see Juan de Mata Carrizo's *Estudio preliminar* in his edition of the *Crónica de don Álvaro de Luna* (Madrid, 1940).

¡O Juan Bocacio! si oy fueses vivo, no creo que tu pluma olvidase poner en escripto la caida deste tan estrenuo y esforzado varon, entre aquellas que de muy grandes principes mencionó. . . . ¿Quién pudiera tal creer, que un hombre espurio, nacido de tan baxa madre, aunque de padre virtuoso e noble, no conocido de aquel hasta la muerte, sin herencia, sin favor, sin otra mundana esperanza, en Reyno estraño, alongado de parientes, desamparado en edad pueril, ser venido en tan gran estado e tan altas dignidades? . . . Por cierto no creo en esta España ninguno de los antepasados sin corona, igual deste se puede hallar: pues miren aquellos que sola su esperanza, pensamiento, e trabajo ponen en las cosas vanas, caducas, e ciegas deste mundo, e con ánimo atento acaten y vean qué fin ovieron todas las honras, todo el resplendor, todo el señorío, todo el tesoro, todo el mando de aqueste tan poderoso, tan rico, tan temido señor. Por cierto si aquella sentencia de Bocacio debemos creer, ninguno verdaderamente se pudo decir más malaventurado que aqueste, como él afirmó: *el mayor linage de malaventuranza es haber seydo bienaventurado.* [15]

We are back on the ground of familiar homilies, ground which the chronicler continues to till in succeeding passages.

The *Crónica de don Álvaro de Luna* is more important than the *Crónica de Juan II* as a source for the plays, because it not only contains the essential information on the historical events but it also includes anecdotal material, literary references (especially to the Bible and to Seneca), and modes of expression (notably, Christological motifs and metaphors) which appear in altered form in the Don Álvaro de Luna tragedies. Equally important, the chronicle itself is a sort of extended prose drama of the rise and fall of the title character, a prose drama viewed by the author as a tragedy, not simply as a morality play. It is for this reason that the chronicle's most recent editor, Juan de Mata Carriazo, observes: "Tiene la vida de don Álvaro empaque de tragedia griega; y su *Crónica* también." [16]

---

[15] *Crónica de Juan II,* p. 691.
[16] *Crónica de don Álvaro de Luna,* p. LXII.

The author of the *Crónica de don Álvaro de Luna,* now almost certainly identified as Gonzalo Chacón who entered Don Álvaro's service as a page in 1446, was as biased in favor of his master as the chroniclers of the *Crónica de Juan II* were prejudiced against him. Thanks to that bias there is a rich coloration in the presentation of characters, especially in the delineation of the Condestable's enemies. Although most of Don Álvaro's enemies come off poorly as envious ingrates — and he, of course, as the innocent victim of their malignity — it is Alonso Pérez de Vivero, the king's *contador mayor* and the Condestable's greatest beneficiary, against whom Chacón's invectives are chiefly directed. According to Chacón, Vivero was primarily responsible for poisoning Queen Isabel against the favorite; he was the principal instigator of the conspiracy that led to Don Álvaro's trial and execution. As a consequence, Vivero, in league with Lucifer, becomes the Spanish Judas Iscariot, a name applied to him at least six times in the chronicle. He is a *perro bermejo* who betrays his creator and master, just as the biblical Judas betrayed his Master in mankind's greatest tragedy of ingratitude:

> ¡Oh iniqua trayçión, ofensora de la Magestad Divina! Comía el traydor de Judas Escariote en el plato del verdadero Dios, Redentor del mundo, e teníale tratada la muerte. Avía otrosí el traydor Alonso Pérez en muchos lugares e por muchas maneras tratado e concertado la muerte de su señor . . . [17]

Even though Chacón insists upon the parallel between the relationship of Don Álvaro — Vivero and Christ — Judas, the Condestable is not the Lamb. He orders the murder of the traitor (which Chacón neither condemns nor condones, although he justifies it *a priori* by emphasizing Vivero's repeated treachery). Moreover, for greater irony, the Spanish Judas meets his death on Good Friday. Aware of Don Álvaro's responsibility for the murder, Chacón can only admire his master's artful pretense when, in apparent distress, the Condestable reports that Vivero fell to his death because of the broken bannister on a balcony:

---

[17] Ibid., p. 338.

Non se puede negar por cierto que en este paso e en este fecho el egregio Maestre mostró e dio a conosçer el gran saber e entender suyo; e segúnd dize el Sabio, "aquel es digno de ser señor que entre otras cosas de virtud, o de prez, e de valor que en él aya, sabe algunas bezes, quando el caso lo requiere, mostrar de sí plazer, aunque no le aya, o tristeza, aunque no la sienta; ca así lo requiere la condición del mundo, e sus mudanças." [18]

Certainly there is nothing Christ-like in the revenge that Don Álvaro takes on Vivero, but after the traitor has been dispatched, the chronicler resumes the Christological and other religious motifs that attend the final days of the doomed favorite. On the eve of his arrest and imprisonment in the castle of Portillo, there is a sort of reenactment of the Last Supper attended by the Condestable and his few remaining followers. Don Álvaro cites a biblical admonition: "... dize la Escriptura, segúnd algunas vezes lo oy contar e razonar, que maldito sea el varón que confía en el hombre." [19] As will be seen later, the admonition acquires major thematic importance in the plays, especially in Mira de Amescua's *La adversa fortuna de don Álvaro de Luna* and *El ejemplo mayor de la desdicha*.

As the execution draws near, just as Christ was denied by His disciples at the Crucifixion, so Don Álvaro is denied by many of his closest adherents (even by his page Morales, whom the ballads depict as ever faithful, but not by Chacón, who remained loyal to his master to the last). [20] But what wonder, because "como sea que el ángel de perdición, Lucifer, dexó e han subçedido en este mundo muchos sequaces suyos, e muchos herederos, segúnd más o menos, de aquel pecado de ingratitud e de anbición

---

[18] Ibid., p. 335.
[19] Ibid., p. 403. Cf. "Thus saith the Lord; accursed be the man that trusteth in man and maketh flesh his arm, and whose heart departeth from the Lord!" (Jeremiah xvii. 5). The biblical admonition carries over into the ballads where it is paraphrased: "Triste el Maestre suspira, / Diciendo que a Dios ensaña / El hombre que en hombre fía"; and, "¡Y cuántas [veces] te dije a solas / Que el hombre que en hombre espera, / Hace, de Dios enemigo, / Dios el hombre, y a sí bestia!" (Agustín Durán, *Romancero general*, BAE, XVI, Nos. 987 and 1004).
[20] *Crónica de don Álvaro de Luna*, p. 422.

en que él pecó, conviene que aquellos den testimonio de sus obras." [21] So it is that Don Álvaro goes to his death as a martyr of Christ:

> Cavalgó pues el bueno e bienaventurado Maestre en su mula, con aquel gesto e con aquel senblante e con aquel sosiego que solía cavalgar los pasados tienpos de su leda e risueña fortuna. La mula cubierta de luto, e él con una capa larga negra. E como de los mártyres se cuenta que iban con el alegre cara a rescibir martyrio e muerte por la Fe de Jesucristo, semejantemente iba el bienaventurado Maestre, sin turbaçión alguna que en su gesto paresciesse, a gustar e tragar el gusto e trago de la muerte, conosçiendo de sí mismo que siendo inocente, e sin cargo nin culpa contra el Rey su señor, e por aver usado todos tienpos de bondad e de virtud e de lealtad acerca dél, le daban la muerte que yba a rescibir. [22]

Ultimately, in the portrait that Chacón gives of his master and in the interpretation that he makes of his death, Don Álvaro de Luna is a tragic hero, not because he is victimized by bad fortune, but because he possesses a flaw common to many tragic heroes — his excessive virtue that blunts his perception of reality and blinds him to the malice of others:

> Vulgarmente se suele dezir, que no ha persona más ligera de engañar, que la que tiene buen coraçón e noble, fundado en virtud, e anda con sana e entera buena fe. Buena es la lealtad e buena es la virtud en sus debidos términos, la qual consiste en el medio, e lo más ya es estremo. [23]

Then, as if he was unmindful of the final catastrophe that overtook Don Álvaro de Luna, Chacón exhorts all favorites to emulate the life and deeds of the Condestable:

> Tomad enxemplo en el nuestro Maestre e muy magnífico Condestable los que oviéredes gran privança o

---

[21] Ibid., p. 414.
[22] Ibid., p. 432.
[23] Ibid., p. 364.

çercanía con los reyes o prínçipes. . . . Acatad en la glo-
riosa vida del nuestro Maestre, e fallaredes que por
aqueste muy çierto e fiel camino lo aya enderesçado la
virtud . . . [24]

It is obvious — but worthy of note — that the example drawn
from the demise of the *bienaventurado* Maestre by Chacón differs completely from the example underscored by the writers of
the *Crónica de Juan II* as they viewed the death of the *malaventurado* Condestable. Although the author of the *Crónica de don
Álvaro de Luna* may be regarded by skeptics as an unabashed
sycophant, the importance of the chronicle as a source for the
Don Álvaro plays — and probably for the ballads too — can
hardly be exaggerated. In general, the dramatists are much more
"objective" in their presentation of the favorite, but in the chronicle they found a conception of tragedy, an ordering of themes,
and modes of expression that helped shape their plays.

Little need be said about Juan de Mariana's *Historia general
de España*, for although it is the closest in date to the composition
of the plays (and probably the history most accessible to the
playwrights), it adds little information to that contained in
the chronicles. For the most part, Mariana is unfavorable in his
view of Don Álvaro de Luna, but he does not hesitate to place
the blame for Castile's disorders on those on whom he thinks it
should fall, whether on Don Álvaro or his enemies. Mariana's
history is most useful for its relatively succinct review of the
major events in the long reign of John II. Perhaps it will be
helpful to include a chronological outline of those events, particularly as they regard Don Álvaro de Luna and are reflected in
the plays. For this purpose I shall draw on the *Crónica de Juan II,*
the *Crónica de don Álvaro de Luna,* and Mariana's history,
although there are discrepancies among them, especially with
regard to dates.

---

[24] Ibid., p. 440.

CHRONOLOGY

1385 (?) Birth of Don Álvaro de Luna in Cañete, in the province
of Cuenca; illegitimate son of Don Álvaro de Luna, *copero
mayor* of Enrique III, and of María de Cañete, called *la
Cañeta;* nephew of Pope Benedict XIII of Avignon.

1405 Birth of Juan II.

1406 Enrique III dies; succeeded by Juan II under the regency
of his mother, Queen Catalina, and his uncle, the Infante
Fernando de Antequera.

1408 Don Álvaro de Luna arrives at the court of Castile.

1410 Don Álvaro becomes a page of Juan II.

1419 Juan II is declared of legal majority; marries his cousin
María, daughter of Fernando I of Aragon. First mention
of Don Álvaro de Luna as the king's greatest favorite:
"mucho privado del Rey" and "el que más tenía la voluntad del Rey" (*Crónica de Juan II*, pp. 379, 380).

1420 The Infantes Enrique and Juan of Aragon, the King of
Navarre, and many Castilian nobles promote disturbances
in Castile. The Infante Enrique seizes Juan II in Tordesillas, but the king, aided by Don Álvaro, escapes to Montalván. The Infante Enrique marries Catalina, sister of
Juan II; Don Álvaro de Luna marries Doña Elvira Porto-
carrero.

1422 Convocation of the Cortes in Madrid. The Infante Enrique
is imprisoned there on the orders of Juan II.

1423 Ruy López de Avalos, the Condestable of Castile, is di-
vested of his titles and holdings; flees from the kingdom.
Don Álvaro de Luna is named Condestable of Castile.

1425 Don Álvaro intercedes to free the Infante Enrique, but
the latter continues to oppose him. Birth of Prince Enrique,
the future Enrique IV of Castile.

1427   First exile of Don Álvaro contrived by the Infantes of Aragon and their Castilian partisans. Incensed by the action taken against his favorite, Juan II orders the arrest of Hermán Alonso de Robles, *contador mayor* and former follower of Don Álvaro, who betrayed his benefactor. Robles later dies in prison.

     Speaking of the king's loneliness during Don Álvaro's exile (which was supposed to last a year and a half), Mariana wrties: "Dél hablaba [el Rey] entre día, y dél pensaba de noche, y ordinariamente traía delante su entendimiento y se le representaba la imagen del que ausente tenía" (p. 86).

1428   Return of Don Álvaro to the court and reunion with the king in Turégano. Ruy López de Avalos dies in exile in Valencia.

1429   Don Álvaro captures Trujillo, patrimony of the Infante Enrique of Aragon.

1430   Juan II orders the confiscation of the Castilian holdings of the Infante Enrique and of the King of Navarre. Don Álvaro is named administrator of the mastership of the Order of Santiago, of which the Infante Enrique is the Maestre. Don Fadrique de Castro, Duke of Arjona and an enemy of Don Álvaro, dies imprisoned in Peñafiel.

1431   Now a widower, Don Álvaro marries Doña Juana Pimentel, daughter of the Count of Benavente; the king and queen serve as sponsors. Campaign against Granada; Juan II and Don Álvaro participate in the victory over the Moors at Higueruela.

1435   Birth of Juan de Luna, son of Don Álvaro and Doña Juana. Juan II and the queen serve as godparents.

1436   Don Álvaro sends provisions to help Joan of Arc (called *la Pucella*) in the war against the English.

1439   Second exile of Don Álvaro but his absence is of short duration.

1440   Don Juan Pacheco, a former friend of Don Álvaro and the favorite of Prince Enrique of Castile, persuades the prince to join the Condestable enemies in their efforts to oust him.

1441   Don Álvaro is sentenced to six years' exile by judges appointed by the king — among them, Queen María, Prince Enrique, and Don Fadrique Enríquez, the Almirante of Castile. The exact duration of Don Álvaro's absence is not known.

1443   Birth of Doña Juana, daughter of Don Álvaro. Again the king and queen serve as godparents.

1445   Victory of Juan II and the Castilians in the battle of Olmedo against the King of Navarre and the Infante Enrique of Aragon; the latter dies of wounds incurred in the battle. Several Castilian leaders are rewarded for their part in the victory: Don Álvaro is named Maestre of the Order of Santiago to succeed the deceased Infante; Don Íñigo de Mendoza is named the Marquis of Santillana and Count of Real de Manzanares.

Death in Toledo of Queen Leonor of Portugal, followed shortly afterwards by the death of Queen María of Castile, wife of Juan II. Some historians repeat the rumor that Don Álvaro ordered both queens poisoned.

1447   Marriage of Juan II to Doña Isabel of Portugal. The king, who planned to marry a French princess, becomes angry with Don Álvaro because the latter arranged the marriage with Isabel without the king's knowledge.

1449   Uprising in Toledo caused by the imposition of new taxes ordered by Don Álvaro. The Condestable participates in the suppression of the rebels led by a wineskin maker of unknown name.

1451   Don Juan Pacheco, now the Marquis of Villena, and his brother Don Pedro Girón, the Maestre of the Order of Calatrava, organize the followers of Prince Enrique to oppose Don Álvaro. A meeting is held in Tordesillas to effect a reconciliation, based on their mutual opposition to Don Álvaro, of the Castilian nobles loyal to Juan II and the partisans of his son, Prince Enrique.

1453   Alonso González, secretary and *contador mayor* of Don Álvaro, and Alonso Pérez de Vivero, *contador mayor* of Juan II and formerly one of Don Álvaro's closest associates, conspire with the Condestable's enemies to bring about his downfall. Don Álvaro murders Vivero or orders him killed. Don Álvaro is arrested in Burgos and imprisoned in the castle of Portillo. Sentenced to death, he is beheaded in Valladolid on June 2.

1454   Juan II dies in Valladolid on July 21.

THE BALLADS

In his brief article, "Un romance de don Álvaro de Luna," Antonio Pérez Gómez makes the following statement concerning the extant ballads on the fallen favorite:

> Todos sin excepción, desde el publicado en 1566 por Sepúlveda, pertenecen a la clase de romances eruditos. Ningún pormenor histórico es en ellos conservado; son puras endechas al Condestable, trenos lamentando su desgracia, juegos de palabras en torno a su apellido, y consideraciones morales sobre lo quebradizo de las glorias humanas. [25]

It is certainly true that the vast majority of the ballads on Don Álvaro are "erudite" rather than "popular" in that they were written more than a century after his death and were inspired by the chronicles (as indicated by the title of Lorenzo de Sepúlveda's collection, *Romances nuevamente sacados de historias antiguas de la crónica de España,* in which the first printed ballad on the favorite appeared). It is also true that unlike the chronicles, which give a rather orderly — albeit biased — account

---

[25] Antonio Pérez Gómez, "Un romance de don Álvaro de Luna," *Romance Philology,* 5, Nos. 2 & 3 (Nov. 1951-Feb. 1952), 204.

of his career and of the major political events in which he was involved, the ballads do not present a balanced historical review of events leading to his rise and fall (although I do not understand on what basis it can be alleged that they preserve "ningún pormenor histórico"). For the most part, the ballads focus on the most "dramatic" and moving moments in the final days of the favorite's life. They do not dwell on his political ascendancy; they do not go into detail concerning the opposition to him. In the main, they deal with the alienation of the king and his favorite, with Don Álvaro's premonitions of his downfall, his trial, the king's anguish on signing the death warrant, Don Álvaro's response to the sentence, his testament, his conduct in the face of death, the execution itself, and the efforts of his page Moralicos to secure alms for his burial. Most of these "dramatic" moments, as will be seen, are incorporated in the Don Álvaro de Luna plays. And it is on the basis of these moments that the dramatists allow their characters to engage in "puras endechas al Condestable, trenos lamentando sus desgracias."

Other influences of the ballads on the plays are evident in the presentation of the character of Don Álvaro (who, to a large degree, is the creature of the poetry written about him rather than an "historical" personage) and in their artistic and affective qualities: the lunar metaphors, as Don Álvaro's rise and fall are rendered in terms of the phases of the moon (or, as Pérez Gómez puts it, the "juegos de palabras en torno a su apellido"); the moralizing tone which characterizes the thematic statements (concerning, of course, the hazards of *privanza*, the inconstancy of fortune, the fugacity of time, *desengaño*, etc.); and the elegiac expression and pervasive sentimentality. And, of course, several of the ballads sound the warning and state the "lesson" that are found in most of the fallen-favorite tragedies — the lesson concerning, in the words of Pérez Gómez, "lo quebradizo de las glorias humanas."

But no matter how the ballads are used — in direct quotation or paraphrase, in dialogue or song, in furnishing stylistic and rethorical patterns, in suggesting thematic elements, in imposing moral attitudes — they provide the basis of some of the most effective scenes of the Don Álvaro de Luna plays. Since so many of the ballads reappear in the plays (in short or longer fragments but seldom in their entirety) it will not be necessary to reproduce any of them here, but they will be commented on as they occur in the Don Álvaro de Luna tragedies.

II. The Plays

In view of the fact that the personality and tragic fate of Don Álvaro de Luna were so deeply embedded in the national consciousness that any discussion of favoritism — Spanish or foreign, past or contemporary — inevitably returned to him, it is surprising that he is not the central character in a greater number of plays. He does not figure at all in Damián Salucio del Poyo's two-part *Próspera* and *Adversa fortuna de Ruy López de Ávalos*, although it is insinuated that he will replace Ruy López as the Condestable of Castile. But, of course, Don Álvaro is the tragic hero in Poyo's *La privanza y caída de don Álvaro de Luna*. He is a major character in Mira de Amescua's *La próspera fortuna de don Álvaro de Luna y adversa de Ruy López de Ávalos* (but notwithstanding the title this is really the latter's play), and he is the protagonist of the sequel, *La adversa fortuna de don Álvaro de Luna*. He also has a prominent role in two later anonymous plays, *Morales, paje de don Álvaro de Luna* and *El paje de don Álvaro*. Both are tragicomedies which dramatize Don Álvaro's downfall but concern themselves primarily with the life of the favorite's page before and after the Condestable's execution.

To be sure, Don Álvaro has a secondary role in several *comedias*, a few of which are of interest because of their imaginative fictions concerning the hero, or their presentation of the theme of *privanza*. As an example of the latter, we have already seen in chapter IV how, in Vélez de Guevara's *El espejo del mundo*, Don Basco de Portugal cautions Don Álvaro against the deceptions of fortune and the dangers of *privanza* to which an unwary favorite is always easy prey. In another of Vélez's plays, *El privado perseguido* [26] (in which the persecuted favorite is the

---

[26] *El privado perseguido* was first printed anonymously in *El mejor de los meiores Libro* (sic) *que han salido de comedias nuevas* (Alcalá, 1651), which is the edition I have used.

Duke of Arjona), Don Álvaro also has a secondary but important role. Of interest here are the circumstances of Don Álvaro's birth, attended by various omens including the eclipse of the moon which presages his demise (but his downfall does not occur in the play). Don Álvaro describes those circumstances to the duke:

> En el vientre de mi madre
> dizen que lloré, y con sueños
> portentosos la afligía;
> la Luna estuvo eclipsada,
> de mi sobrenombre agüero.
> A esta imitación saqué
> una Cruz de sangre al pecho,
> y a manera de cuchillo
> otra señal en el cuello.
> Murió de parto mi madre,
> y después de sentimiento
> mi padre también...
>
> (Act I, pp. 215-16)

Examples of Don Álvaro's participation in other *comedias* could be added, [27] but our concern rests with those plays in which the favorite's tragic fall is of major substance. For that reason I have limited the following study to Poyo's and Mira de Amescua's tragedies and to the anonymous *Morales, paje de don Álvaro*. I have not made an analysis of *El paje de don Álvaro* because it is nothing more than a weak imitation of *Morales*. [28]

---

[27] Mention should be made of *El milagro por los celos y don Álvaro de Luna*, in which, notwithstanding its title, Don Álvaro has only a minor role. It does contain, however, a dramatic confrontation between the favorite and Queen Isabel, who makes known her determination to bring about Don Álvaro's destruction. This play has been attributed to both Lope de Vega and Tirso de Molina. It is printed in Lope's *Obras*, ed. M. Menéndez Pelayo, vol. X (Madrid, 1899). In her edition of Tirso's *Obras dramáticas completas* (Madrid, 1952), II, 864-66, Doña Blanca de los Ríos makes the following points: *El milagro por los celos y don Álvaro de Luna* is an imitation or *refundición* of Tirso's *Doña Beatriz de Silva*, printed in his *Parte IV* (Madrid, 1635); it was printed as a *suelta* c. 1734 by a Madrilenian bookseller with the title *Comedia Famosa. Favorecer a todos y amar a ninguno. Doña Beatriz de Silva*. Later editors or printers simply dropped the name of Doña Beatriz de Silva from the title, leaving it *Favorecer a todos y amar a ninguno*.

[28] See n. 65 of this chapter.

A.   DAMIÁN SALUCIO DEL POYO, *La privanza y caída de don Álvaro de Luna*

It has already been remarked (in chapter IV) that Poyo's play on the rise and fall of Don Álvaro is the first real tragedy of *privanza* in that, unlike Poyo's plays on Ruy López de Avalos, the hero suffers an ignominious death. Although *La privanza y caída de don Álvaro de Luna* violates the unities of place and time and does not have a chorus *per se*, it is probably, whether by accident or design, the most "Aristotelian" of all fallen-favorite plays from a structural point of view. Also, it is one of the most Aristotelian of all Spanish tragedies written for popular entertainment in the seventeenth century. [29] Its most notable Aristotelian elements may be summarized briefly.

The subject matter of Poyo's tragedy is, of course, historical rather than of the author's invention. Its plot is single in its issue in that it contains but a single change of fortune and that change is from good to bad. The plot is complex rather than simple in that it involves both a reversal of the situation and recognition on the part of the protagonist. The hero is not too "eminently good and just," but he is "better rather than worse"; and his misfortune is brought about, "not by vice or depravity, but by some error or frailty." There is a final scene of suffering, and the whole is intended to arouse pity and fear in order to achieve the catharsis of these emotions. One might add that the play is "classical" also in its sustained sobriety, having almost no comic elements.

Of course, the fact that Poyo's play contains numerous elements that Aristotle recommended for the tragedy (whether Poyo deliberately "followed" Aristotle or not) does not necessarily make it a good — or bad — tragedy. In point of fact, the play has several technical and artistic deficiencies (among them, a lack

---

[29] There were, of course, a few seventeenth-century Spanish tragedies written for the purpose of "illustrating" Aristotle's theories or modernizing Seneca, but even these academic exercises generally turned out to be a compromise between classical theory and Spanish practice. See Edwin S. Morby, "The *Hercules* of Francisco López de Zárate," *Hispanic Review*, 30 (1962), 116-32.

of fluidity, an awkward articulation of scenes, clumsy dialogue, rather pedestrian poetry, and an infelicitous prolongation of the action beyond the climax); nevertheless, it is a convincing tragedy and, above, all, a very earnest one. [30]

But the major contribution of Poyo's *La privanza y caída de don Álvaro de Luna* to the fallen-favorite tragedies does not lie in its Aristotelianism nor in its earnestness; it lies, rather, in his "discovery" of a new structural principle — a structural principle developed by combining the traditional medieval concept of the "formula of four" of the Wheel of Fortune and the lunar metaphors suggested by Don Álvaro de Luna's surname. As Howard Patch points out, the "formula of four" was commonly used in medieval pictures in which the figures on Fortune's Wheel are "inscribed respectively, Regno, Regnavi, Sum sine Regno, and Regnabo." [31] Not surprisingly, some European dramatists seized upon the "formula of four" of the Wheel of Fortune as a structural device around which the changing fortunes of the hero and other characters were proportioned. [32] But Poyo had at hand an analogue to the Wheel of Fortune: the lunar metaphors which occur repeatedly in the chronicles (especially in the *Crónica de don Álvaro de Luna*) and which abound in the ballads. It occurred to him to use the lunar imagery, not simply as a rhetorical device as it had been employed before him, but as a structural principle analogous in function to the Wheel of Fortune. So it is that the changing fortunes of his Don Álvaro de Luna correspond to the major phases of the moon: crescent (Don Álvaro's ascendancy), full (his fulfillment), and waning (his decline) — and

---

[30] However, A. F. von Schack, *Historia de la literatura y del arte dramático en España*, trans. Eduardo de Mier, 5 vols. (Madrid, 1885-87), III, 313, could find nothing good to say about Poyo's Don Álvaro play: "Pocos asuntos se han manejado tanto por los dramáticos españoles como la historia de D. Álvaro de Luna; pero la verdad es también que acaso la comedia más débil, que desenvuelva este argumento, es la de nuestro Damián Salustrio del Poyo." I strongly disagree with Schack, although I must admit that my qualification of the play as a "convincing tragedy" is as ambiguous as a critical opinion as Schack's judgment is wrong.

[31] Howard R. Patch, *The Goddess Fortuna in Medieval Literature*, p. 164.

[32] Cf. George L. Geckle, "Fortune in Marston's *The Malcontent*," *PMLA*, 82 (1971), 202 ff. I am indebted to Professor Geckle's article for calling to my attention the use of the "formula of four" as a structural principle in drama.

one can add the eclipse (his death). We can now see how the plot of *La privanza y caída de don Álvaro de Luna* is constructed on the basis of Poyo's "new" principle.

Early in the first act, as the king continues to heap honors and titles on Don Álvaro, three courtiers (Don Fadrique, Don Alonso, and Don Pedro de Girón) comment on the favorite's good fortune, but each predicts his fall. Here, as throughout the play, the three courtiers perform a function similar to that of the Greek chorus, interpreting each event and heightening the tension by intimating that the favorite's every gain is but a step toward his ruin. Don Álvaro's ascendancy, they remark, will follow the pattern of the crescent moon which, inevitably, will decline and perhaps undergo eclipse.

Later in the first act, the king and Don Álvaro encounter a LOCO, who claims to be the famous necromancer, the Marqués de Villena. The LOCO asks which of the two is the king, a question he justifies by observing, "que hay más reyes en Castilla/ que en juegos del ajedrez" (vv. 553-34). [33] After the king reveals his identity, the LOCO addresses Don Álvaro:

> ¿No sois vos Luna, pariente?
> Pues guardaos para adelante,
> porque ha de ser la menguante
> mayor que fue la creciente; ...
> que está dos dedos y medio
> de la privanza el cuchillo.
>
> (Act I, vv. 539 ff.)

Shaken by this warning, Don Álvaro prepares to leave; but the LOCO whispers in his ear that he should beware of *cadahalso*, which the favorite takes to mean the town of Cadalso de los Vidrios in the province of Madrid. Superstitious like most of fortune's favorites (who, in both Spanish and foreign plays, fre-

---

[33] Citations are to the only known edition of the play, printed in the *Parte tercera de las comedias de Lope de Vega, y otros avtores* (Barcelona, 1612). There were several reprintings of this *Parte,* and I have used the Valencia printing of 1614 which is unpaginated. I am preparing an edition of the play, and cite the line numbers of the quoted passages.

quently consult astrologers and soothsayers), Don Álvaro is upset by the warning, resolving never to set foot in Cadahalso. [34]

But as the first act ends, Don Álvaro would seem to have no cause for alarm, even though a tribunal dominated by the Infantes de Aragón sentences him to six years' exile. In response the king exiles the Infantes from Castile, leaving it up to Don Álvaro to determine the duration of his absence — a month or less, suggests the king. The friendship between the king and his favorite appears to be inviolable.

Whereas the first act of *La privanza y caída de don Álvaro de Luna* dramatizes the favorite's ascendancy, the second centers upon incidents which show him at the height of prosperity — incidents which, at the same time, reveal that he has become rash in his use of power. Summoned from exile by the king, Don Álvaro is named Condestable of Castile — and once again the trio of courtiers comment on his certain decline: "que si como luna crece,/ que ha de menguar como luna" (Act II, vv. 1013-14). Now for the first time Don Álvaro commits a series of acts that provoke the king's displeasure, although in every case there is an apparent reconciliation between the two. The most fateful of these acts is Don Álvaro's secret arrangement of the marriage between his royal master and Isabel of Portugal, an act which infuriates the king because of his desire to marry Princess Rosiunda ᶜ France. But, as Don Álvaro remarks to Vivero (who, for personal advantage, later exploits the misunderstanding between the king and his favorite): "no es el rey / más de lo que quiero yo" (vv. 1332-33). The Condestable's arrogance has peaked, a fact underscored by the three courtiers in commenting on his arbitrary act.

Fortunately for Don Álvaro, so it seems, the king accedes to his choice and is happy with the bride. And, ironically, the new queen tells the favorite that he will now have two sovereigns to "reward" him. As a token of her esteem, she invites him, against Castilian custom, to dine at the royal table, an invitation that moves him to apostrophize fortune:

---

[34] The *equívoco* involving the word *cadahalso* occurs in Mariana (p. 139) and in Mira's *La adversa fortuna de don Álvaro de Luna*, Act I.

¡Ah, fortuna, estáte queda,
no seas mudable y soez!
¡Oh quién pudiera esta vez
echar un clavo a tu rueda!

(Act II, vv. 1725 ff.)

Don Álvaro's position on the Wheel of Fortune is approaching the figure of "Regno"; the crescent moon is waxing rapidly.

Things continue to go well for the favorite. He puts down a citizens' revolt in Toledo; he routs the Infantes of Aragón in the battle of Olmedo but earns their gratitude, he thinks, by letting them go free. Juan II rewards him with new honors and titles, even though Don Álvaro earns his disapproval momentarily by killing a disrespectful soldier in his presence. The act ends with Don Álvaro's investiture as the Maestre of Santiago, the culmination of his many triumphs. In an elaborate ceremony (much more elaborate than the ceremony of the knighting of Rodrigo in Guillén de Castro's *Las mocedades del Cid*), the king girds on his sword, the queen puts on his spurs, and all the participants are given new offices and titles in honor of the new Maestre. The moon is full.

Act III deals with four principal events: the arrest, trial, and execution of Don Álvaro, and, anticlimatically, the king's siege of the Castle of Escalona, defended by Don Álvaro's widow, in order to capture the Condestable's fabled wealth. From the opening scene the conspiracy against Don Álvaro gains momentum, leading to a confrontation between him and Vivero, the king's *contador mayor*. Don Álvaro kills Vivero, but he has no worry because, he assures himself, "es el rey mi gallo" (v. 2273). The king, however, orders his arrest. Again the courtiers comment on the turn of events:

Paciencia; dejar pasar
los tiempos tras su fortuna,
que ya está llena esta luna,
y por fuerza ha de menguar; . . .
que la luna no padece
eclipse hasta que está llena.

(Act III, vv. 2367 ff.)

Rapidly the moon begins to wane. The king, vacillating between severity and leniency, accuses Don Álvaro of creating disorder in Castile. The queen persuades her husband to allow him to be brought to trial. Don Diego de Avellaneda, one of the Condestable's few remaining followers, appears with a half-moon which he affixes to Don Álvaro's residence. He means it as a sign of loyalty, but the legend on it reads, "Luna no llena." On seeing it as he goes to trial, Don Álvaro is upset by the portentous symbolism. The trial scene, typical of modern courtroom drama, is one of the longest in the Spanish theater, as the attorneys for the prosecution and the defense argue over the legal technicalities (many couched in Latin) involved in the charges. Found guilty, Don Álvaro is sentenced to be executed. The king is unable to sign the death warrant until the queen lends a helping hand.

Alone in prison, Don Álvaro awaits the verdict but he has a presentiment of the judgment. Again he addresses fortune, complaining of the cloud that obscures his lunar light and punning on his title *condestable*:

> ¿Qué es esto, varia fortuna?
> ¿Qué me has hecho? Triste estoy.
> ¿Qué nube es ésta de hoy
> que se ha puesto ante mi luna?
> ¿Que yo soy el condestable?
> ¿Que el condestable soy yo?
> El conde, sí; estable no;
> porque en mí no hay cosa estable.
>
> (Act III, vv. 2947 ff.)

Don Álvaro's page, Moralicos, comes to comfort his master and sings "his" song ("aquel romance... que hizo tu señoría extremado"). One of the best known ballads on Don Álvaro de Luna (No. 1001 in Durán's *Romancero general*), it begins:

> Los que priváis con los reyes,
> mirad bien la historia mía;
> catad que a la fin se engaña
> el hombre que en hombres fía.

And it includes the significant lines that underscore the favorite's gravest fault: Don Álvaro de Luna, the moon, outshone the sun, the king himself: "Por mí la luna en el mundo / más que el sol resplandecía."

Penitent but still climbing, Don Álvaro mounts the scaffold from whence he will be elevated to eternal life, for in this moment of recognition he realizes that man's existence is indeed comparable to the life cycle of the moon which is reborn only after its decline:

> No diga el mundo que tuvo
> hoy don Álvaro caída,
> porque si subió en la vida,
> también en la muerte subo ...
> Si estrella fuera, y faltara
> de mi luz, me diera pena;
> mas siendo luna ya llena,
> no me espanto que menguara.
>
> (Act III, vv. 3127 ff.)

On the scaffold (appropriately called also *teatro* in Spanish, because it is the stage where so many favorites act out the final scene of their life's drama), Don Álvaro does not kiss the blade that will take his life (as Sir Walter Raleigh is reputed to have done) but he tests its cutting edge. "¡Qué buenos filos le has dado!" he says to the executioner who promptly — and in public view — carries out his duty. As Joseph of Arimathea claimed the body of the crucified Christ, so Moralicos claims the body of his master, but it is carried away by the guards.

Historically, as well as in this play, Juan II did not wait in Valladolid for the execution of his favorite; rather, he left to lay siege to Don Álvaro's castle in Escalona. But his deep melancholy tells him that his favorite is dead. An unnamed page arrives to sing of Don Álvaro's death; the song is the familiar ballad (No. 1011 in Durán) which bears the refrain,

> "Dadme por Dios, hermano,
> Para ayudar a enterrar este cristiano."

The king permits Don Álvaro's widow to keep half of her husband's wealth, one of Juan's few noble deeds actually seen in the play, although Poyo refers in the final lines to the king's *altas grandezas.* Perhaps Poyo, for all his sobriety, was capable of indulging in sarcasm.

It has been the purpose of the preceding pages to show how the main events in the rise and fall of the protagonist in *La privanza y caída de don Álvaro de Luna* group themselves around the metaphors of the changing moon. The same metaphors will not only serve as a structural principle in the later Don Álvaro de Luna plays but also in other tragedies of *privanza* in which Juan II's favorite has no part. Most of the later dramatists, however, go further than Poyo in exploiting the lunar imagery, and especially the relationship between sun and moon, to underscore the nature of Don Álvaro's fatal error. It is nature's law that the moon derives its light from the sun, but, so the ballad sung by Moralicos tells us ("Por mí la luna en el mundo / más que el sol resplandecía"), Don Álvaro outshone the sun itself, thus creating an imbalance in nature and in the body politic. [35] Therein lies Don Álvaro's fateful imprudence and unforgiveable fault: he allowed the king to languish in his shadow. Poyo does not insist upon the image or the fault (as later dramatists do), but his tragedy is based on the premise that Don Álvaro de Luna absorbed the rays of the too willing sun and burned himself out by shining too brightly.

Since *La privanza y caída de don Álvaro de Luna* is the first of the Spanish fallen-favorite tragedies, something should be said about its use of other elements of the genre. Poyo's tragedy employs most of the common themes of the tragedies of *privanza* (the instability of fortune, the brevity of life, the vanity of human glory, *desengaño*), but its thematic statements are, in general, more perfunctory than forceful. Only the theme of envy and ingratitude incite the dramatist — and, in turn, his characters — to passionate feeling and expression. As mentioned in chapter IV, Don Álvaro de Luna and his great friend Don Juan Pacheco, aroused by the calumnies and machinations of the Condestable's enemies, spend almost a quarter of an act in denouncing envy

---

[35] Another ballad (Durán, No. 1000) puts it differently. Here Don Álvaro says: "Siendo luna crecí tanto / Que quise igualar al sol; / Mas como fue sol de hebrero / A lo mejor me dejó— ... Esto Don Álvaro dijo / Saliendo de la prisión, / Donde mediante la muerte / Su luna llena eclipsó."

("cáncer del alma sangriento"). But what wonder that envy should afflict the world of men when, through Lucifer, it menaced the divine order and led to the crucifixion of Christ ("por ella fue en la cruz puesto")? Metaphorically, in keeping with the relationship of sun and moon, the envious grandees become the clouds that threaten to come between the two heavenly bodies and cut off the moon's light. [36] Early in the play Don Álvaro is confident that the clouds can never reach his height:

> Yo a mí me estoy alumbrando
> con el sol de mi fortuna;
> que esos que me están turbando
> son nubes que van pasando
> por debajo de mi luna.
>
> (Act I, vv. 182 ff.)

Later in the first act, after his enemies demand his exile, Don Álvaro is troubled, but he is still convinced that no envious cloud can deprive him of the sun's rays:

> Si soy Luna y español,
> ¿qué nube es ésta importuna
> que se pone ante mi luna
> y el rey don Juan, que es el sol?
>   Desharánla, ¡vive Dios!,
> los rayos de su poder,
> porque nube no ha de haber
> que se ponga entre los dos.
>
> (Act I, vv. 743 ff.)

Ultimately, however, the clouds dim Don Álvaro's splendor; and in his view, it is envy, not his own actions, that leads to his death:

---

[36] In Renaissance poetry envy is often rendered as a cloud that obscures the light of sun and moon or that comes between them. Cf. the ballads: "De invidia una escura nube / Vuestros reflejos eclipsa" (Durán, No. 989); "Las invidiosas tinieblas / De tu sol las confianzas / En la fe de mi nobleza, / Mi luna dio tanta luz / Con la tuya acá en la tierra, / Que de invidia se turbaron / En tu cielo mis estrellas..." (Durán, No. 1012). The "envious clouds" also occur in Shakespeare's *Richard II* (Act III, sc. 3): "See, see, King Richard doth himself appear, / As doth the blushing discontented sun / From out the fiery portal of the east, / When he perceives the *envious clouds* are bent / To dim his glory and to stain the track / Of his bright passage to the occident" (italics mine).

> pero ¡por aquel Dios omnipotente!,
> por el paso que espero,
> como muero inocente,
> que la envidia me mata solamente.
>
> (Act III, vv. 3024 ff.)

Ingratitude is prominent in the play, not so much in explicit statement, but in the examples of the defections and betrayals of Don Álvaro's former friends and beneficiaries. There is one notable exception — a direct reproof of ingratitude: when the queen urges her husband to have his favorite brought to trial, the king chides her:

> Ya veo
> vuestra ingratitud, que es tal
> que sólo pudo caber
> —por ser al fin de mujer—
> reina, en vuestro pecho mal.
> Mas ¿qué digo ni qué hago?
> Esto y más merece al justo,
> pues que me casó a su gusto
> con quien le da tan mal pago.
>
> (Act III, vv. 2422 ff.)

But Juan's sarcasm is unavailing. He is no match for his wife who, employing the common simile that the kingdom is like the human body, persuades him that he, the head, must protect the health of the body politic by amputating the diseased member — Don Álvaro.

One of the recurring experiences of man's history is the defection of friends of those who are publicly condemned. It is an experience which every writer on favoritism — whether philosopher, historian, or poet — must seek to communicate. In *La privanza y caída de don Álvaro de Luna* there are numerous defectors (Vivero, the queen, the king himself) but none so poignantly human as Don Juan Pacheco. Poyo takes great care in depicting the warm friendship that binds Pacheco and Don Álvaro; Pacheco is the Condestable's confidant, his constant companion. On many occasions and at considerable personal risk he comes to the defense of his friend, but after the king and queen turn against Don Álvaro, he is perplexed: "¿Qué he de hacer? Viva quien vence" (v. 2542).

But Pacheco does not yet join the crowd; even after Don Álvaro has been sentenced to die, he still claims that his friend is innocent. After the Condestable's execution, however, he can no longer hold out: the king buys his acquiescence by naming him the Marqués de Villena, the very title which Don Álvaro had promised him early in the play. And after Pacheco joins the king's forces in wresting from Don Álvaro's widow the castle of Escalona, he is rewarded with his friend's title, the Duke of Escalona. However, Poyo does not condemn Don Juan Pacheco; he merely shows in dramatic action that defection is one of the ways of the world, especially of the world of *privanza*.

As a tragedy, *La privanza y caída de don Álvaro de Luna* has various shortcomings other than the technical deficiencies previously mentioned. For the most part, these shortcomings are owed to Poyo's failure to vivify the tragic sense of life that lies beyond the external conflicts dramatized in the play. His tragedy is simply too literal, too matter-of-fact. This is not to say, however, that either character or meaning is sacrificed to action, as happens in many other Spanish plays that involve tragic themes. We are given occasional glimpses into the inner being of Don Álvaro de Luna, but he does not seem to understand fully his own significance as a tragic hero. He does not understand that his destiny has importance beyond his own immediate circumstance. He is too imperceptive to see himself other than as a pawn in the game of power politics.

But the meaning of Poyo's play emerges as clearly as the allegory of the Fall of man. Whatever Don Álvaro's intentions, he seeks to make his way in the world armed only with ambition, pride, and human resourcefulness. His disaster serves as testimony to the moral that those arms are not enough, not merely to contend with the complexities of this life, but more importantly, they count for nothing in the eternal scheme. Such is the message of Poyo's tragedy, a message that will be repeated time and again in the later tragedies of *privanza*.

B. Antonio Mira de Amescua, *La próspera fortuna de don Álvaro de Luna y adversa de Ruy López de Ávalos* and *La adversa fortuna de don Álvaro de Luna*

Some twenty years elapsed between the first known performance of Salucio del Poyo's *La privanza y caída de don Álvaro de Luna* and the appearance of Mira de Amescua's two plays on Don Álvaro. [37] Those years, corresponding approximately to the reign of Philip III, were climaxed by the dismissal of the Duke of Lerma as the king's first minister and by the execution of Don Rodrigo Calderón. Curiously, during the long interval separating Poyo's and Mira's Don Álvaro plays, the theme of favoritism remained quiescent in Spanish drama. The playwrights, so it seems, were waiting to see the dénouement of the political infighting that roiled the court before venturing their own "imitations" of their leaders' actions.

However, as early as 1604, when Lerma's position was unchallenged, Poyo himself wrote the two-part play *La próspera* and *Adversa fortuna de Ruy López de Ávalos,* which, when viewed in retrospect, seems to be a prophetic rendering of the events leading up to Lerma's removal. Indeed, if Poyo's Ruy López plays had been written after Lerma's dismissal, there is little doubt that they would have been thought to have been inspired by that worthy's fall. But if Poyo's plays on Don Álvaro and Ruy López de Ávalos had no immediate successors, they have the distinction of serving as models for Mira de Amescua's tragedies of *privanza*.

Although generally acknowledged to deserve inclusion among the masterpieces of Spanish drama, Mira's two plays on Don Álvaro de Luna (hereafter called *La próspera fortuna* and *La adversa fortuna*) have received far more attention because of the uncertainty that has long attended their authorship than because of their artistic merits. Neither the problems concerning the authorship of the two plays nor the date of their composition and

---

[37] As indicated in chapter IV, n. 6, Poyo's play may have been performed in 1601. The only firm date associated with Mira's Don Álvaro plays is the *aprobación* for performance, dated October 17, 1624, written on Mira's autograph of *La segunda de don Álvaro.*

of their first performance have been fully resolved, but on the
basis of the evidence now available, it will be assumed here that
Mira de Amescua was the principal, if not the sole, author of
both plays. Our chief concern rests with their literary and dramatic qualities as fallen-favorite plays.

To Margaret Wilson, who believes that Tirso de Molina
probably collaborated in the writing of Act II of *La próspera
fortuna,* we are indebted for a penetrating study of the first
play. [38] Among other things Miss Wilson studies the sources (the
chronicles of Juan II and Don Álvaro de Luna, Mariana, and
especially Poyo's two plays on Ruy López de Ávalos); and she
also analyzes the structure, characterization, imagery, and themes.
Notwithstanding the fact that Don Álvaro's name appears first
in the title of Mira's play, Miss Wilson rightly points out that
"The play remains essentially the story of Ruy López — Álvaro
is a shadowy figure who scarcely comes to life; yet his sudden
rise to *privanza* and to the position of Constable gives us the
measure of Ruy López's fall." [39] In other words, unlike Poyo's
plays which deal with the fortunes of a single favorite, *La próspera fortuna* offers an example of the structural principle indicated
by Anibal: "the simultaneous balanced and graduated rise and
fall of two characters."

The character of Ruy López is highly idealized by Mira de
Amescua, who, following Poyo's lead, presents him as loyal, wise,
generous, and the "embodiment of moral rectitude" [40] — in short,
one whose major concern is *obrar bien.* The last section of Miss

---

[38] "*La próspera fortuna de don Álvaro de Luna*: An Outstanding Work
by Mira de Amescua," *Bulletin of Hispanic Studies,* 33 (1956), 25-36.

[39] Ibid., p. 30.

[40] Ibid., p. 32. Miss Wilson observes that, contrary to the idealized
portrait of Ruy López de Ávalos given by Mira de Amescua, the histories
reveal him to have been "a typical factious noble, thirsty for power, jealous
of those preferred before him; manoevring for the favour of Don Álvaro, of
the Infante Don Enrique, of whoever was supreme at the time; but heedless
of the King, who wielded no real power, even disrespectful of his person
and disobedient to his commands" (p. 29). I think that it is significant to
note that in presenting Ruy López in such a favorable light, Mira was
greatly influenced by the example of Salucio del Poyo, whose wife, Doña
Beatriz de Ávalos Lara y Soto, was a descendant of the Condestable. See
Justo García Soriano, "Damián Salucio del Poyo," *Boletín de la Academia
Española,* 13 (1926), 269.

Wilson's study is devoted to the nature and intensity of Ruy
López's calamity. Unjustly accused of treason, he is stripped of
his office and possessions and exiled by the king. The old man,
whose loyalty to the king — to all kings — amounts to veneration,
is crushed, because as the code of honor pertains to the relations
of king and vassal, denunciation by the king is the gravest of
catastrophes. For that reason he laments,

> En la honra me ha tocado
> un rey de España.

Although in the end Ruy López is vindicated, in this first part
of Mira's two-part play "*pundonor* is ... used as the mainspring
of great tragedy." [41]

We shall return to *La próspera fortuna* in a moment, but first
we shall review briefly the criticism that has been devoted to
the second play. *La adversa fortuna* has received far more critical
attention than the first play. It has been studied at some length
in the editions of Nellie E. Sánchez-Arce, Luigi de Filippo, and
Doña Blanca de los Ríos (who contends that Quevedo collaborated
with Tirso de Molina in their composition). [42] In particular, it has
been the subject of a masterful analysis by I. L. McClelland of
the human relationships involved in the course of Don Álvaro's
rise and fall. [43] It has also been studied in a more cursory way
in articles and general works concerning the dramaturgy of Mira
de Amescua and Tirso de Molina — depending, of course, on
whether the critic considered Mira or Tirso to have been the
author (for example, Anibal in his study of Mira's theater, Bernard
Gicovate in his article, "Observations on the Dramatic Art of
Tirso de Molina"). [44]

Gicovate's comments on the Don Álvaro plays are especially
pertinent because they focus on them as tragedies and on Don

---

[41] Wilson, p. 36.

[42] Ed. Tirso de Molina, *Obras dramáticas completas,* I, 1845 ff.

[43] I. L. McClelland, *Tirso de Molina: Studies in Dramatic Realism*
(Liverpool, 1948), pp. 90-128. In her study Miss McClelland assumes that
Tirso is the author of the play.

[44] *Hispania,* 43 (1960), 328-37.

Álvaro as a tragic hero, a tragic hero whose *hamartia* — or, the nature of whose *hamartia* — remains open to question:

> If we consider the two plays on Don Álvaro de Luna as one, the full circle of the *privado*'s rise and fall becomes a perfect example of Aristotelian tragedy. But the best analysis of the play, an almost scene by scene account of its psychological complexity, fails to find the "hamartia" or flaw of classical poetics. As a consequence, I. L. McClelland is almost ready to accept a secondary position for these plays in the hierarchy of tragedies. Possibly too narrow a conception of the tragic flaw has been responsible for an inability to understand the towering figure of Álvaro de Luna. In a more generous conception, Aristotle's "hamartia" is "not necessarily wrong-doing, much less moral weakness: it may be simply a matter of being a strong character in an exposed position." The magnetic superiority of the *privado* becomes his undoing. Tirso chose this lamentable episode of Castilian history to show greatness at its greatest, the unexplained superiority of a great heart and a keen mind destroyed by fate. [45]

One might question Gicovate's assertion that *La adversa fortuna* is a "perfect" example of Aristotelian tragedy (although I should like to think that Aristotle would have approved of it), but it will probably be more rewarding to examine the character of Don Álvaro as a tragic hero and the nature of his *hamartia*. In this regard, Nellie E. Sánchez-Arce has pointed out that the hero's catastrophe, rather than being unexplained or owed solely to fate, is brought about by one of his own acts:

> Ilusionado con su destino político, rasgo genuinamente humano en don Álvaro, se ciega y comete una seria equivocación que le cuesta la vida. El Condestable sufre las consecuencias de la imposición de su voluntad sobre Juan II, instándole al matrimonio con Isabel de Portugal, y yerra... Así, su flaqueza humana en este instante le acarrea su desastrado desenlace; Álvaro halla su fatalidad irrevocable por vía de su carácter sagazmente autoritario; y, al ser instrumento de su propio daño, se aproxima al concepto clásico del héroe trágico. [46]

[45] Ibid., p. 335.
[46] Nellie E. Sánchez-Arce, ed. *La segunda de Don Álvaro*, pp. 20-21.

It is my conviction, however, that the author of the two Don
Álvaro plays not only complies with Aristotle's observation on
hamartia as an essential element in the fall of the tragic hero but
that he explains it amply by various means available to the
dramatic poet. Moreover, Don Álvaro's *hamartia*, far from being
a sporadic or accidental element in his characterization, is
developed carefully throughout both plays. In the following
pages, as we go through the plot of the plays, I hope to show
that at the heart of Don Álvaro's *hamartia* is his unrelenting urge
to play God. [47]

Act I of *La próspera fortuna* is a busy one indeed. It introduces the principal characters, lays the ground for the conflict
between the king and Ruy López de Ávalos, and states explicitly
several important themes of the play: fortune, friendship, ingratitude, and playing God. By terms of his father's will, Juan
must wait until his fifteenth birthday to ascend to the throne of
Castile. Impatient to secure the crown, he asks Ruy López to
persuade the grandees to advance the date of coronation by six
months. Moved to tears by his memory of the deceased King
Enrique, the Condestable is distraught rather than deliberately
evasive when he fails to give the young king a satisfactory
answer. Juan is angry. By way of contrast, in the following scene
Don Álvaro is introduced to the *rey niño*, who is immediately
attracted to his new page, as he tells his sister:

> Miralde bien, que me hallo
> tan inclinado a su amor
> que no le tendrá mayor
> ningún rey a su vasallo.
>
> (267a)[48]

---

[47] As noted in the Preface, much of the following discussion is based
on my article, "Tragic *Hamartia* in *La próspera y adversa fortuna de don
Álvaro de Luna*," *Hispania*, 47 (1964), 82-90.

[48] Page and column references are to Emilio Cotarelo y Mori's edition
of the two plays in the *Comedias de Tirso de Molina*, Tomo I, *NBAE*, IV
(Madrid, 1906). Later, as will be indicated, some passages not contained
in the *NBAE* edition will be quoted from Sánchez-Arce's edition, and
occasionally defective passages will be corrected with her text.

Struck by the king's compulsive attachment to the youthful Don Álvaro, other courtiers predict that the page will enjoy phenomenal success. Ironically, however, their predictions foreshadow the tragic fate of the favorite, as the present and future indicative of verbs is qualified by the contingency of subjunctives. Moreover, Doña Elvira, Don Álvaro's future wife, employs his family name in the now familiar imagery of the moon's eclipse, a metaphor for the mutability of fortune and impending doom:

> Luna sois, palacio os vea
> siempre con luz no eclipsada:
> felice ha sido la entrada,
> ansí la salida sea.
>
> (Ibid.)

At this early stage of the play the theme of friendship and fortune are already linked.

The theme of ingratitude is first introduced in scene ix (according to Cotarelo's scenic division), when the Infante of Aragón solicits Don Álvaro's intercession in his suit of the king's sister: "Tú podrás lo que deseas; / vencerás humanas suertes" (267b). In answer, Don Álvaro himself has recourse to the uncertainty of the subjunctive, alluding to the ingratitude which will obsess him in the second play: "Plega Dios en eso aciertes, / aunque tú ingrato me seas" (Ibid.).

In the following scene the king attempts to assuage his favorite's apprehensiveness caused by Elvira's remark ("felice ha sido la entrada, / ansí la salida sea"), but the king's vows of undying friendship are also tinged with the irony of the well-worked subjunctive: "Si tú en mi gracia has entrado, / no temas que pueda el hado / quitarte la gracia mía" (268a). In view of the fate that awaits him many years in the future when he makes his final exit from the king's palace, Don Álvaro has reason to be apprehensive; but at this juncture in the play, when the moon is ascending, the favorite's premonitions seem to be ill founded.

Overhearing the conversation between the king and his favorite, Ruy López muses upon the propensity of kings to create *hechuras* in their own image:

> ... que sus hechuras
> tiene cada rey, y quiere
> parecer a Dios, y gusta
> de hacer de nuevo los hombres
> a su imagen ...
>
> (Ibid.)

The Condestable's observation applies to the God-complex of kings, but in the second play Don Álvaro delights in playing God — and king — and in a sense Juan II becomes his *hechura*.

In the same scene Ruy López incurs the king's wrath when he reports that the nobles are unwilling to advance the date of the coronation. Don Álvaro promises to appease the king, but the Condestable replies:

> Obrar bien es lo que importa,
> don Álvaro; no me turban
> accidentes, que Dios tiene
> en sus manos la fortuna.
>
> (269a)

Fittingly, Act I concludes with this expression of Christian Stoicism (which will stand Ruy López in good stead as his fortunes continue to wane), because it constitutes one of the important lessons of the two plays. The message is lost on Don Álvaro on this occasion, however, because he learns only the words, not the meaning. *Obrar bien* becomes his motto, the justification for his later self-righteous but arbitrary acts; it is not until the final act of the second play when he confronts his own death that he discovers, with the aid of his wife, the true meaning of the Condestable's speech.

In Act II the theme of fortune is given new impetus by the intervention in scene ix of the Cordoban poet Juan de Mena, who arrives at court to dedicate his latest book to Juan II. The book in question is *El laberinto de fortuna,* about which the poet tells the king,

> En él
> no sé si con dicha alguna
> las mudanzas de fortuna
> escribo, César novel.
>
> (272b)

As noted in chapter II, *El laberinto de fortuna* was finished and dedicated to Juan II in 1444, nine years before the execution of Don Álvaro de Luna, but one of the most striking changes of fortune contained in the book concerns the king's favorite. He is first shown at the height of prosperity, completely dominating fortune; but later a resuscitated corpse predicts his downfall:

> E del condestable judgando su fecho
> assí determino su fado e pregono:
> será retraído del sublime trono
> e aun a la fin del todo desfecho . . . [49]

The apparently trivial role of Juan de Mena may provide a "bit of unhistorical clowning," [50] but the dramatist also had Don Álvaro's sharp reversal in mind when he introduced the poet and his famous book.

At the end of the second act when he is accused of treason by his secretary Juan García, Ruy López is placed under house arrest on orders of the king. His honor impugned, the old man cries out in anguish to fortune, employing the common metaphor of man as a tree that is withered by winter's winds:

> ¡Ah, fortuna! ¿De qué sirve
> que en estos siglos pasados
> me dieses honra y riquezas,
> si de un golpe me has quitado
> el honor a la vez,
> cuando suelen los ancianos
> tener ya su honor seguro
> y vencidos los naufragios
> de la juventud ociosa?
> Bien dicen que el hombre es árbol:
> hojas y flores produce;
> su belleza son los ramos,
> sus riquezas son las flores,
> compitiendo con los rayos
> del Sol y los arreboles
> de las nubes del ocaso
> en colores y hermosura.

---

[49] See chapter II, n. 8.
[50] Gicovate, p. 335.

Sopla el cierzo, sopla el austro,
y antes de llegar el fruto,
pimpollos verdes y blancos
derriban en la campaña
verdes blasones de Mayo.
¡Ay, honor! ¡Ay, vejez mía!
(277b) [51]

Then, as the result of an imagined dialogue with Christ, Ruy López is made to perceive the truth. Like Poyo's Don Álvaro before him and Mira's Don Álvaro after him, he has erred in serving earthly kings rather than the Queen of Heaven and the saints:

"Ruy López... —Señor, ya tiemblo,
Rey eterno, de escucharos.
—¡Ojalá hubieras servido
a mi Madre y a mis santos
como al Rey: tu fueras *bueno,*
como el mundo te ha llamado!
—Señor, si los corazones
veis vos solo, y los humanos
reyes no los pueden ver,
sólo a vos, Rey justo y santo,
servir debemos los hombres."
(Ibid.)

In Act III, after Don Álvaro suffers an ominous fall on the king's coronation day, evidence of Ruy López's disloyalty mounts. Reflecting on the Condestable's disgrace, Don Álvaro borrows from the old man's words for part of his soliloquy. It is one of the most significant speeches of the first play:

Corazón, temamos esto;
sírvanos de ejemplo grave
la desdicha de Ruy López.
Mas el mismo Condestable,
"obrar bien es lo que importa"
dijo una vez; semejante
es mi parecer. Fortuna,

---

[51] Wilson, p. 33, calls attention to the close parallel between this speech and Wolsey's speech in Shakespeare's *Henry VIII* (Act III, sc. 2).

o ya firme o ya inconstante,
obremos bien y subamos:
yo he de poner de mi parte
obrar bien; tú, de la tuya,
haz aquello que gustares.

(280a)

It is well for Don Álvaro to resolve to emulate the Condestable
in *obrar bien,* but not until his own final moments does he learn
from Ruy López's example. Moreover, there is an essential difference between the two men's attitude toward vying with
fortune. Ruy López said, "... no me turban / accidentes, que
Dios tiene / en sus manos la fortuna." Don Álvaro makes no
appeal to God. He challenges fortune to work against him. This
is part of his tragic *hamartia.*

On learning that letters incriminating him were written by
Juan García, his trusted secretary whom he always regarded
more as a son than as a servant, Ruy López is dismayed. Like
other *privados* before and after him, he is quick — and vain
enough — to see an analogy between his betrayal and Christ's:

A Cristo parezco yo,
que siendo Dios, le vendió
el que en su plato comía.

(281b)

But shaking off his self-righteousness, Ruy López soon realizes
that Juan García acted as God's agent in bringing about his
punishment for his secular preoccupations: "Dios castiga mi
pecado. / Instrumento fue el traidor / de mi castigo" (Ibid.).

Finally, before he goes into exile in Aragón, Ruy López
pronounces another speech in which he resigns himself to God's
will. The speech also serves to underscore the difference between
Don Álvaro's humanitarianism and Ruy López's Christian Stoicism, as well as their different attitudes toward fortune:

Cuarenta años he vivido
con dicha y honra infinita,
y aunque apriesa,
destas pompas he caído,
si Dios las da y las quita,
no me pesa.

Al ataúd y a la cuna
una misma forma dimos:
nuestra muerte
fue línea de la fortuna:
¡qué mucho! Todos nacimos
de una suerte.

(282a)

As remarked earlier, *La próspera fortuna de don Álvaro de Luna y adversa de Ruy López de Ávalos* is essentially Ruy López's play. It is he — not Don Álvaro — whose character and view of life have undergone fundamental change during the course of the play. It will be a long time before Don Álvaro learns that his supposed self-sufficiency and good intentions are not enough to compete with fortune. It remains to be seen how he responds when he too, at the end of the second play, is forced to ponder the meaning of the *cuna-ataúd* motif.

The theme of playing God gains momentum early in the first act of *La adversa fortuna*. After the baptism of the new-born heir to the throne of Castile, at which event Don Álvaro (now Condestable) acts as godfather, the quack astrologer Linterna offers to cast the prince's horoscope. The king will not permit it because

Émulo no debe ser
de su Criador la criatura.

(288a)

In the context of the situation the king means that man should not usurp the role of God in trying to divine the future. In the general context of the play, the words mean just what they say. Either way, Don Álvaro pays no heed. After the king leaves, he asks Linterna to read his horoscope. The quack predicts *sucesos notables* for him, but

Con desdichas y embarazos
todos aquellos a quien
hará en este mundo bien,
le serán ingratonazos.

(288b)

Linterna also prophesies that Don Álvaro will die "en cadahalso," which (as every commentator on the play has been
quick to point out) the Condestable understands to mean the
town of Cadahalso. He who has declared himself to be undaunted
by fortune very humanly resolves to avoid the place at all costs.

But of greater moment is Don Álvaro's concern with the
ingratonazos that Linterna predicts will plague him. Ingratitude
(later related with his God-complex) becomes his major obsession.
Obrar bien (which he learned from Ruy López) means several
things to Don Álvaro, but above all it means creating *hechuras*.
He cannot refrain, however, from demanding that his beneficiaries
be grateful. The sequence of his speeches to his *hechuras* is
significant. After appointing Robles *tesorero general,* he says: "lo
que quiero solamente / es que agradecido seas" (289a). Informing
Vivero of his appointment as *contador mayor,* he tells him, "sólo
os quiero agradecido" (Ibid.); but at the same time he assures
himself, "Mi ambición es solamente / hacer bien" (Ibid.). [52] Then,
filled with exaltation over his own powers, he cautions himself:

> No seáis sólo para vos,
> Álvaro, en dichas seguras,
> porque esto de hacer hechuras
> tiene un no sé qué de Dios.
> (Ibid.)

Don Álvaro now frankly enjoys playing God. The role has
always been difficult for mortals, and in his grand, inconsistent
humanity the Condestable finds it so. After saving the life of the

---

[52] After quoting this verse, Sister Mary Austin Cauvin, "The *comedia
de privanza* in the Seventeenth Century," comments: "This line is significant.
The favorite is seen to be acting always from patriotic motives, as well as
generous with friend and foe" (p. 89). Referring to Don Álvaro's previous
statement to Robles, she says: "Again, Don Álvaro sensing insincerity, in-
terrupts Robles to remark that he only hopes the latter will be loyal to him.
This is one of the most excellent incidents the dramatist inserts to show
that the intellect or reason guides Don Álvaro's actions; he is not impressed
by sentimental volubility" (p. 90). And she adds the following note (159):
"In these typical dramas of *privanza,* the *valido* expects gratitude and
complains when it is not forthcoming." I agree with the latter statement,
but obviously my interpretation of Don Álvaro's insistence upon gratitudes
differs greatly.

Infante of Aragón, he repeats his familiar exhortation, but adds a revealing statement:

> Sólo pido que agradezcas
> mi voluntad, porque yo
> hago bien sólo con esta
> condición.
>
> (291b)

The repetition of *sólo* as a qualifying adverb serves to emphasize his human inability to carry out the role.

When (still in Act I) Don Álvaro's *hechuras* begin to turn against him, it is not surprising to hear him liken his situation to God's, because the Creator Himself was repaid by the ingratitude and revolt of his most beautiful creature:

> Quien hace bien a un villano,
> quien a un traidor favorece,
> esta ingratitud merece.
> Mas ¿qué mucho si en aquel
> divino y santo vergel
> labró Dios una figura
> que, en mirando su hermosura,
> se rebeló contra él?
>
> (293b) [53]

At the end of the act, Don Álvaro goes into exile to spare the king further trouble with the nobles who complain of his domineering ways. Returning from exile in Act II, he is greeted by Robles, one of the chief conspirators against him. Now aware of his *hechura*'s treachery, the Condestable pronounces one of the longest speeches in the play, a speech in which the theme of ingratitude finds its most elaborate statement, as human ingratitude is contrasted to the loyalty of animals. But if this wry comment on the human condition points to a disorder in nature, the *luna*

---

[53] These verses are not found in the autograph. The theatrical director or rewrite man who added them was apparently sensitive to Don Álvaro's God-complex and wanted to enhance it. As we have observed on numerous occasions, the Lucifer motif is common in the fallen-favorite plays and in the chronicles, especially in the *Crónica de don Álvaro de Luna.*

still receives its light from the *sol* (or "steals" its light), as the king tells his favorite on welcoming him back:

> Yo, amigo, podré decirte
> que la luna contemplaba
> muchas veces cuando hermosa
> hurtó al sol rayos de plata,
> por ser tu nombre, y decía:
> "Si yo soy el *sol* de España
> y he de iluminar mi *luna*,
> ¿qué mar, qué tierra pesada
> se ha puesto en medio y no deja
> que penetre esferas altas
> su luz?
>
> (296b)

Historically, Don Álvaro de Luna had long since stolen (for patriotic reasons, let it be granted) the light of the Spanish sun. In the play, the exploitation of the imagery of theft or usurpation now begins in earnest, even if in an apparently frivolous way. Again entrenched at court, the Condestable sets about running the king's business with renewed vigor. For reasons of state but without consulting his master (as recorded in the chronicles and dramatized in Salucio del Poyo's Don Álvaro play), he gives his word that the king will marry Doña Isabel of Portugal. Unknown to Don Álvaro, Juan has his heart set on marrying a French princess, and even a royal heart has its reasons. Understandably the king complains when he awakens to find that Luna has stolen the *sol* of France (the portrait of the French princess over whose loveliness he had fallen asleep): [54]

> ¿Qué occidente o mar helado,
> qué nube sin arrebol
> hurtó de mi mano el sol,
> y la sombra me ha dejado?
> (299a)

The king is angry: "¿Cómo, don Álvaro, vos / me casáis a mí sin mí?" (299b). But rather than embarrass his favorite, who

---

[54] For Mira de Amescua's indebtedness to Poyo for the non-historical parts of this episode, see Cauvin, pp. 68-70 and 96-97.

threatens to go into exile, Juan agrees — reluctantly — to marry
Isabel: "Sí, que me caso, / sin mi gusto y por el vuestro" (300a).
Unmindful of the cost of his victory (as noted earlier, the *Crónica
de Juan II* tells us that "después de esto [el rey] lo desamó
mucho más enteramente"), [55] the *privado* exults:

> Hoy ve el curso de mi vida
> con esto fija a mis pies
> a la fortuna, si es
> Isabel agradecida.
>
> (Ibid.)

Don Álvaro is now at the height of his prosperity, he thinks, *if*
(as the dramatist pointedly says) Isabel only turns out to be
grateful.

As the Condestable leaves to command a military campaign
against the rebellious Infante of Aragón in Trujillo, it is time for
a restatement of the several themes and issues involved. They are
united in Doña Juana's farewell speech to her husband, a speech
that begins and ends with a reference to fortune and touches
upon *privanza*, the tragic fall, the *luna-sol* motif, envy, and the
outcome of human glory:

> Tributario de bárbaros despojos
> te mire la fortuna tan triunfante,
> que aun el tiempo sentirse apenas pueda
> en los vuelcos fatales de su rueda.
> Ni recele, ni sienta tu privanza
> golpe infeliz de mísera caída,
> ni se mire tu luna con mudanza
> de los rayos del sol instituída;
> ni adquiera en tus sucesos su venganza
> la envidia de los hombres, ni en tu vida
> nos dejen experiencias las historias
> de lo que pueden las humanas glorias.
> Pasmo del mundo tu fortuna sea.
>
> (300b)

The fierce irony of Doña Juana's final verse with its ambiguous
subjunctive alerts us to the fact that Don Álvaro's duel with

---

[55] *BAE*, LXVIII, 63.

fortune is about to take a critical turn. First, however, the dramatist holds out a final triumph for the Condestable. He wins back Trujillo from Juan's dissident cousin, the Infante of Aragón. The king comes to congratulate his favorite, underscoring the unnatural phenomenon that he (the *sol*) now lives in the shadow of Luna: "no puedo vivir sin verte, / tu sombra soy y testigo" (302b).

At this point, as elsewhere in the play, we can blame Juan II (as many writers did) for allowing his favorite to eclipse him, but in tragedy the hero must share in the responsibility and suffer the consequences when matters get out of hand. It is not enough that his intentions are good; most tragic heroes' intentions are. Nor can the tragedian tell the hero what he should or should not do; that is the business of the didactic writer. As mentioned earlier, in his play *Cómo ha de ser el privado*, Quevedo had occasion to reflect on the relationship of Juan II and his favorite — and perhaps on Mira's play. [56] His conclusion, expressed by the Marqués de Valisero, places the blame on the king; but also, employing the *sol-luna* imagery that we have traced, it points up the unwitting error of Don Álvaro:

> MARQ.   Fue gran rey
> el rey don Juan; mas le dan
> culpa todas sus historias.
> REY   ¿Cuál?
> MARQ.   Haberse sujetado
> con extremo a su Privado...
> Sí, Señor, porque un Privado,
> que es un átomo pequeño
> junto al Rey, no ha de ser dueño
> de la luz que el sol le ha dado. [57]

Friendship between politicians is always subject to the constant strain of political imperatives. Juan II and Don Álvaro cannot escape the truism. As the third act begins, the Castilian nobles call for the *privado*'s blood. The troubled king refuses him his hand. Don Álvaro appeals to his *hechuras*; he is thrice denied

---

[56] See chapter III, pp. 56-57, 62, and n. 13.
[57] Ed. Miguel Artigas, p. 10.

—by Vivero, by the Infante of Aragón, by the queen. As he speaks to himself more than to the retreating queen, his God-complex asserts itself momentarily; but no, not he but heaven itself is responsible for her imperfections:

> Yo os hice sólo en un día
> majestad de señoría;
> reina os hice, ¡vive Dios!
> El ser me debéis, y ansí
> veros ingrata es consuelo,
> pues sé que es obra del cielo,
> y que no nace de mí.
>
> (304b)

Then Don Álvaro has a moment of recognition: he is cast in the role of tragic hero in mankind's eternal tragedy of envy and ingratitude. He has been ordained by heaven to be an exemplary victim:

> Los mismos cielos envían
> a un magnánimo este mal
> para ejemplo universal
> de los hombres que confían
> en los hombres, y si vengo
> a ser ejemplo del mundo,
> aun cayendo en lo profundo,
> hoy singular dicha tengo. . . .
> yo mismo labré mi daño;
> gusano de seda fui.
>
> (Ibid.)

Although the last two verses suggest a new awareness on the part of Don Álvaro, they are not followed by the hero's reconciliation to his fate that we have come to expect in tragedy. He is too intent on acting out his role as the innocent victim of other men's wrongdoing. No showman like Shakespeare's Richard II, he seeks solitude to stage a miniature drama of self-justification, speaking both parts of the dialogue. With an off-stage musician he engages in a sequence of alternating song and gloss, of thematic statement and personal application. The "scene" begins with the opening lines of the ballad (Durán, No. 1001) that Poyo employed in a similar situation in *La privanza y caída de don Álvaro de Luna*:

MÚSICA: "Los que priváis con los reyes
         notad bien la historia mía:
         mirad que a la fin se engaña
         el hombre que en hombres fía."
D. ÁLV. Servíle treinta y dos años,
         y siempre bien me ha querido;
         ¿cómo ahora se ha creído
         de mentiras y de engaños?...
         No lo entiendo, estoy turbado;
         no lo entiendo, estoy perdido.
                                    (305b)

Finally Don Álvaro's wife comes to arouse him from his confusion and self-pity. Her words (which recall Ruy López de Ávalos' earlier expressions of Christian Stoicism) state one of the didactic, not the tragic, lessons of the play:

         ... el varón fuerte
         no tiene cólera alguna
         con el tiempo y la fortuna,
         con la vejez y la muerte.
         Lo que importa es que en el trance
         de cualquiera de estos cuatro
         se exponga el hombre al teatro
         del vivir sin que le alcance
         culpa alguna, y que balance
         su virtud y acciones de hombres;
         porque cuando más le asombre
         fortuna o muerte atrevida,
         quitaránle estado y vida,
         mas no borrarán su nombre.
                                    (306a) [58]

Don Álvaro is still not resigned to his fate, however. He makes a final pathetic plea to the king to spare his life, reminding

---

[58] McClelland, pp. 122-24, comments perceptively on Doña Juana's role and characterization as an authentic wife, a rarity in the Golden Age theater. Doña Juana also functions, it seems to me, as both *raisonneur* and chorus, but certainly not a disinterested chorus. Various of her speeches summarize the issues, unite the principal themes, and express an ideal point of view.

him "que son ya treinta y dos años / los que os serví con lealtad, / más de amigo que vasallo" (307a). Overcome with emotion, the king cannot answer. Overcome with emotion, the king cannot sign the death warrant until the queen (whose marriage to Juan was to "fix" the *valido*'s fortune forever, "si es Isabel agradecida") guides his trembling hand.

Don Álvaro's passion now reaches its culmination. Fittingly, it is introduced by Moralico's song (which, as in Poyo's *La privanza y caída de don Álvaro de Luna*) climaxes the *sol-luna* imagery:

> "Aquella luna hermosa
> que sus rayos le dio el sol,
> hoy con un mortal eclipse
> pierde luz y resplandor
> en lo más alto subida
> del cielo de su favor..."
>
> (308b)

Informed of the death sentence, the Condestable reacts with every ounce of his humanity: [59]

> ¿Quién oyéndola nombrar
> no ha gemido y no ha temblado?
> ¡Válgame Dios! ¡trance fuerte!
> ¡miseria fatal del hombre!
> Si me espanta sólo el nombre
> ¿qué será la misma muerte?
>
> (Ibid.)

---

[59] In the midst of his passion Don Álvaro, like Christ on the cross, thirsts; however, it would be unavailing to push the analogy between the two "scenes" too far. Nevertheless, in view of the numerous Christological motifs observed in the literature of *privanza*, including the plays, I think that there is a stronger case for seeing in them an allegory of the Passion of Christ than in some other plays in which such an allegory has been said to exist. Cf. Victor Dixon's review of Elizabeth Auvert Eason, ed. Lope de Vega, *El Duque de Viseo*, *Bulletin of Hispanic Studies*, 48 (1971), 354: "...Dr. Eason's main thesis is that *El Duque de Viseo* (and *El caballero de Olmedo*) may be interpreted in part as an allegory of the Passion of Christ.... She might have strengthened her case by referring to the Christ-analogies seen by Terence May in *El castigo sin venganza* and by Alan Soons and W. C. McCrary in *El caballero de Olmedo*..."

But it is in the face of death itself that Don Álvaro finds a measure of equanimity of spirit that Ruy López knew and that his wife urged upon him. Like his predecessor he ponders the meaning of the *cuna-sepulcro* motif, resigning himself to nature's law and God's decree. Still, however, he can find no cause for self-reproach in his relations with the king; again like Ruy López, he has offended only God:

> Ea, alentad, corazón;
> temor no debéis sentir,
> porque el nacer y el morir
> actos semejantes son. . . .
> La cuna es bien y es trabajo,
> porque sin distancia alguna,
> cuando está hacia arriba es cuna,
> tumba cuando está hacia abajo. . . .
> Bien sabéis, rey verdadero,
> pues sois el original
> de mi rey, que es rey mortal,
> que por su ofensa no muero;
> por las vuestras, sí, y asombre
> vuestra gran piedad, mi Dios,
> que ofenderos pude a vos
> sin hacer ofensa al hombre.
>
> (309a)

As he is led away to the execution block, Don Álvaro states again his awareness of his leading role in the tragedy of man:

> Bien sé que atalaya soy,
> que subí desde la cuna
> al monte de la fortuna,
> y avisos al hombre doy,
> porque se guarde y asombre,
> diciendo con voz incierta:
> "Alerta, humanos, alerta,
> no confiéis en el hombre."
>
> (Ibid.)

This is part of the final message of the play: "no confiéis en el hombre." However, in Mira de Amescua's autograph manuscript Don Álvaro's speech does not end here; the following *redondilla* is added:

(¡Síruaos yo de exemplo a vos
quando doy auisos tales!
"Alerta, alerta, mortales,
confïad en sólo Dios!") [60]

This *redondilla* states the correlative to the preceding one:
"confïad en sólo Dios." Taken together, the two quatrains spell
out a message as old as the Old Testament, a lesson relearned
during the Counter-Reformation and the Baroque. The quatrains
hark back to the biblical admonition, "accursed be the man that
trusteth in man and maketh flesh his arm, and whose heart
departeth from the Lord"; and they also recall the ballad lines,
"Triste el Maestre suspira, / Diciendo que a Dios ensaña / El
hombre que en hombre fía" and "Que el hombre que en hombre
espera, / Hace, de Dios enemigo, / Dios el hombre, y así
bestia." [61] Clear as it is, the meaning of *La adversa fortuna de
don Álvaro de Luna* will be disconcerting to those who are
comfortable with the tradition of humanistic tragedy, which so
often reaffirms the worth of man as a human being, not only as
a creature of God.

Looking back over the play, it is evident that it contains most
of the essentials of Aristotelian tragedy — plus baroque trimmings
and substance. It also contains the three moments of the tragic
rhythm of action (as defined by Kenneth Burke and Francis
Fergusson): [62] Purpose (Don Álvaro's reasoned purpose to emulate
Ruy López in *obrar bien*); Passion (his suffering when his purpose
goes awry and his *hechuras* conspire in his death); Perception
("no confiéis en el hombre"; "confïad en sólo Dios"). It has long
been evident, however, that Don Álvaro's purpose was distorted
from the outset. This, of course, is true of many tragic heroes
who, nevertheless, emerge from their suffering with full vision
of the truth. Not so with Don Álvaro, however, whose final

---

[60] Ed. Sánchez-Arce, vv. 2899 ff.

[61] See n. 19 of this chapter.

[62] Kenneth Burke, *A Grammar of Motives* (New York, 1945), pp. 38 ff.;
and Francis Fergusson, *The Idea of a Theater* (Princeton, 1949; New York,
1953), Chapter I, "The Tragic Rhythm of Action." Burke's well-known for-
mulation of the tragic hero's — *poiema, pathema, mathema* — was translated
by Fergusson as "purpose," "passion," "perception."

perception is incomplete because his *hamartia* remains with him to the last. The nature of his *hamartia* is stated explicitly by Ruy López in the first play, although he is speaking of himself, not Don Álvaro:

> ¿Con qué furor, con qué extremos
> de soberbio y loco error
> nos engaña el propio amor,
> y nunca nos conocemos.
> Nadie sus defectos ve;
> amor propio es amor ciego:
> bien dice el proverbio griego,
> que la mayor ciencia fue
> el conocerse a sí mismo.
>
> (270a)

Don Álvaro could never make this speech about himself because it involves a "science" he never learns.

In his final moments, as he confronts his death, Don Álvaro turns outward, not inward, to find the cause of his tragedy. He has learned much about the treachery of other men, little about himself. This stubborn Aragonese, who has forced fortune, played God, and eclipsed his king, is certain that he must die because of the errors of his fellows, not his own. He has acquired little self-knowledge, yet he becomes reconciled to his mortality. Tragedy's ineluctable Moment of Truth yields him nothing more.

Although Mira de Amescua's *Próspera* and *Adversa fortuna de don Álvaro de Luna* will not satisfy those who insist that tragedy must be ultimately optimistic — that from the suffering and evil endured by the hero must emerge a liberating awareness, reconciliation, and a reaffirmation of life — probably no Spanish play complies to a greater degree with Hegel's "cosmic justice" and Schopenhauer's "eulogy of failure" which they saw as the supreme goals of tragedy. It is probable too that no Golden Age secular play dramatizes more convincingly the tragic vision of life, as that vision was apprehended and expressed by poets and playwrights of the Spanish Baroque. Just as Lisarda, the hapless heroine in Mira's *comedia de santo, El esclavo del demonio,* proclaims as she assesses her ravaged life,

> La vida, el mundo, el gusto y gloria vana
> son junto nada, humo, sombra y pena (Act II)

so Don Álvaro de Luna, the greatest of all Spanish favorites, falls back on the same trope to express his bitter disillusionment:

> Si humo, nada, polvo y viento
> es la vida, ¿qué será
> el bien que el mundo nos da?
> También vendrá a ser tormento.
>
> (305b)

The tragic vision of life underlying Don Álvaro's disenchantment and renunciation is the distinctive mark of Mira de Amescua's tragedies of *privanza*. To a lesser degree it is also the mark of the other fallen-favorite plays.

C. ANONYMOUS, *Morales, paje de don Álvaro de Luna*

Virtually unknown by students of Spanish drama (it is not mentioned in La Barrera's *Catálogo* or in other similar listings), *Morales, paje de don Álvaro de Luna* survives in a late seventeenth- or eighteenth-century manuscript located in the Biblioteca Nazionale of Naples. The manuscript contains no indication of the identity of the author, nor is there any bibliographical evidence on which to base the date of composition. I would venture to say, however, that it was written soon after Mira de Amescua's plays held the boards, because it seems likely that the author of *Morales* intended to capitalize on the popularity of Mira's plays, especially on the final moving scenes of *La adversa fortuna de don Álvaro de Luna* in which the favorite's page has a poignant role.

The sources of *Morales* include those ballads in which the page attends his master immediately before and after the execution, [63] and also Poyo's and Mira's plays on the rise and fall of Don Álvaro. Sister Mary Austin Cauvin, who has made the only previous study of *Morales*, [64] suggests that it is based on *El paje de don Álvaro*, but I think that the reverse is true. [65] Since

---

[63] The ballads which most influenced the composition of the play are Nos. 989, 990, 998, 1004, 1011, and 1019 in Durán, *BAE*, XVI.

[64] Cauvin, pp. 140-44.

[65] As noted by Antonio Restori, "La collezione CCIV. 28033 della Biblioteca Palatina-Parmese," *Studi di Filologia Romanza*, 6 (1893), 144, an

Morales is largely fictitious and contains no historical elements not found in the ballads or in the previous plays, it is doubtful if the author made use of the chronicles.

As the title indicates, *Morales, paje de don Álvaro de Luna* is concerned primarily with the vicissitudes in the life of the page after he enters the service of Don Álvaro and is caught up in the intrigue, both political and amorous, of the Spanish court.

---

eighteenth-century manuscript copy of *El paje de don Álvaro* is located in the Palatinate Library in Parma. On the title page one reads: *Comedia Famosa. / El Paxe de Don Álvaro. / De Don Pedro Calderón.* This play has also been attributed to Luis Vélez de Guevara, to Juan Vélez and to Lope de Vega, in addition to Calderón (see F. E. Spencer and R. Schevill, *The Dramatic Works of Luis Vélez de Guevara* [Berkeley, 1937], p. 233 and n. 7). In the preface to his edition of the *Verdadera quinta parte de comedias del célebre poeta español don Pedro Calderón de la Barca* (Madrid, 1682), Juan de Vera Tassis includes *El paje de don Álvaro* among the list of apocryphal plays attributed to Calderón.

It would be difficult to establish the priority of *Morales, paje de don Álvaro de Luna* and *El paje de don Álvaro* without making a detailed comparison, which I do not think is necessary here. Suffice it to say that unlike *Morales*, which manages to maintain a tenuous connection between its political and amorous plots, *El paje de don Álvaro* is devoid of political dimensions. Its plot is primarily concerned with solving the complications that thwart the love of Morales and Elvira — and again the complications are not the result of political issues but of familial problems and misunderstandings. Don Álvaro intervenes in a few scenes in the first act, but his role is more important for his services as a go-between in affairs of the heart than for his acts as the Condestable of Castile in matters of state. There is no explanation, much less dramatization, of the opposition against him. Neither Vivero nor the queen appears in the play, as they do in *Morales*. There is not a single scene in which the king and his favorite appear together. In sum, *El paje de don Álvaro* represents the utter deterioration of the theme of *privanza* as material for tragedy. Its only moments of tragic mood are supplied by ballad sequences (Durán, Nos. 989 and 1011 *Doble*) interpolated in two scenes, one at the end of the first act, the other at the beginning of the second as a witness to Don Álvaro's execution describes the event. Apparently the author thought that he had a good story, worthy of a second part, although he was commendably self-conscious about the quality of his verse, as the final lines indicate:

> Cumplimientos
> cessen para que se acabe
> la comedia, que su autor,
> supuesto que ésta os agrade,
> promete con grande afecto
> escriuir segunda parte,
> que aunque no lo sean los versos,
> la historia será agradable.

The structure of the play differs substantially from that of most tragedies of *privanza*, in that it does not dramatize the rise of the favorite, only his fall. And, of course, it does not involve the changing fortunes of two favorites, the old and the new. *Morales* is essentially a romantic tragicomedy, and, as such, is structured along the lines typical of many Spanish *comedias*.

It comprises two plots which are more or less inseparable: a political (or "tragic") plot concerning Don Álvaro's loss of favor, leading to his execution, and the grave problems confronted by the page as a result of his steadfast loyalty to his master; a romantic plot which ends happily when Morales succeeds in overcoming all obstacles and wins the hand of his beloved. Not only are these plots intermingled throughout the play but also interlarded in the three acts are humorous scenes involving male and female servants and an assortment of minor characters — an innkeeper, a soldier, a student, and a Breton. The alternation of serious and comic scenes provides the variety of dramatic situations and of changing mood and tempo that we have come to expect in the *comedia*. This is not to say, however, that the common elements of the tragedy of *privanza* are lacking; they are merely diluted. Special attention will be given to these elements in the following summary of the play, although this will necessitate giving greater emphasis to the political plot at the expense of the love intrigue.

En route to Valladolid to seek a position at the court, Morales encounters the hunting party of Juan II. The king and Don Álvaro are engaged in a race on horseback or, more precisely — as the dramatist pointedly indicates — they are *corriendo parejas*. As a result of his efforts to keep pace with the king, the Condestable is thrown from his horse. The augury of Don Álvaro's fall is not lost on the youthful Morales, who, after helping him to his feet, lectures him on the folly of trying to match the king:

> Pues, no pongáis en olvido
> que corriendo una pareja
> con el rey, habéis caído; ...
> que con el rey no es segura
> la igualdad, pues que no dura
> mientras pasa la carrera.
>
> (Act I, fol. 7 r.)

In appreciation for his help, Don Álvaro takes Morales into his service and later the king rewards him handsomely. Vivero, however, regards Don Álvaro's fall with poorly concealed glee. Playing on the meanings of *luna* as both "moon" and "mirror glass," he regrets only that Luna was not shattered in the fall:

> (¡Oh, si en parte dividida   *(Aparte.)*
> la luna hubiera quedado!
>   Es luna que al sol excede;
> condestable llegó a ser,
> mas menguar la luna puede
> y el condestable caer.)
>   (Ibid.)

Aware of the ill-will that Vivero bears toward Don Álvaro, the king also employs the glass-metaphor as he admonishes the envious courtier:

> Dad gracias a la fortuna
> que la luna quedó entera;
> que a estar quebrada la luna,
> quizá en su cristal se viera
> con muchas caras alguna.
>   (Act I, fol. 7 v.)

In keeping with the mirror-image as initiated here and developed later in the play, Vivero and Don Álvaro's other *hechuras* exist only as reflections of Luna. If he cracks, so will his creatures — into many fragments. And, by means of a double-edged conceit, Luna the *espejo* is also a mirror for favorites, a paragon among men. [66] But at this stage of the play we are only reminded of

---

[66] The mirror-image, common in Renaissance literature, occurs in one of the ballads on Don Álvaro (Durán, No. 1019):

> Del rey mi señor he sido
> Luna de un precioso espejo,
> Que el hacerle buena cara
> Era hacerme el rostro bueno.
> Llegó a mí torcido el rostro,
> Pensó ser mío el defecto,
> Tiró el espejo, la luna
> Era vidrio, saltó luego.

The same image occurs several times in Vélez de Guevara's *El espejo del mundo,* in which Don Álvaro has a minor role. On one occasion the

the fragility of glass; forewarned, we can expect the mirror to be broken.

Vivero and Morales engage in a sharp exchange over Don Álvaro's stewardship of the kingdom, but their conflict shifts from the business of politics to an affair of the heart when Doña Elvira appears upon the scene. Elvira is distressed by the ardent attentions of Vivero, but noting her displeasure, Morales rebukes the amorous courtier. Only the timely return of the king prevents them from duelling. At their first meeting, Elvira and Morales feel strongly attracted to each other, whereas their servants, Nuño and Beatriz, initiate a contest of repartee.

Later at the palace, the queen urges her husband to heed the grandees who complain of Don Álvaro's tyranny and ask that he be banished from the kingdom. The king, however, attributes their grievances to envy, and reminds the queen that she owes her position to the favorite. The king then overhears a conversation between Morales and Don Álvaro, in which the latter speaks of his great love for his royal master. Moved by Don Álvaro's devotion, Juan rewards him with more titles and honors.

Nuño brings Morales a letter from Elvira, but Vivero, recognizing the handwriting, tries to gain possession of it. Again the rivals start to duel but are interrupted by Don Álvaro, who reprimands them for fighting in the palace. Morales warns his master that Vivero, motivated by self-interest and envy, is conspiring to destroy him; and again he employs the metaphor of the mirror, as well as that of the "envious clouds" used so frequently in the earlier Don Álvaro plays:

---

protagonist, Don Basco de Portugal, tells Don Álvaro of the misfortunes that have befallen him:

> desdichas han sido mías,
> no tengo yo del Rey quexas.
> Tú Condestable famoso,
> atento te mira en ellas,
> porque a tu próspera dicha,
> espejo y exemplo sean.
> Mírate en mí como espejo,
> verás mi fortuna en ella,
> que eres Luna, y serlo y todo
> de aqueste espejo pudieras.
>
> (Act III)

> Mirad, señor, si algún polvo,
> si algún vaporcillo empaña
> la luna del claro espejo
> y más incapaz de manchas,
> ved que los descuidos leves
> de la condición humana
> turban al cristal más puro . . .
> Luna sois, si algún defecto
> hay que la ofusque, limpiadla
> de las nubes de la envidia,
> del polvo de la esperanza.
>
> (Act I, fols. 17 v.—18 r.)

Don Álvaro is grateful for Morales' concern, but Nuño scolds him for his long-winded moralizing and — satirically — for speaking the truth at court:

> Aquí es necio, loco y vano
> quien avisa o contradice,
> y ansí te has de ir a la mano,
> que el que más lisonjas dice
> es el mejor cortesano.
> Di mentiras y favores;
> la corte es tierra que ya
> no da fruto sino flores.
> Decir verdades es allá
> para los predicadores.
>
> (Act I, fol. 18 v.)

As the second act begins, Elvira, now a lady-in-waiting to the queen, tells Morales that because of the queen's insistence she has consented to marry Vivero, even though she despises him. By a curious turn of feminine logic she blames her inconstancy on the instability of fortune (thereby providing a tenuous thematic connection between the tragic and the romantic plots):

> Si la fortuna no sabe
> ser firme, ¿quién hay que pueda
> ser fiel con una rueda
> donde fe cierta no cabe?
>
> (Act II, fol. 24 v.)

However, in order to assuage Morales' grief, she prays that a sudden accident ("algún súbito accidente") will prevent the marriage from taking place on the morrow.

Elvira's player is answered sooner than she could reasonably expect: Don Álvaro rushes in to announce that he has just thrown Vivero from a balcony and needs a horse to make his escape. But Morales' and Elvira's love is not yet free from obstacles, because Don Juan Pacheco, who has learned of Vivero's death, lets it be known that he intends to ask the queen for Elvira's hand. Pacheco then informs Elvira of the circumstances of Vivero's "accident": Don Álvaro learned that Vivero had turned the grandees against him by writing incendiary tracts, whereupon the Condestable pushed his former follower from the balcony. Pacheco now fears for his friend's safety because the queen and the nobles are calling for his blood — and "el rey es fácil sin duda" (fol. 27 v.). It is Elvira who then proclaims a variation of the thematic statement found in the earlier Don Álvaro plays: "¡Y hay hombres que en hombres fían!" (Ibid.).

In the following scene the king pronounces a long soliloquy (some 150 verses) in which he first grieves over the absence of his favorite, then steels himself to weigh the issue that confronts him: Should he take the side of friendship or of justice? As in Poyo's *La privanza y caída de don Álvaro de Luna* in which the queen persuades her husband to have Don Álvaro brought to trial because the king is the head of the body politic and must control its members, so Juan II in *Morales* employs a similar simile (extended to sixty verses) to convince himself that he must maintain order by dispensing justice:

> Es el rey el corazón
> del reino, porque es la fuente
> de donde manan los miembros
> los espíritus que beben,
> repartiéndolos a todos
> tan proporcionadamente
> que, igualmente desiguales,
> ninguno de ellos se queje . . .
> (Act II, fol. 30 r.)

After the king orders Don Álvaro's arrest, Don Álvaro returns unexpectedly to the palace in order to plead his cause; but before

he sees the king, Morales tries to convince him that the king has
changed and that the grandees will prevail. [67] Don Álvaro will
not listen because he is confident that he is the rock against which
his enemies ("ola frágil") will batter themselves in vain:

> ¿Viste escollo burlarse de la furia
> con que ola frágil su firmeza infuria,
> que ella se desvanece, el que la espera
> inmóvil en sí mismo persevera? . . .
> La que yo miré ola
> volverá leve espuma.
> Estable roca soy; ¿qué maravilla
> si soy el condestable de Castilla?
>
> (Act II, fol. 36 v.)

Don Álvaro's supreme self-confidence (his tragic flaw in this
play) does not desert him even after the king rejects his pleas
and walks out on him, saying: "Don Álvaro, otro soy ya"
(fol. 38 v.). The Condestable (the "estable roca") will not change,
even though his friends abandon him: "Que yo siempre he de
ser yo, / aunque ellos se hayan mudado" (Ibid.). But above all,
Don Álvaro has faith in his king who created him out of nothing
and who, like God, will intervene to save his creature no matter
how great his imperfections are. Morales remains unconvinced,
warning his master that he should not expect too much from
mortal kings:

> . . . no aseguro
> el que espera de hombre puro
> las finezas de hombre Dios.
>
> (Act II, fol. 40 r.)

As Act III begins, Don Álvaro has already been executed.
Nuño relates the circumstances of the execution ("el más trágico
dolor / que lloró teatro humano") to Morales' father Don Francisco de Morales, who has just arrived at court. The scene is
described in terms of a religious sacrifice in which Don Álvaro

---

[67] At this point in the play Nuño quotes a *truhán* as saying that Don
Álvaro will die "en cadahalso" and that the Condestable, therefore, should
avoid the place.

is the innocent, expiatory victim — the victim, as in the other Don Álvaro plays, of his misplaced trust in men:

> El semblante era tal que su inocencia
> llevaba escrito entonces en el frente
> con dos ojos al margen que decían:
> "Ved en qué paran los que en hombres fían."
> ... ...
> Luego empezó el ministro de la muerte
> a disponer la víctima escogida,
> si bien fue edificada injustamente,
> convocada también a mejor vida.
> Ya el alma heroica del varón más fuerte
> desea el golpe o la fatal herida;
> devoto, afable, alegre se dispuso . . .
>
> (Act III, fol. 42 r.)

It is obvious that the Don Álvaro of this play greets death in a far different way than Mira de Amescua's hero whose final moments of piety do not lessen his reluctance to leave the world.

Nuño urges Don Francisco to go comfort his son who has stayed behind to mourn over his master's body, but the father is displeased because Morales has chosen to remain loyal to a criminal executed on the king's orders. He agrees, however, to accompany Nuño to the main square where, in concealment, he observes his grieving son decrying the ways of fortune. Don Francisco can stand no more; he reproaches his son: "que el criado / que así le abona, parece / que es cómplice con su amo" (fol. 45 r.). But so torn by grief is Morales that he does not recognize his father. Employing the familiar ballad lines, he begs for alms: "Dadme, por Dios, hermano, / para ayudar a enterrar este cristiano." [68] Don Francisco is incensed at his son's misplaced piety. After identifying himself, he denounces and disowns Morales, but the youth does not waver:

> Pues, si no os mueve mi llanto
> ni me conocéis por hijo,
> ni como padre he de hablaros,
> "Dadme, por Dios, hermano,
> para ayudar a enterrar este cristiano."
>
> (Act III, fol. 46 v.)

---

[68] The refrain occurs three times in the ballad (Durán, No. 1011 Doble).

After Don Francisco leaves, the king comes in disguise to observe the scene of the tragedy. Remorseful for not having intervened to save his favorite, Juan II asks Morales how the populace has reacted to the king's action in bringing Don Álvaro to justice. Morales' reply is blunt: "Los votos han sido vanos, / pero hay muchos que le culpan," and, "Que me espanto / que fuese un rey tan mudable / y al mayor amigo ingrato" (fol. 48 v.). The abashed monarch warns him that his words may reach the king's ears, but Morales answers with the refrain, "Dadme, por Dios, hermano, / para ayudar a enterrar este cristiano." Later the king orders Don Juan Pacheco to have Morales brought to the palace.

At an inn outside of Valladolid Don Francisco has had a change of heart; he decides to return to the city to aid his son. Before he leaves, however, Morales and Nuño arrive, but they can order nothing to eat because they are penniless. Don Francisco, unobserved by the two men, orders the innkeeper to feed them. He then overhears a debate between Morales and a student over the trial and execution of Don Álvaro — a debate in the form of a scholastic dispute and couched in terms of Latin grammar. Because of its curiousness, I include an example of the student's speeches (obviously a satire on students' propensity for pedantry):

> Tal fue el dativo de pena
> y acusativo de culpa,
> pero si la luna engendra
> envidias con sus crecientes,
> yo no me espanto que tenga
> nominativo de luna
> tal genitivo de menguas.
> Mala gramática ha sido.
>
> (Act III, fol. 54 r.)

But if Morales accepts the student's description of Don Álvaro's execution as a "bad grammatical show," he cannot tolerate the remarks of a Breton that the favorite was disloyal to the king. He threatens to go to Brittany and cut out the slanderer's tongue if he should ever speak ill of Don Álvaro. And once again Don Francisco becomes annoyed on hearing his son defend so ardently the culprit of the king's justice. His fears are realized when Don Juan Pacheco comes to arrest Morales.

Meanwhile at the court, the king tells Elvira that she must marry Pacheco to please the queen. In reply Elvira gives him a written petition that he promises to read later. When Pacheco arrives with Morales, the king closets himself with the page, demanding to know what the youth had said about him. Morales repeats his words of criticism: "Dije que fuiste mudable / y aun ingrato al condestable" (fol. 57 v.). The king's reply is unexpected; rather than rebuking Morales, he criticizes him for not having spoken more harshly. He then praises the page for his loyalty to Don Álvaro.

After this turn of events, it is no surprise when the king grants Elvira's petition that she be allowed to marry Morales instead of Don Juan Pacheco. When Don Francisco de Morales, expecting the worst, arrives prepared to beg that his son's life be spared, he is overjoyed to learn that Morales is to be rewarded with the habit of Santiago. And it so happens that Don Francisco has a lovely daughter who, so thinks the king in his superior wisdom, will make a perfect match for Don Juan Pacheco. The dramatist does not say if there will be a double wedding.

Reviewing the three acts of *Morales, paje de don Álvaro*, it becomes clear that we have moved from the narrow confines of the tragedies of *privanza* into the expansive boundaries of the Spanish *comedia*. Some of the properties of the "authentic" fallen-favorite plays remain: the problem of favoritism and its risks are often mentioned but never thoroughly explored; the usual themes — the instability of fortune, envy, ingratitude, the inconstancy and corruptiblity of man, disillusionment — are all touched upon but seldom stressed; the language, images, and rhetorical devices are employed in a perfunctory way. But the author of *Morales* should not be faulted for what he did not attempt to do; his work should be judged on its merits as the sentimental tragicomedy that it was meant to be.

Above all, the play was written to extoll the loyalty of the page who, in contrast with his fickle elders, never swerves in his devotion to his master; in that the play succeeds. It also succeeds in a more limited way in dramatizing the conflicts that Morales experiences as a result of his loyalty — conflicts with Vivero, the king, and especially with his father. The play fails, however, in bringing Don Álvaro to life. It fails in its few feeble efforts to stage dramatic confrontations between Don Álvaro and his adversaries (suprisingly, Don Álvaro and the queen exchange not a word in the entire play). And most of all it fails because the author was so intent on showing and rewarding Morales' piety that he neglected to communicate any real sense of tragedy arising from the favorite's death. But *Morales* does not represent the ultimate stage in the deterioration of the rise and fall of Don Álvaro de Luna as material for tragedy; that distinction belongs to the derivative play, *El paje de don Álvaro.*

CONCLUSION

Whether they viewed him as a tyrant deserving of his disgrace or as the innocent victim of other men's malignity, the chroniclers of Don Álvaro de Luna agreed on several points: he was a singular man of prepossessing qualities; his rise and fall could only be regarded as a paradigm of tragedy; his death should serve as a moral example to others to set small store on worldly glory. But the author of the *Crónica de don Álvaro de Luna* went beyond the usual moral; he gives a highly idealized portrait of the Condestable, replete with Christological motifs, and urges his readers to emulate the *bienaventurado* Maestre as a martyr of Christ. The balladeers, inspired by the chronicles, enhanced the sentimental view of the favorite and of the pathos of his death. They also concretized some of the themes implicit in the chronicles, and refashioned their rhetorical elements to comply with the requirements of "poetry."

Well read in the chronicles and the ballads, Salucio del Poyo wrote the first play on Don Álvaro — and the first fallen-favorite tragedy — *La privanza y caída de don Álvaro de Luna.* Although he avoids the excessive sentimentality of the ballads, Poyo fails to bring Don Álvaro to life. But notwithstanding his lack of skill as a dramatist, Poyo's play is notable for having brought together all the elements — structural, thematic, and rhetorical — of the *tragedias de privanza.* It is also notable for having structured the fortunes of Don Álvaro — his rise and fall — around the cyclic phases of the moon as an analogue to the traditional Wheel of Fortune.

Written some twenty years after Poyo's tragedy and deeply indebted to it, Mira de Amescua's *Próspera* and *Adversa fortuna de don Álvaro de Luna* represent the artistic culmination of the fallen-favorite tragedies. Absorbing in its plot, penetrating in its thought, and measured in its expression, Mira's two-part play vivifies the risks of *privanza* and communicates its terrible cost in terms of human suffering and loss. But of all the commendable qualities of these two plays, it is probably the characterization of Don Álvaro de Luna that is most rewarding. Not that Don Álvaro is an "original" character in the sense, say, that Hamlet is; rather, he is a "received" figure, one who came to Mira de Amescua largely formed by the earlier chronicles and ballads, by the legends and lore that had grown up around him. In this sense Mira's Don Álvaro is a ritualistic and "metatheatrical" character, one who is conscious throughout the plays that he is playing a role already determined for him and who also knows that he is meant to serve as an example to mankind:

> (¡Síruaos yo de exemplo a vos
> quando doy auisos tales!
> "Alerta, alerta, mortales,
> confïad en sólo Dios!")

Morales, paje de don Álvaro de Luna is typical of many Spanish *comedias* in that it has two plots of more or less equal importance, one romantic, the other political but tragic in its issue. Don Álvaro has a prominent role in the first two acts, but after his execution (in the description of which he is depicted as a Christian martyr, much as in Chacón's chronicle) it becomes Morales' play. The page richly deserves the happy ending which he is granted.

In summarizing the Don Álvaro de Luna plays, one is tempted to fall back on the lunar metaphors which inform them all. The whole cycle is present: crescent (Poyo's *La privanza y caída de don Álvaro de Luna*); full (Mira de Amescua's *Próspera* and *Adversa fortuna de don Álvaro de Luna*); waning (*Morales, paje de don Álvaro de Luna*). And if we wish to adhere to a lunar "formula of four," there is the total eclipse, *El paje de don Álvaro*, which we earlier relegated to a footnote.

VI

THE FAULTLESS FAVORITES: BELISARIUS AND DUARTE PACHECO

Viéndote sobre el cerco de la luna
triunfar de tanto bárbaro contrario,
¿quién no temiera, ¡oh noble Belisario!,
que habías de dar envidia a la Fortuna?
... ...
Quisiéronte cegar tus enemigos,
sin advertir que mal puede ser ciego
quien tiene en tanta fama tantos ojos.
(Francisco de Quevedo, "A Belisario")

... ...
"O' Belisario, disse, que no coro
Das Musas serás sempre engrandecido,
Se em ti viste abatido o bravo Marte,
Aqui tens como quem podes consolar-te!

"Aqui tens companheiro, assi nos feitos
Como no galardão injusto e duro;
Em ti e nelle veremos altos peitos
A baxo estado vir, humilde e escuro:
Morrer nos hospitais, em pobres leitos
Os que ao Rei e à lei servem de muro!
Isto fazem os reis cuja vontade
Manda mais que a justiça e que a verdade."
(Luiz Camões, on Duarte Pacheco in
Os Lusíadas)

Although separated by a millennium, the sixth-century Byzantine hero Belisarius and the sixteenth-century Portuguese
general Duarte Pacheco Pereira had several things in common.
Both were primarily soldiers who made their reputations on the

battlefield and in long service overseas; both were rewarded for their successes by being paraded in triumph on their return to their national capitals; both enjoyed the friendship and respect of their monarchs before being caught up in the intrigue of the court; both fell victim to their enemies and ended in deep misfortune and disgrace. In spite of the difference in their stature as national leaders (Belisarius was by far a greater force in his country) the parallel between the lives and fortunes of the two men was readily apparent to Portuguese writers who often called Duarte Pacheco the Lusitanian Belisarius.

As remarked in chapter IV in the discussion of the tragic hero, José Maravall observes that the authors of the *tragedias de privanza* sought variety in their plays by bringing together kings and favorites of diverse character and in all possible combinations: the good king and the good *privado*, the good king and the bad *privado*, the bad king and the good *privado*, etc. In the case of Belisarius and Duarte Pacheco the identical combination is at work: both are good *privados* whose fate it is to serve, not evil kings, but rash, impetuous men who act before they think. Unfortunately for the favorites, they are destroyed before the remorseful sovereigns can repair the damage. But are Belisarius and Duarte Pacheco really "faultless" as I have termed them? Only in a moral sense, not in an intellectual one. As a matter of fact, both of them are as imprudent and imperceptive in their way as the rulers they serve; both at times are hopelessly naive. It is interesting to note, however, that their creators — Mira de Amescua and Jacinto Cordero — do not scorn them for their naïveté and imprudence; rather (which is rare in the Baroque) they pity them for their guilelessness. But Duarte Pacheco has another — and very human — fault: he is a terrible bore. Long-suffering though he is (I later liken him to Job), he tries the patience of all who will listen to his prolix recitals of his tribulations. That is an unforgiveable fault in drama.

In the following pages it will be seen that there are numerous thematic and a few textual parallels between Mira de Amescua's Don Álvaro de Luna tragedies and his Belisarius play, *El ejemplo mayor de la desdicha*. It should be noted now that those plays and Jacinto Cordero's Duarte Pacheco plays share a com-

mon message. That message is spelled out in the ballads on Don
Álvaro de Luna and summed up in two verses in *La adversa
fortuna de don Álvaro de Luna*:

> "Alerta, humanos, alerta,
> no confiéis en el hombre."

A. MIRA DE AMESCUA, *El ejemplo mayor de la desdicha*

The greatest general of the Byzantine Empire, Belisarius
entered the service of Justinian when the latter succeeded to the
throne in 528, and he continued to serve his emperor at home
and abroad for almost forty years. He secured Justinian's
sovereignty in the East by defeating the Persians at Dara; after
he returned home he quelled an insurrection in Constantinople.
He invaded Africa, captured Carthage, and destroyed the kingdom
of the Vandal Gelimer. Called the Third Africanus by his
countrymen because of his victories in Africa, he returned again
in triumph to Constantinople; but he soon set out for Sicily and
Italy where he defeated the Ostrogoths and became master of
Rome. Recalled by Justinian, he was sent to Syria where he
repulsed the marauding Persians; but on his return to the imperial
court, he was degraded by the emperor's wife, the spiteful
Theodora. Years later he was called upon again to repel the
Huns who threatened to overrun the empire.

Less than two years before his death, Belisarius fell into
disgrace. Accused of having conspired against Justinian's life, he
was summoned before the imperial council for a hearing.
Although he denied the charges against him, he was placed
under house arrest and his possessions were confiscated. Six
months later he was exonerated and his honors and property were
restored to him, but broken in health and spirit, he died within
a year. Traditionally Belisarius has been regarded as one of
history's most striking examples of a magnanimous man cast
down by bad fortune and by the ingratitude of an impetuous
ruler. It was inevitable that he should become the subject of a
Spanish tragedy of *privanza* as well as several foreign tragedies. [1]

---

[1] I have not made a thorough study of all the Belisarius plays, but the
earliest to come to my attention is *Belisar* (1607) by the German Jesuit

The principal source of *El ejemplo mayor de la desdicha*, as indicated by Valbuena Prat, was the *Historia Arcana* of Procopius of Caesarea, translated by Nicholas Allemanus from the original Greek into Latin in 1623. [2] Since Procopius was Belisarius' personal secretary and his companion on several campaigns, it is not surprising that he gives an idealized portrait of his patron and a laudatory account of his accomplishments. If anything, Mira de Amescua exceeds Procopius in portraying Belisarius as a man of surpassing generosity and altruism. To Procopius are also owed the names and traits of character of other historical persons in the play, but Mira took many liberties in delineating the characters and in developing the plot. Procopius is not responsible for the legend, which has no basis in fact, that Belisarius was blinded on the orders of Justinian and was forced to beg for bread on the streets of Constantinople. However, this legend acquired currency in the late Middle Ages, and it is small wonder that the Spanish dramatist saw fit to include its piteous circumstances as the culminating misfortune in *El ejemplo mayor de la desdicha.*

It is not known when Mira de Amescua finished the autograph of his tragedy because he did not affix the date of its completion, but the manuscript bears an *aprobación* for a performance (probably its first performance) signed by Lope de Vega in July of 1625. [3] Presumably Mira completed his tragedy shortly before that time — or less than a year after the *aprobación*, dated October 17, 1624, that appears on the autograph of *La adversa fortuna de don Álvaro de Luna.* Notwithstanding the great difference in quality between the Belisarius and Don Álvaro plays (the latter are much superior in almost every respect), they have much in common other than generic similarities, indicating that Mira borrowed from the earlier Don Álvaro plays to compose

---

Jakob Bidermann, who wrote several school dramas in Latin. Two French tragedies, Desfontaines' *Bélisaire* and Jean Rotrou's *Bélissaire* (printed 1644) are both based on Mira de Amescua's play (Henry C. Lancaster, *A History of French Dramatic Literature* [Baltimore, 1929], Part I, II, 338).

[2] Mira de Amescua, *Teatro*, II, ed. Ángel Valbuena Prat, *Clásicos Castellanos*, vol. 82 (Madrid, 1947), p. x. All citations to *El ejemplo mayor* are to this edition.

[3] Ibid., p. 250.

El ejemplo mayor de la desdicha. There are a few textual parallels that suggest that Mira had the Don Álvaro plays at hand — or very much in mind — while he was composing his tragedy on Belisarius (henceforth referred to as Belisario).

The similarities between the rise and fall of Don Álvaro de Luna and Belisario are obvious, but they are more superficial than significant. Both men serve their sovereigns for almost forty years; both men hold their countries together against the designs of domestic and foreign foes. Both not only become privy to their rulers but they also enjoy their intimate friendship (although in presenting the relationship between Belisario and Justiniano as rivaling that of Castor and Pollux, Mira violates all historical evidence in favor of poetic license). Both favorites are envied and conspired against; both are maligned by a vindictive queen. When Don Álvaro and Belisario are accused of disloyalty, they are denied by their friends and condemned by their royal masters. Moved by the pleas of Don Álvaro's wife, the king regrets his hasty decision, but he acts too late to halt the execution. Only Don Álvaro's wife and page remain loyal to the deposed favorite until the very end. Similarly, Justiniano begins to repent after he has ordered Belisario's eyes plucked out, but he does not fully realize his error until the favorite's sweetheart Antonia (historically, his wife Antonina) reveals how the emperor has been deceived. Only Antonia and his servant Floro remain faithful to Belisario to the last.

But the fact that *El ejemplo mayor de la desdicha* owes much to Mira's Don Álvaro de Luna plays does not save it from being a poorly executed tragedy. The reasons are simple: even though it has an earnest message concerning the pitfalls of *privanza* and the doleful inconsistencies of human behavior, the plot becomes so bogged down in intrigue that it never succeeds in extricating itself. Moreover, Belisario, upon whom the thrust of the play so largely depends, never becomes a believable hero, because he too is sacrificed to the intrigue.

The intrigue centers upon the motif of the *reina enamorada* — but with a new twist. [4] Before her marriage to Justiniano,

---

[4] As stated earlier, Sister Mary Austin Cauvin, "The *comedia de privanza* in the Seventeenth Century," employs the terms *rey enamorado* and

the Empress Teodora loved Belisario, but he remained politely cool to her advances. He is now in love with her cousin Antonia. Bent on revenge, Teodora forbids Antonia to communicate with Belisario; and she also commissions, successively, three courtiers to kill him. In each case, however, the would-be assailant, having discovered that Belisario has generously befriended him, refuses to murder his benefactor. Each man warns the favorite that a woman has instigated the plot against him, but not until well along in the third act does Belisario learn whether it is Antonia, whose strange silence makes her suspect, or Teodora who wishes to kill him. As a consequence, much of the play is consumed in pondering the ways of women rather than the significant questions of favoritism as a way of life. [5]

The intrigue is rounded out with several customary devices of cape-and-sword drama: eavesdropping, mistaken identities, sleep talking, and intercepted letters. It is an unaddressed love letter, meant for Antonia but confiscated by Teodora, that leads to Justiniano's conviction that Belisario has betrayed his trust. The jealous emperor than orders his favorite to be blinded for having laid eyes on his wife: "Los ojos han de pagar / lo que pecaron los ojos" (Act III, vv. 2312-13). The theme of "seeing and not seeing" is fundamental to the meaning of *El ejemplo mayor de la desdicha*, but its tragic significance is diluted because its ultimate and ironic representation — Belisario's blinding — is the result of the machinations of a vengeful female.

No tragic protagonist can escape unscathed from such heavy interlarding of intrigue; Belisario is no exception. Apparently Mira de Amescua intended to depict him as a model favorite and a paragon of virtue, but if the intrigue does not wholly

---

reina enamorada for the kings and queens whose amorous proclivities provide the basis of the intrigue in several plays of *privanza*.

[5] Of course, the play contains several statements on the unhappy fate of *privados*, including the following one:

> Desde César, el imperio
> todo es tragedias y muertes
> de varones principales.
> Por invidia o por venganza,
> teatros son de la mudanza
> los palacios imperiales.
>
> (Act II, vv. 1148-53)

destroy his credibility, his consummate goodness does. Belisario has only one ambition: to do good — *hacer bien, obrar bien.* He is also convinced that his good works will protect him from harm:

> Yo, Floro, por muchos modos
> tengo de hacer bien a todos,
> y esto me habrá de guardar.
>
> (Act I, vv. 150-52)

But if this should not be the case, "haga yo bien siempre, y sea / quien quisiere mi enemigo" (Act I, vv. 155-56).

Time and again the favorite reiterates his faith that good works are never wasted, because, if for no other reason, virtue is its own reward:

> Mas si el hacer bien me guarda,
> pensamiento, no temamos;
> hagamos bien, porque al fin
> esto no podrá faltarnos.
>
> (Act I, vv. 911-14)

And, "no se pierde el bien que se hace" (Act II, v. 1231).

Like Don Álvaro de Luna, Belisario insists that his militant charity is not motivated by personal ambition ("Hago bien sin ambición" — Act II, v. 1243), but unlike the Spanish favorite, he is not concerned whether or not his beneficiaries are grateful:

> El bien obrar
> por sí mismo se ha de amar,
> y no porque lo agradezcan.
>
> (Act II, vv. 1224-26)

Indeed Belisario is a Christ-like figure, one capable of asking that his enemies be forgiven because they know not what they do. But he is also human enough to become apprehensive of his good fortune (like many other favorites) when the emperor continues to lavish favors on him:

> Fortuna, tú que me subes
> hasta la región del fuego,
> y como el Olimpo griego
> me has coronado de nubes,

si me levantas ansí
para desdicha mayor,
o niégueme tu favor
o ten lástima de mí.

(Act I, vv. 775-83)

Throughout the play Belisario is shown to have something of
a martyr-complex, but when he is condemned for a crime he
did not commit, his sense of outrage and instinct for survival
assert themselves. His admonition to Justiniano, as he pleads for
his life, is similar to Don Álvaro's final plea to John II:

BELISARIO	DON ÁLVARO DE LUNA
¿Por qué allí me habéis honrado	Si me las disteis, señor,
con magistrados y oficios,	por darme lugar más alto
si era el subirme tan alto	de que arrojarme, pregunto:
para mayor precipicio? ...	¿fueron mercedes o agravios?
Cruel sois haciendo bien,	¿Por qué me hicisteis tan rico
avaro en el beneficio,	para hacerme desdichado?
tirano dando la vida;	Cruel sois haciendo bien,
engañoso es vuestro estilo.	dando vida, sois tirano.
(Act III, vv. 2496 ff.)	(Act III, p. 207b) [6]

And just as Don Álvaro asks that his life be spared ("Acordaos de mí, acordaos; / no borréis la imagen vuestra" [Ibid.]), so
Belisario ends his plea: "¡No deshagáis vuestra imagen!" (Act III,
v. 2554). Before they are led away, both favorites sound a final
warning to mankind: "Alerta, humanos, alerta, / no confiéis en el
hombre," says Don Álvaro de Luna (Act III, p. 308a). "Mortales,
alerta; alerta," exclaims Belisario (Act III, v. 2708). The message
of *El ejemplo mayor de la desdicha,* a message which is clear
enough, is aptly summed up in the words of the censor who
approved the play for presentation in 1625: "[Esta comedia] no
tiene inconveniente, sino aviso y escarmiento de las confianzas
humanas." [7]

Belisario, a man who fights the sins of the world with the
arms of a saint, is the most faultless — the most morally faultless
— of all favorites. In the final scene, as he stands with the blood

---

[6] Ed. Cotarelo y Mori, *NBAE,* IV.
[7] Ed. Valbuena Prat, p. 250.

gushing from his empty eye sockets, he is also the most pathetic, if not the most tragic, of all the fallen favorites. In his blindness, he now sees that he must have offended God to deserve such punishment (vv. 2658-61) — but no, not really, because unlike other favorites he can find no cause for self-reproach. As he begs the bystanders for alms, he can truthfully say that his punishment is completely unmerited:

> Señores, si el mal lastima
> cuando no se ha merecido,
> dad limosna a quien castiga
> la fortuna por leal.
>
> (Act III, vv. 2544-47)

Unmerited punishment is, of course, a major source of tragic pathos. But a "good" moral and a "good" hero and "good" pathos do not necessarily make a good tragedy. Even though Mira de Amescua's play avoids the easy moral of poetic justice, it is hard to forget that the hero's catastrophe and the lesson to be learned from it were produced by the scheming — during three acts — of a spiteful woman. [8]

B. JACINTO CORDERO, *La primera y segunda parte de Duarte Pacheco*

Author of some twenty plays written in Castilian, the Portuguese ensign Jacinto Cordero (Cordeiro) made his debut as a dramatist at an early age. His play *De la entrada del rey en Portugal*, written to commemorate the state visit made by Philip III to Portugal in 1619, was published two years later when the author may have been only fifteen. [9] His precocity was

---

[8] Speaking of Mira's play and of Rotrou's adaptation, Lancaster, p. 339, observes: "Neither author noticed the absurdity of the emperor's readiness to accept the evidence offered against his favorite by the discredited empress. . . . Theodora's extraordinary vindictiveness is insufficiently explained by the fact that she had once failed to win the general's love."

[9] Biographical, bibliographical, and critical material concerning Jacinto Cordero is minimal. He is mentioned only in passing, if at all, in the histories of Portuguese literature (probably because he wrote almost exclusively in Castilian); however, La Barrera devotes two columns to him in his *Catálogo bibliográfico y biográfico del teatro antiguo español* (Madrid,

not attended by originality, however, if one may safely judge from his *privanza* plays. *De lo que es privar,* printed in the *Segunda parte* of Cordero's plays (1634), is a run-of-the-mill *comedia de privanza,* heavily laden with intrigue but brought to a happy ending when the maligned favorite proves his mettle. *La primera y segunda parte de Duarte Pacheco* (also known as *La próspera* and *Adversa fortuna de Duarte Pacheco*) are highly derivative plays, made up of episodes, dramatic situations, and incidents purloined from earlier works. Only the hero, the historical setting, and the tone are really new.

The historical Duarte Pacheco Pereira gained fame as a soldier in the wars in India in the first decade of the sixteenth century when he successfully defended the kingdom of Cochin, an ally of Portugal, against the encroachments of neighboring princes. [10] History has it that he scored victories over five Indian kings, including the powerful Samorin of Calicut, whose army of sixty thousand was decimated by a small band of Portuguese and their Cochin allies under the command of Pacheco. So grateful was the King of Cochin that he wanted to reward Pacheco liberally, but the latter refused all gifts because his only ambition was to serve God and his king. But rewarded he was when he returned to Lisbon in 1605. He was warmly received by King Manuel, paraded in triumph, and pensioned for life. Years later he was named governor of São Jorge de Mina on the west coast of Africa — and there his troubles began. Accused of feathering his own nest at the expense of the royal treasury, he was brought home in chains and imprisoned. Although he was eventually exonerated, Pacheco, according to legend, wandered homeless and forsaken before dying in extreme penury. In a moving tribute

---

1860), pp. 99-100, and Domingo García Peres, *Catálogo razonado biográfico y bibliográfico de los autores portugueses que escribieron en castellano* (Madrid, 1890), pp. 122-23, gives a more complete bibliographical description of his works. Both La Barrera and García Peres give 1606 as the year of Cordero's birth; but Heitor Martins, "Jacinto Cordeiro e *La Estrella de Sevilla,*" *Actas do V Colóquio Internacional de Estudos Luso-Brasileiros,* vol. IV (Coimbra, 1966), pp. 10-11, believes that he was probably born several years earlier.

[10] Historical information on Duarte Pacheco Pereira, especially on his later years, is scanty. Aubrey F. G. Bell devotes a chapter to him in *Portuguese Portraits* (Oxford, 1917), pp. 79-101.

to the hero of Cochin in *The Lusiads,* Camoens refers to him as
the Lusitanian Achilles; but, recalling his later misfortunes, the
poet compares him with the ill-starred Belisarius because of
the cruel treatment he also received from an ungrateful monarch. [11]

Influenced by Camoens's vision of Duarte Pacheco, Jacinto
Cordero dramatizes the rise and fall of the luckless soldier as a
Portuguese Belisarius. Pious and patriotic, his only ambition is to
serve his faith and his country. Innocent of wrongdoing, his only
fault lies in boring his listeners with repeated and lengthy
recitals of his past deeds. Pathetic and sentimental (an example
incarnate of Portuguese sentimentality), he far exceeds Mira de
Amescua's Belisarius in the magnitude of his self-pity. [12] Duarte
Pacheco's trials are many, but he is also a very trying person.

Although *La primera y segunda parte de Duarte Pacheco*
owe much to earlier plays for their themes and structure, they
have two features which distinguish them from most other two-
part tragedies of *privanza*: (1) Pacheco's fortunes start going badly
as early as the second act of the *Primera parte,* and he is not at
the summit of his prosperity at its conclusion. Indeed, he barely
manages to escape with his life, and even though he is reconciled

---

[11] After narrating Pacheco's deeds on the battlefield and extolling him
above the heroes of Greece and Rome, Camoens devotes stanzas XXII–XXV
of Canto X of *Os Lusíadas* to the injustices with which the hero was repaid.

[12] It is difficult to say whether or not Jacinto Cordero knew and used
Mira de Amescua's Belisarius and Don Bernardo de Cabrera plays (although
the similarities between them and *La primera y segunda parte de Duarte
Pacheco* are numerous) because we do not know the date of composition
of the latter. The first known edition of the Duarte Pacheco plays was
printed in his *Seis comedias famosas* (Lisbon, 1630); however, he seems to
have been working on them as early as 1621. In the *Prologo ao Leyctor*
of *La entrada del rey* (Lisbon, 1621), Cordero states: "Se a que offereço
for recebida como a beneuolencia que mereçe a singeleza de meu animo,
empregaloey como o cabedal que me fica *em acabar alguas obras que tenho
comesadas de Heroes valerosos, que na India me conuidaraõ cõ o belicoso
som de suas valerosas Proezas*" (italics mine). The italicized words almost
certainly refer to the Duarte Pacheco plays. The earliest date associated
with Mira's *El ejemplo mayor de la desdicha* is 1625; the date of composition
of his *Próspera* and *Adversa fortuna de don Bernardo de Cabrera* (first
printed in 1634 in the apocryphal *Parte veintenueve* of Lope de Vega's
comedias) is not known. No one has ever suggested that perhaps Mira de
Amescua knew and used Cordero's Duarte Pacheco plays.

temporarily with the king, their relations remain strained. (2) The usual formula of having a new *privado* ascend to prosperity as the old favorite falls from favor is not present. Instead, the *Segunda parte* dwells on the hero's calamities, and to make matters worse, the misfortunes of the father are visited on his son, Juan Fernández Pacheco.

The initial scene of the *Primera parte* takes place in Cochin, where, as in history, Duarte Pacheco refuses the many gifts offered him by the grateful king. In order to make sure that we do not miss the irony, Cordero has Pacheco say repeatedly that his own king will reward him well. Returning to Lisbon, Pacheco is welcomed by King Manuel and honored with a public procession; but his hour of triumph is marred by an unseen *Voz* that sounds a series of ominous warnings, ending with the prediction: "Tú te verás presso en hierros" (Act II, fol. 8 r.).[13] Shaken by the augury, Pacheco pronounces a soliloquy of four *décimas*, a soliloquy that unites the familiar themes of the inconstancy of fortune, the brevity of life, the vanity of human glory, the precariousness of *privanza*, and the necessity of doing good works (*obrar bien*). Two of the *décimas* follow:

> Poco a poco, altiuas glorias,
> en cuyo engaño cifrado
> veo que el bien es prestado,
> que ofrecen vuestras memorias;
> no os animen las vitorias
> de vuestro breve sumario:
> porque es el mundo contrario
> a los hombres de opinión,
> testigo desto es Cypión,
> Xergues (sic) y el gran Belisario....
> Mas poned de parte vuestra,
> alma, siempre el bien obrar,
> para poder acertar
> como el exemplo nos muestra:
> de las potencias maestra
> sed siempre, y acertaréys,

---

[13] Citations to *La primera parte de Duarte Pacheco* are to a *suelta*, without place or date, consisting of twenty numbered folios. The *suelta* is located in the Biblioteca Nacional in Madrid.

como esta intención lleuéis,
no os desvanezca esta gloria,
quando en la humana memoria
tantos exemplos tenéys.

(Act II, fol. 8 r.)

Because of his strength of character and his awareness of the dangers of his situation, Duarte Pacheco would seem to be competent to guard against the fluctuations of fortune, but he cannot protect himself against the envy and malice of others. Lisardo, his rival for the hand of Beatriz and the king's secretary, poisons the king's mind against him by insinuating that Pacheco has been disloyal. The irate king confronts Pacheco, drawing his sword and challenging him to fight. The favorite refuses to draw against his sovereign, and, as an act of obeisance, places his sword at the king's feet. King Manuel is temporarily appeased.

Chagrined to learn that Pacheco has been pardoned by the king, Lisardo (a typical villainous Machiavellian secretary), then hires three assassins to kill his rival. Pacheco puts them to flight, however, but spares the life of Lisardo, whom he admonishes: "Mira no seas ingrato / a la piedad que he tenido" (Act II, fol. 13 r.). But Pacheco realizes that his very generosity has earned him an implacable enemy: "Este será mi enemigo: / o el mundo miente, o me engaño" (Ibid.).

At the end of Act II, King Manuel, who oscillates between frivolity and fury throughout much of the play, teases Beatriz by telling her that she must marry Lisardo. Distressed by this match, Beatriz dresses in mourning for the ceremony, but she is overjoyed when Duarte Pacheco turns out to be the bridegroom. Lisardo, however, is not amused. He renews his determination to destroy his rival.

Years later as the third act begins, Duarte Pacheco, accused of trying to usurp the rule of São Jorge de Mina, is brought back to Lisbon in chains. In the presence of the king he proclaims his innocence, but the king walks out on him, and one by one his former friends desert him. Left alone, he apostrophizes fortune, decrying his abandonment:

Ya, fortuna, puedes
con el baybén de tu rueda

atropellar mis mercedes;
todos se van poco a poco. . . .
todos solo me han dexado,
mas pobre y preso no tiene
ni consuelo en sus trabajos,
ni amigo en sus accidentes:
¡Qué solo es un pobre honrado!

(Act III, fol. 14 v.)

As in *La adversa fortuna de don Álvaro de Luna* Pacheco's wife comes to encourage him (though her news that all his property has been confiscated is hardly calculated to cheer him up). Like other favorites before him Pacheco now realizes that his error lay in serving earthly kings too well, the Divine King too little; but like Belisarius he is confident that heaven will protect him in his innocence. His faith is shaken, however, when he is found guilty and imprisoned.

There follows a scene reminiscent of the one in *La Estrella de Sevilla* in which Sancho Ortiz de la Roelas, unjustly jailed, goes mad with grief. [14] Here Duarte Pacheco goes berserk, fancy-

---

[14] Because of the similarity between the jail scenes in *La primera parte de Duarte Pacheco* and *La Estrella de Sevilla* in which the protagonist becomes delirious with grief and engages in wild flights of fantasy, and because of numerous grammatical, linguistic, and literary similarities between Cordero's other plays and *La Estrella de Sevilla*, I once entertained the notion that the Portuguese dramatist should be considered as a serious candidate for the authorship of the famous Spanish play which is still in search of an undisputed father. Among other things that disturbed me then — and continue to disturb me — is the fact that if Cordero was indeed born in 1606, he was simply too young and inexperienced to write a play as skillful as *La Estrella de Sevilla*, believed to have been composed in 1623. At any rate, I communicated my notion to my former colleague, Heitor Martins, and urged him to investigate the matter further. In his monograph "Jacinto Cordeiro e *La Estrella de Sevilla*" (see note 9), Martins adduces additional evidence to support Cordero's authorship. Among that evidence is the fact that in addition to the delirium scene in *La primera parte de Duarte Pacheco*, two other of Cordero's plays (*La entrada del rey* and *El fabor en la sentencia*) also contain delirium scenes. The one in *El fabor en la sentencia*, in which the protagonist imagines he is in hell, is remarkably similar in detail to the scene in *La Estrella de Sevilla*. Of course we need additional evidence before we can consider Cordero to be the long-lost author of *La Estrella*, because the inclusion of a delirium scene in jail offers no conclusive proof. Luis Vélez de Guevara, whom Anibal suggested as a candidate for the authorship of *La Estrella de Sevilla*

ing himself at the head of his troops and reenacting the battles that brought him fame. Also as in *La Estrella de Sevilla* his servant Gonzalo humors him in his wild fantasy until he recovers his senses:

> Ya buelvo en mí, loco he estado,
> mas ¿cómo no hará locuras
> quien passa entre sinrazones
> el rigor destas injurias?
>
> (Act III, fol. 18 r.)

An offstage musician sings of Belisario, whose misfortunes reflect on Pacheco's situation and enhance his somber mood:

> "Buen exemplo es Belisario,
> en cuya aduersa fortuna,
> parece que la desgracia
> de su valor hizo burla,
> vencedor de mil batallas,
> fue tal su suerte oportuna,
> que le sacaron los ojos."
>
> (Act III, fol. 18 v.)

Duarte Pacheco sees himself as another Belisario — as another example for the edification of mankind: "de lo que canta, que en mí / se ve el exemplo..."

At the end of the *Primera parte de Duarte Pacheco* Lisardo's fellow conspirators in São Jorge de Mina confess by letter their plot against Pacheco. Lisardo is killed in a duel by Don Rodrigo de Melo, Pacheco's one friend who has not deserted him; and Pacheco himself is pardoned by the king. Still proud in spite of his many ordeals, Pacheco is reluctant to be pardoned for crimes that he did not commit, as he pointedly tells King Manuel: "...bien puedo / escussar esos perdones / en delitos que no he hecho" (Act III, fol. 20 r.).

If the *Primera parte de Duarte Pacheco* adds few new dimensions to the literature of *privanza*, the *Segunda parte* adds even

---

("Observations on *La Estrella de Sevilla*," *Hispanic Review*, 2 [1934], 1-38), includes a similar but unimportant scene in the third act of *El conde don Pero Vélez y don Sancho el Deseado*.

fewer. It need not detain us long. Much of the action centers upon the rivalry of Duarte Pacheco's son Juan Fernández Pacheco and of Prince Juan for the love of Elena. She reciprocates the love of Juan Fernández, but the prince, as arbitrary and unpredictable as his father, orders his rival not even to look at her.

The vicissitudes of the young lovers are punctuated by the lamentations of Duarte Pacheco, who continues to importune the king with written petitions and personal appeals. Again, after being rejected by the word-weary king, Pacheco expresses his *desengaño*:

> Tal es nuestra humana vida,
> el exemplo en mí se vio,
> pues el Rey me levantó
> para dar mayor caída.
> No me admira su mudança,
> ni su inconstancia me admira,
> quel mundo es una mentira
> y una engañosa esperança.
>
> (Act I, p. 12) [15]

But later, in a conversation with his son (to whom he once again recounts his former exploits), Duarte Pacheco has a moment of insight: his misfortunes have been ordained by heaven because he once struck a priest, and the consequences of his sin have been visited upon his hapless son:

> Ofendí a aquel Sacerdote,
> y aunque razón me sobrasse,
> al Cielo tengo ofendido
> en mi atrevimiento fácil. . . .
> y hasta en vos veo señales
> que pagáis daquesta offensa
> tributos por ser mi sangre.
>
> (Act I, p. 31)

---

[15] Citations to the *Segunda parte* are to a *suelta* which bears the title *La Gran / Comedia de la Segunda Parte / de la Adversa Fortuna de / Duarte Pacheco. / El Alferez Iacinto Cordero. / Representóla Salazar Mahoma.* Because of the pagination this so-called *suelta* seems to have been torn from Cordero's *Seis comedias famosas* (Lisbon, 1630), but I cannot be sure since I have worked with microfilm ordered from the Biblioteca Nacional in Madrid and have not seen the text in the *Seis comedias*.

And, as if his afflictions were not enough, Duarte Pacheco suffers another blow. As Act I ends, he hears an offstage *Voz* predict that he will die in an asylum for the poor.

Things continue to go bad for father and son. Juan Fernández saves the prince's life and earns — temporarily — his gratitude, but soon after he is imprisoned for communicating with Elena. In Act III, after Prince Juan has replaced his deceased father on the throne, the climax of Duarte Pacheco's trials is capped. He goes to see the new king to plead his cause, but Juan, engrossed in documents confirming the disloyalty of his secretary Barroso, does not look up. Thinking that Pacheco is Barroso, he upbraids him and orders him to leave Portugal in perpetual exile. Poor Pacheco can stand no more; he cries unashamedly as he says to Gonzalo:

> Bien sabes tú mi valor,
> y si estoy deshecho en llanto,
> no te cause, amigo, espanto
> mi llanto, pena, y dolor;
> llora el alma con amor,
> viendo lo poco que medras,
> llora dexar mis dos yedras,
> y que llore, no te asombre,
> que poco importa ser hombre,
> que no son los hombres piedras.
> (Act III, p. 79)

Predictably, after Duarte Pacheco goes to take leave of his family, Gonzalo parodies his master's speech. Typical of the *gracioso,* Gonzalo will remain faithful to Pacheco by accompanying him into exile, but he bemoans his hunger:

> la sangre falta en las venas,
> pança, viendo que no medras;
> si el vino y pan son tus yedras,
> que yo llore, no te asombre,
> que poco importa ser hombre,
> que no son los hombres piedras.
> (Act III, p. 80)

Here, as in so many other Spanish plays, pathos is not allowed to remain unrelieved; parody is its antidote.

Meanwhile, Juan Fernández has been freed from prison because Elena has promised to marry a man of the king's choosing. She, however, gains the king's permission to enter a convent. Juan Fernández is not happy with the bargain, but impotent to act, he can only philosophize on his wretched lot: Life is a clock which not only ticks off the minutes of man's declining existence but which also measures hours of misery for the unfortunate.

Duarte Pacheco takes leave of his family with a long farewell of six tearful pages, in which he again recalls his deeds of yesteryear and compares himself with Belisario. And once again Gonzalo parodies his master's speech, taking almost three pages to bid farewell to those whom he holds most dear:

> ¡Ay, panadera; ay, tauernero mío,
> no lo sintáis, y no lloréis conmigo,
> de que a vno lleue el pan, y al otro el vino.
> (Act III, p. 98)

Sometime later the king learns that he mistakenly exiled Duarte Pacheco, not Barroso, but it is too late to correct his error. Gonzalo returns to report that Pacheco, after wandering homeless and friendless, died in a poorhouse in Valencia de Aragón (as the *Voz* had predicted). To make amends the king bestows Elena's hand on Juan Fernández and endows her with Barroso's estate.

Because of the uncertainty of the date of composition of the Duarte Pacheco plays and their priority in relation to Mira de Amescua's tragedies of *privanza*, it is impossible — and perhaps unimportant — to know by which, if any, of Mira's plays Jacinto Cordero was influenced. Several things are clear, however. Cordero conceived of Duarte Pacheco as a Portuguese Belisarius, a faultless, pathetic figure much like the Byzantine hero in Mira's *El ejemplo mayor de la desdicha* — but very different from Mira's willful Don Álvaro de Luna, who continually reaches beyond his grasp. He also conceived of Duarte Pacheco as a Portuguese Job, who endures his many sufferings, not stoically, but loquaciously as he maintains his justice before king and court. And, like the biblical character, he constantly urges patience on his family and himself, but he will not stop talking about his miseries. Job-like characters do not make good tragic heroes because their self-righteousness tends to diminish their righteousness and to obscure the injustices done to them by the gods and fortune.

In the *Segunda parte de Duarte Pacheco* the usual themes of the *privanza* plays (prominent enough in the *Primera parte*) are diluted in tears, as father, mother, son, and servant bemoan their unhappy lot. Because of its domesticity, its sentimentality and pathos (often bordering on bathos), the *Segunda parte* anticipates the French *comédie larmoyante* of the eighteenth century.

Taken together, Mira de Amescua's *El ejemplo mayor de la desdicha* and Jacinto Cordero's Duarte Pacheco plays evince two major problems, one of which is peculiar to them alone, the other of which pertains to most, and especially the later, fallen-favorite tragedies. I shall deal first with the second problem, which may be put in the form of a question: To what extent can amorous intrigue be introduced into a tragedy (whose chief concern is not romantic love) without destroying the tragic mood? It is a question which long harassed many writers of tragedy but which Spanish dramatists often ignored because they did not regard tragedy as sacrosanct. The question does not arise with regard to Mira de Amescua's Don Álvaro de Luna plays because the love intrigue is minimal; nor does it arise with regard to *Morales, paje de don Álvaro* because the anonymous author intended it to be a romantic drama. But in *El ejemplo mayor de la desdicha* and especially in the *Segunda parte de Duarte Pacheco*, both clearly meant to be tragedies, the amorous intrigue is so prominent, albeit desultory, that the tragic mood is constantly threatened, if not destroyed. The problem continues to reassert itself in most of the later tragedies in which the intrigue attendant upon amorous adventure occupies an increasingly disproportionate share of attention.

The first problem, peculiar to the Belisarius and Duarte Pacheco plays, concerns the nature of the tragic heroes themselves. It is difficult to write convincingly about faultless heroes for the simple reason that they are almost always right. They seldom recognize any moral ambiguities; they are seldom torn by having to choose between right and wrong. And when they are faced with a dilemma not of their own making, they never look for an expedient way out. Certainly they complain when they are unjustly persecuted, but so overly scrupulous are they that they depend only on their rightness to defend them. Their wills are seldom engaged in the struggle.

Later, the opposite breed of tragic heroes — the Machiavellian villains — will be considered, but it can be said now that their dedication to evil makes them almost as intractable as the saintly ones. But first a pair of flamboyant French dukes, who are neither saintly nor satanic, must be dealt with.

VII

THE FRENCH DUKES: BIRON AND MONTMORENCY

On voyait près de lui [le roi] briller tous ces guerriers,
Compagnons de sa gloire et ceints de ses lauriers:
D'Aumont, qui sous cinq rois avait porté les armes;
Biron, dont le seul nom répandait les alarmes;
Et son fils, jeune encore, ardent, impétueux,
Qui depuis ... mais alors il était vertueux...
(Voltaire, *La Henriade*)

J'ai demandé ma grâce, hélas! c'était en vain,
Malheureux que je suis! Quel destin est le mien!
En vain je suppliais; et le fils, et le père,
Tout était contre mois, pour moi tout était pierre.
(Gérard de Nerval, "Le Duc de Montmorency
fut condamné par Louis XIII a être décapité
devant la statue de Henri Quatre")

In the aftermath of the execution of Don Rodrigo Calderón, Spanish dramatists remained alert for other striking examples of the tragic fall of royal favorites. It was small wonder, then, that two of them should turn their attention to France where favorites and old-time feudal lords continued to embroil the court and the provinces. But something more than the pros and cons of favoritism was being tested, for at issue was the question of the royal authority itself, which had been challenged during the reign of Henry IV and was to be challenged again during the reign of Louis XIII. The result was the execution within a span of thirty years of two of the challengers, the Duke of Biron who was beheaded in 1602 and the Duke of Montmorency who met the same fate in 1632. Scions of two of the most illustrious families of the realm and distinguished in their own right, both were found guilty and punished for the supreme crime — *lèse majesté*. It was inevitable that their fall should be reenacted on the Spanish stage.

Juan Pérez de Montalbán, fond of dramatizing the risky adventures of conspiratorial favorites (Sejanus in *Amor, privanza y castigo*, and Philippa of Catania in the collaborative play, *El monstruo de la fortuna*), found a natural subject for a fallen-favorite tragedy in the person of the French soldier and diplomat Charles de Gontaut, Duke of Biron. Son of the honored Marshal Biron and a kinsman of Henry IV, young Charles, partly because of his father's many services to the crown and partly because of his own deeds on the battlefield, was quick to gain his sovereign's favor. Within a few years (1592-1598) he rose to become admiral, marshal, governor of Burgundy, and, finally, Duke of Biron. He was also entrusted with various diplomatic assignments, including a delicate mission to Queen Elizabeth's court.

Brilliant but impulsive, audacious and arrogant, Biron began creating trouble for himself by making secret deals in order to enhance his own power. The climax of his conspiracies against the crown (and the only instance of his treachery dramatized in Montalbán's *El Mariscal de Birón*) came as the result of his military victory in Savoy in 1601. When the Duke of Savoy, a devious character himself, came to Paris to negotiate a truce, he had already measured his conqueror's appetite and thrown out his bait. He was ready to support Biron in his bid for the sovereignty of Burgundy and, in the bargain, he would give him his daughter in marriage, a marriage that would ensure Biron's ascension to the dukedom of Savoy. In exchange, the Frenchman was to impede the defense of Amiens, soon to be attacked by an army of Savoy, and to turn over to Savoy's Spanish allies certain towns in the south of France. Biron swallowed the hook. Apprised of Biron's conspiracy, Henry confronted his vassal who denied the charges and stubbornly refused to ask for pardon, even though the king assured him of clemency. Tried and condemned, Biron went into a frenzy on the scaffold because of his horror of so disgraceful a death. Only the executioner's blade could silence his ranting.

Far different from Biron in temperament, achievements, and reputation was Henri II, the Duke of Montmorency. Godson of Henry IV, Montmorency was noted chiefly for his successes against the Spanish in the Italian wars and for his moderation as governor of Provence. His rebellion against the royal authority and the dictatorial power of Richelieu was motivated, not so much by reasons of personal ambition and self-aggrandizement, but in protest against the treatment of Louis XIII's exiled brother, Gaston of Orleans, who after all was also a son of Henry IV. Captured and brought to trial, Montmorency freely admitted his error; but notwithstanding the appeals of the nobility and the populace that his life be spared, Richelieu and the king determined to make an example of him, as Henry had made of Biron, because factious feudal lords could not be tolerated. En route to the place of execution, Montmorency was led by a statue of his godfather, the great Henry IV himself, which he regarded with deep emotion. On the scaffold, he conducted himself with the same piety and dignity that Don Rodrigo Calderón had displayed almost a dozen years earlier.

Whereas Biron and Montmorency were linked in common disaster because of their opposition to royal authority, they were also linked together in the minds of seers and poets. Remarkably — but perhaps not so strangely for those who find their truths in astrological workings — Nostradamus is said to have predicted in his *Centuries* the fate of both favorites almost half a century before Biron was executed and many years before Montmorency was born. [1] Be that as it may, several French Romantics of the nineteenth century took morbid delight in retelling their fall as a single tale of woe. [2] And not so remarkably, an obscure Aragonese author, Martín Peyrón y Queralt, leaned heavily on Montalbán's *El Mariscal de Birón* to write *Las fortunas trágicas del Duque de Memoransi*, first printed in Zaragoza in 1640.

---

[1] See Jean Richer, *Nerval, expérience et création*, 2nd. ed. (Paris, 1970), p. 329, who quotes Nostradamus's prophecies.

[2] Ibid., pp. 577, 587-88.

A. Juan Pérez de Montalbán, *El Mariscal de Birón*

The primary source of Montalbán's play (first printed in *Parte XXV* of the *Comedias de diferentes autores,* Zaragoza, 1632, and later included in *Parte I* of his collected plays, Madrid, 1635) was the *Historia trágica de la vida del Duque de Birón,* the Spanish translation made by Juan Pablo Mártir Rizo of part of Pierre Matthieu's *Histoire de France et des choses memorables advenues aux Provinces estrangères durant sept années de Paix.* The Spanish translation, printed in Barcelona in 1629, is notable for three things which influenced Montalbán's treatment of his subject: (1) following Matthieu, it has little to say about Birón's many services to his king and country; (2) it repeatedly underscores his restless spirit and extreme arrogance; (3) it gives a detailed and rather lurid account of Birón's execution.

In the interests of dramatic economy Montalbán also devotes little attention to Birón's distinguished service to Henry IV (hereafter called Enrique). As the play begins, Birón is already caught up in his conflicting impulses — his driving ambition, his irrepressible spirit *(brío),* and his sense of loyalty to the king:

> No sé qué espíritu en mí,
> o me arreuata o me lleva
> a que aspire, a que me atreua
> al Sol, cuyo rayo fui,
> si bien en passión tan loca,
> como al fin el Rey lo es mío,
> quanto fabrica mi brío,
> mi nombre lealtad reuoca.
>
> (Act I, fol. 111 v.) [3]

So great is Birón's megalomania that he refuses to parade with the defeated Duke of Savoy in the streets of Paris, not just because he scorns a loser but mainly because he is unwilling to share the stage with anyone. And later, at a private reception at

---

[3] Citations are to the *Primer tomo de las Comedias del Doctor Ivan Pérez de Montalván* (Alcalá, 1638). The foliation in *El Mariscal de Birón* is askew, but I have followed the numbering of the folios as the slumbering printer designated them. I have also supplied accents.

court, he boasts of his valor and engages the Spanish Count of Fuentes (historically, his secret ally) in a round of threats. Their verbal battle is silenced only by the king's intercession.

Also in the first act Montalbán invents a romantic intrigue that promises to involve king and vassal in fateful rivalry. Both Enrique and Birón, without the other's knowledge, are in love with Blanca, who reciprocates the favorite's love and seeks to elude the amorous king. [4] Blanca tells her maid of an ominous dream that troubled her sleep: she dreamed that Carlos (Birón), seeing in Enrique a threatening rival, laid hand upon his sword as if to kill him, but the king, reacting quickly, dealt Carlos a mortal blow and he died in her lap. [5] Although distraught by the dream, Blanca cannot comprehend the full meaning of the omen (which, of course, portends the death of Birón as the result of his treason, symbolized by his threatening gesture of drawing his sword against his king). A conflict over Blanca is averted, however, when the king, learning of Birón's love for her, generously withdraws. Moreover, to show that he bears no resentment toward his favorite, Enrique names him the Duke of Birón and a Peer of France. It is only later, when Birón's conspiracy is discovered, that the king will remind his vassal that among the many favors he bestowed upon him, he also gave him his *dama*. Such sacrifices a French king is not likely to forget.

At the end of the first act Birón agrees to take up arms against his sovereign in exchange for his marriage to the sister of the Duke of Savoy (not the daughter as in the source) and the as-

---

[4] Sister Mary Austin Cauvin, "The *comedia de privanza* in the Seventeenth Century," p. 415, n. 44, points out that Henry IV was a natural subject for the *rey enamorado* theme, since his amorous activities were a matter of public scandal. She cites the case of Philip III's sister, the Princess of Condé, who fled to Flanders with her husband in order to escape from Henry's importunities.

[5] Perhaps a passage in Mártir Rizo's translation suggested to Montalbán the idea of Blanca's ominous dream, although the dream and the source-passage are dissimilar in details. Because of Birón's habit of speaking disrespectfully about the king, "Vno de sus amigos fue entonces el oráculo de su suerte, deziendo que si no mudaua estilo en estas licenciosas palabras que después se arrepentiría. '¿Qué me puede suceder?' respondió él. . . . [Su amigo] le dixo entre burlas y veras, que El Rey le haría cortar la cabeça" (fol. 11 r.).

surance that he will acquire possession of the duchy. Birón is aware of his disloyalty to both Blanca and the king, but he is a "superior" man who cannot let sentimental loyalty or conventional morality stand between him and his destiny. He must risk all, because

> me llama
> mi brío a mayor poder;
> César o nada he de ser,
> breve vida o grande fama.
> (Act I, fol. 118 v.)

Whereas the first act of *El Mariscal de Birón* is notable for its depiction of the tragic hero's character — in particular, his boundless *brío* that promises to enmesh him in a web of his own spinning — the second act is distinguished by one of the tautest scenes in all the tragedies of *privanza*, as King Enrique and Birón are joined — and unevenly matched — in direct confrontation. Aware of Birón's defection, the king summons his favorite and asks for an accounting of his dealings with the Duke of Savoy. Birón denies the charges against him. The king promises to grant him clemency no matter how great his crimes, but at the same time he demands of Birón an act which he knows full well that the proud duke is incapable of performing: humiliating himself by begging for pardon. It is a game of cat and mouse, in which a cunning cat toys with the smaller creature:

> Yo, imitando a Dios en todo,
> blando, piadoso, y benigno
> os las [culpas] quiero perdonar,
> con condición, que rendido
> me pidáis perdón de todas...
> (Act II, fol. 133 v.)

Birón's response is predictable. Like a child caught in a lie, he becomes more defiant in proclaiming his innocence — and arrogance:

> soy
> de natural tan altiuo,
> que quiero más de su enojo
> prouar constante el cuchillo,

que no gozar el perdón
estando a sus pies rendido.
(Act II, fol. 138 r.)

The king puts an end to Birón's blustering by bidding him
good night and walking out on him, but in an aside he discloses
his intention: "Yo le cortaré los bríos" (ibid.). So ends this scene,
a scene charged with tension and embarrassment, the embarrassment one feels when he is made to witness an adult throw a
childish tantrum. But the confrontation between Enrique and
Birón, dramatic as it is, has a broader significance than the
revelation of the contrasting character of the cool-headed king
and the hot-blooded vassal. At issue in their encounter is the
ideological question of the authority of the monarch when challenged by an individualistic, feudal-minded subject who thinks
that he is a law unto himself. Though Montalbán does not focus
sharply on this question, it is implicit in the meaning of the play.

Many tragic heroes think that they are immune to the whims
of fortune when they are at the height of their prosperity, but
are quick to acknowledge their vulnerability when they are cast
down. Not so with Birón, who is of a different breed. Imprisoned
in the Bastille as the final act begins, Birón takes issue with
Suisón (the Count of Soissons) who moralizes: "Sombras son de
la fortuna/ la privança y la caída" (Act III, fol. 138 v.). Un-
repentant, Birón insists that his predicament was brought on by
his own deliberate acts, not by fortune who would not dare
intrude upon his "sphere":

No ha sido fortuna en mí,
Conde, lo que agora passo,
que la fortuna es acaso,
y esto yo lo pretendí:
porque viendo que al privar
se sigue siempre el caer,
lo que el hado auía de hazer
me quise yo negociar,
para que no se alabara
de que se atrevió a mi esfera,
pues si yo no me cayera,
la fortuna no me echara.
(Act III, fol. 135 r.)

In his confident assertion of his superiority over fortune, Montalbán's Birón is reminiscent of George Chapman's Byron, who rejects the notion that astral influence could affect his life, even though his horoscope indicates that he will be beheaded:

> Spite of the stars and all astrology
> I will not lose my head; or if I do
> A hundred thousand heads shall off before.
> I am a nobler substance than the stars,
> And shall the baser overrule the better?
> Or are they better, since they are the bigger?
> I have a will and faculties of choice,
> To do, or not to do: and reason why
> I do, or not do this: the stars have none . . .
>
> (Act III, sc. 3, ll. 106-14) [6]

But for all his self-assurance (or is it bravado?), the Birón of the Spanish play never attains the exaltation displayed by Chapman's hero in his famous speech:

> Be free, all worthy spirits,
> And stretch yourselves for greatness and for height,
> Untruss your slaveries; you have height enough
> Beneath this steep heaven to use all your reaches; . . .
> There is no danger to a man that knows
> What life and death is; there's not any law
> Exceeds his knowledge; neither is it lawful
> That he should stoop to any other law.
> He goes before them, and commands them all,
> That to himself is a law rational.
>
> (Act III, sc. 3, ll. 130 ff.)

The remainder of the third act of Montalbán's tragedy is devoted largely to Birón's reaction to the death penalty that has been imposed upon him. At first he refuses to believe that the king will permit the sentence to be carried out, but as the hour of execution draws near, he acknowledges to himself that he brought on his doom. But if die he must, he proclaims, let his body be kept whole, for the very sight of it on the battlefield will put

---

[6] *The Conspiracy and Tragedy of Charles Duke of Byron*, in *The Plays of George Chapman*, ed. Thomas M. Parrott (New York, 1961).

France's enemies to flight. Finally, wearied by his own acting and his spirit broken, the proud Birón performs the act to which he thought he could never bring himself: he kneels at his sovereign's feet and pleads that his life be spared. Like other favorites before him, he recites a long speech (266 verses) recalling that he had once saved Enrique's life and had suffered many wounds in the defense of Enrique's crown. But if the king insists that he pay the penalty for his crimes, let not the execution serve as a public spectacle because he cannot tolerate the infamy of his body being exposed to the jeering crowd:

> No es miedo, no, de la muerte,
> señor, el que me apasiona,
> sino miedo de la infamia
> que a bueltas della se compra....
> abráseme vna ponçoña
> las entrañas, y vn estoque
> venas y arterias me rompa,
> o déxeme en vna cueua
> la más triste, y la más honda,
> sin comer, porque la hambre,
> que nuestro calor sufoca [sic],
> me vaya dando garrote
> con vna congoxa y otra.
>
> (Act III, fol. 127 r.)

Birón's plea is not only marked with self-pity, but, consistent with the self-dramatization that has characterized his life, it is also tinged with self-justification, as he misconstrues the commonplaces of the tragic fall:

> y en mi postrimera hora
> miren como en vn espejo
> los que supieren mi historia,
> de la priuança mayor
> la caída más costosa,
> de la más alta fortuna
> la mudança más traidora,
> de la mayor presunción
> la humildad más prodigiosa,
> del Monarca más piadoso
> la ingratitud más notoria,
> y del hombre más valiente

que tuuo Grecia, ni Roma,
la muerte más desdichada,
y la vida más heroica.

(Ibid.)

The king is moved — "mas ya la misericordia/ no tiene lugar
aquí;/ perdóneme el amor agora" (fol. 127 v.). Birón is left alone
to ponder his fate. He vacillates: "que yo prometo a mi brío/
morir con tan religiosa/ bizarría, que parezca/ que el morir no
me congoxa...," but no, "... porque pienso/ según la pena me
ahoga/ que antes que salga a la plaça,/ si el cielo no me reporta,/
he de matarme yo mismo" (Ibid.).

We do not see Birón again. As he feared, the execution is
carried out in public, and implausibly (as most commentators on
the play have pointed out) it is Birón's sweetheart Blanca, addressing the king and queen, who describes the spectacle as she
witnessed it. Nature itself provided the scenic effects for this
tragedy of *privanza:*

Al espectáculo grande
del mayor teatro, en cuya
tragedia representaua
sus mudanças la fortuna,
manchado de sangre el Sol,
cubierta de horror la Luna,
vestido el día de assombros,
llena la noche de dudas,
ciego el ayre, sordo el viento,
y en su variedad confusa
diuidido el vulgo en olas,
partido en votos la turba,
a ser lástima y exemplo
de las priuanças, que duran
lo que la vida en la rosa,
lo que en la flor la hermosura,
llegó el Duque a vn cadahalso...

(Act III, fol. 129 r.)

Unlike the historical Biron, who (so Pierre Matthieu and other
historians tell us) went into an uncontrollable frenzy on the scaffold and threatened the executioner, Montalbán's Birón faces
death with composure and dignity — but not without a show

of the theatrics to which he was given. He refuses to be blind-
folded; he refuses to be bound in a chair. He will, he promises,
receive the fatal blow standing up. He does — unflinchingly. Then
the headless trunk remains erect for several moments, surveying
the audience like a triumphant actor after a rousing performance.
To the last Birón refuses to be upstaged.

In spite of its considerable merits, *El Mariscal de Birón* falls
short of being a great play because Moltalbán failed to follow
through in the exploitation of those very elements which he
prepared so skillfully — the motivation of the characters, the
dramatic situations, and the thematic potential. Birón's conflicting
impulses of loyalty to the king and his lust for power (which
should provide the substance of a wrenching psychological crisis)
are touched on in an early speech but neglected in the rest
of the play. The conflict between Enrique and Birón is sharply
drawn, affording some tense moments; but Montalbán tends to
deal with Birón's treason as if it were a matter of personal disloyalty to a friend rather than an attack on the authority of
the monarchy. And, just as he fails to make clear the thematic
significance of Birón's conspiracy (though the theme of the insidious results of disorder is mildly insinuated throughout the
play), so the dramatist fails to explore beneath the surface of
Birón's character. As a consequence, Birón emerges as an "interesting" personality — a courageous but swaggering man who
is given no great speeches but who compensates by overacting
his role. But even so, of all the favorites in the tragedies of
privanza, he will be remembered as the supreme actor. It is a
pity that, unlike Chapman, Montalbán chose to tell of Birón's
final performance on the scaffold instead of permitting him to
show off his talents.

B. MARTÍN PEYRÓN Y QUERALT, *Las fortunas trágicas del Duque
de Memoransi*

Little is known about Martín Peyrón y Queralt, the Aragonese
licentiate who borrowed time from the practice of law to write
poetry and a single extant play: *Las fortunas trágicas del Duque
de Memoransi*, printed in *Parte XXXII* of *Comedias de diferentes
autores* (Zaragoza, 1640) and reprinted in *Parte XLIV* of the

same collection (Zaragoza, 1652). [7] Perhaps the fact that the play was included in two different volumes of the same series, both of which were published in Zaragoza, indicates that the play met with popularity in its day and that the author enjoyed considerable prestige in his native city.

Although from an artistic point of view *Las fortunas trágicas del Duque de Memoransi* is a pedestrian play — indeed, no better than one would expect from a mildly talented amateur — it is not devoid of interest. Part of that interest stems from purely extrinsic factors; part of it results from the fact that the play is sort of a patchwork of themes, situations, and devices drawn from earlier plays, the general literature on *privanza,* and from the contemporary scene. Written within a few years after the execution in 1632 of Henri II, Duke of Montmorency, it is more nearly contemporaneous with the events that it dramatizes than is the case with any other tragedy of *privanza.* To be sure, the execution of Don Rodrigo Calderón was the immediate cause that inspired several plays, but the dramatists were always circumspect enough to veil their allusions to contemporary events by choosing as a tragic hero a favorite several decades — or centuries — removed from the political scene. The readers of Peyrón y Queralt's play (and the spectators too, if it was ever performed) could respond to it with the excitement that people often feel toward the reenactment of recent sensational events.

Like most authors of "historical" plays, Peyrón y Queralt claims to have based his tragedy on historical sources, as he makes clear in the final lines (which also underscore the moral of the play):

> Y aquí la historia dé,
> y los Anales de Francia
> exemplo a los siglos den,
> que no ay Grande que lo sea
> quando se opone a su Rey.
>
> (Act III, p. 40)

---

[7] The name of the dramatist is spelled Peiron by Félix de Latassa y Ortín, *Biblioteca antigua y nueva de escritores aragoneses, de Latassa; aumentadas y refundidas en forma de diccionario bibliográfico-biográfico por don Miguel Gómez Uriel* . . . 3 vols. (Zaragoza, 1884-86), II, 488-89. Latassa gives a sketch of his life and works in the same volume. Citations to the play are to the text of the 1652 edition.

In spite of the author's claim, however, no one has yet identified any written sources, published between 1632 and 1640, which could have been available to him for the composition of his tragedy. Chances are that it was based largely on oral reports and hearsay.

But if the sources of *Las fortunas trágicas del Duque de Memoransi* remain in doubt, there is no question concerning the origin of the dramatic conception that governed the composition of the play, for it is clearly modelled on Juan Pérez de Montalbán's *El Mariscal de Birón,* [8] first printed in the very year that Montmorency met his death. Not only did the Aragonese writer borrow incidents and devices from the earlier play but he was also influenced by Montalbán's depiction of the fiery Biron. For that reason, though not historically, Peyrón y Queralt's hero approaches Birón in his self-dramatization and in his display of flamboyance.

The dramatist's inexperience is most noticeable in the first two acts of *Las fortunas trágicas del Duque de Memoransi,* acts which are burdened with expository speeches and stilted dialogue. As the play begins, Cardinal Ruchili (Richelieu) urges the king to send the Count of Chambert (Schomberg) to Languedoc to put an end to the revolt of Gastón de Borbón, Duke of Orleans and the king's brother, who is aided by Memoransi. Following a love scene between Memoransi and Clorinda, Chambert arrives to demand the surrender of the rebels. Memoransi refuses to capitulate. In Act II Chambert relates to the king the circumstances of the capture of Memoransi, who killed single-handedly twenty men before being subdued. Later Memoransi is visited in prison by Clorinda, who swears to take revenge on his former friends who deserted him in his hour of greatest need. The duke attempts to dissuade her, but like other favorites before him, he is moved to cynicism by the ingratitude of his debtors who have turned against him:

---

[8] Victor F. Dixon, "The Life and Works of Juan Pérez de Montalbán, with Special Reference to His Plays" (Unpublished Ph. D. dissertation, University of Cambridge, 1959), p. 218, n. 2, remarks that Peyrón y Queralt's play is "undoubtedly modelled" on Montalbán's tragedy, but he does not specify the similarities, other than to say that both plays contain reminiscences of the execution of Don Rodrigo Calderón.

Quien quisiera assegurarse
de enemigos lisonjeros,
no haciendo bien a ninguno,
viuirá seguro, y quieto.

(Act II, p. 18)

The third act bristles with intrigue, omens, and bloodshed. Clorinda, who previously disguised herself as a German knight and as the English ambassador in order to see her sweetheart, now pretends to be a country lass whose sister was allegedly abducted by Memoransi. She persuades the queen to give her a ring that will permit her to enter the prison where she will upbraid the culprit. Meanwhile, after further pleas that he be granted clemency are denied, Memoransi attempts to dispell his fears by assuring himself that the Wheel of Fortune may turn again:

A qué furia, a qué rabia me prouoco,
si considero la desdicha mía:
mas, Duque Memoransi, poco a poco,
enfrenad essa altiuez demasía [sic],
y quien rindió reueldes esquadrones,
no se dexe rendir de sus passiones.
Animo, corazón, aunque suceda
trágico fin, sucesso lamentable,
de la fortuna la inconstante rueda
se muda de contraria en fauorable...

(Act III, p. 32)

But portents of disaster pour in upon the hapless prisoner —among them, one of the commonest devices of neo-Senecan revenge drama employed to presage the demise of the protagonist. To while away the time, Memoransi chooses at random one of the books that his jailers brought him; it is Lucan's poem on the death of Pompey. He casts the book aside and picks up another and another; every book he opens concerns the violent death of a former great. But like the proud Birón, Memoransi refuses to be unnerved by mere omens:

Mi valor, mis alientos, mi osadía,
mi presumpción, desprecio, y arrogancia
han podido postrar estos agüeros;
ruego al cielo no sean verdaderos.

(Act II, p. 33)

Finally, he comes across a volume of poems by the Count of Villamediana. He opens it at random and begins to read a sonnet. It is Villamediana's famous sonnet on the death of Don Rodrigo Calderón, beginning:

> Este, que en la fortuna más subida
> no cupo en sí, ni cupo en él su suerte,
> viuiendo pareció digno de muerte,
> muriendo pareció digno de vida....
>
> (Act III, p. 34)

Memoransi can no longer delude himself; his *desengaño* tells him that his own death is imminent:

> Don Iuan de Thassis fue graue sujeto,
> estos fúnebres son; mi desengaño
> he visto, muerto soy, que este soneto
> está avisando mi presente daño;
> claro auiso me da, mudo, discreto;
> salgamos esperanças del engaño,
> mi muerte se apresura.
>
> (Ibid.)

The omens do not cease. Memoransi hears a musician singing offstage of the incarceration of Birón, whose crime parallels his own:

> Preso tiene Enrico Quarto
> al Mariscal de Virón,
> porque aleue a su Corona
> enemigos conspiró.
>
> (Ibid.)

Memoransi's courage wanes: "El aliento desmayado,/ ... passos a mi muerte doy" (Ibid.). No sooner said than the written sentence, condemning him to die for *lèse-majesté*, is brought to his cell. He places the sentence on his uncovered head as a sign of respect, because it bears the signature of the king to whom he still professes vassalage. He then pronounces a long soliloquy which bears on the theme of the brevity of life, a soliloquy — as so often in the Baroque — in which human life is compared with the ephemeral existence of flowers. Part of his speech (which is more notable for its earnestness than for the quality of its poetry) follows:

> La existencia de las cosas
> desta vida sombras son,
> que las destruye, y ahuyenta
> del Alba el primer Albor...
> Emula de los jazmines
> la neuada ostentación
> del almendro, a vn tibio soplo
> toda su pompa perdió.
> A la Reina de las flores,
> del clavel emulación,
> quitó la vida el arado
> de vn rústico labrador.
> Porque la vida del hombre
> es sombra, es almendro, es flor,
> y acaban su lozanía,
> arado, soplo, y albor.
> Prosperidades del mundo,
> sueños, y apariencias son;
> desdichado quien las busca,
> dichoso quien las dexó.
>
> (Act III, p. 35)

The tragic tone of *Las fortunas trágicas* runs its course with the recitation of Memoransi's soliloquy — but all is not yet done with the play. Thanks to the ring that the queen gave her, Clorinda succeeds in having a final interview with her lover who rebukes her for daring to criticize the king for not pardoning him: "quando blasfemias pronuncias,/ prouocas mi indignación" (p. 37). Later, disguised as a man, Clorinda attends the execution where she kills two captains of the royal guard. Captured and brought into the presence of the king and queen, she discloses that the captains were Memoransi's *hechuras* who turned against him. She then reviews the duke's many services to the crown (as in Montalbán's *El Mariscal de Birón*), and moralizes on the ugliness of human ingratitude. She is pardoned when the queen intercedes in her behalf.

Although the third act of Peyrón y Queralt's play is cluttered up with gratuitous incidents (especially Clorinda's strategems), [9] it has moments of tension and brooding tragic sentiment. Much of that sentiment is owed to the author's intrusive conviction that Memoransi's punishment was out of proportion to the nature and motive of his crime; but as observed earlier with regard to Mira de Amescua's *El ejemplo mayor de la desdicha*, unmerited or undue punishment remains one of tragedy's most accessible ingredients to arouse pity. The Aragonese amateur should not be faulted for employing a recourse which most great dramatists have been ready to exploit.

---

[9] It is improbable that Clorinda's intercessions in behalf of her lover were suggested to Montalbán by the intense loyalty demonstrated by Montmorency's wife toward the doomed favorite. A sort of French Dido (before Dido met Aeneas), Montmorency's wife, Marie-Félice des Ursins (Orisini), built a magnificent mausoleum to house the remains of her deceased husband (see Richer, pp. 586-87).

VIII

THE MACHIAVELLIANS: SEJANUS AND PHILIPPA OF CATANIA

> "Él [Seyano] quedará para siempre
> por exemplo prodigioso de suma
> maldad y ambición; y su trágico
> fin nos muestra, que nunca paró
> bien el poder mal adquerido. . . .
> Que la privança ganada por méritos,
> o por ventura, se conserva con la
> modestia, y que la más assegurada
> ha de reconocer su grandeza de
> mano de su Príncipe."
>
> (Vicencio Squarçafigo, *Vida de Elio Seyano*, 1621)

> "Qué estraña bizarría de la fortuna,
> vna labandera manda absolutamente vn
> Reyno, compuesto de tantos grandes,
> de ricas y nobles familias: vna vil
> muger violenta el espíritu de vna
> gran Reyna, y le tiene como incapaz
> y enfermo, qué se puede dezir? Mas
> qué no se dize?"
>
> (Juan Pablo Mártir Rizo, *Historia de la prosperidad infeliz de Felipa de Catanea*, 1625)

Biron and Montmorency fall short on several counts of being Machiavellian types, but principally because their villainy (at least in the plays just considered) consists of a single act: Biron's conspiracy against the crown and Montmorency's open revolt against the royal authority. Needless to say, there is nothing

"Machiavellian" about open revolt. On the other hand, Lucius Aelius Sejanus conforms squarely to the stereotype of the Machiavellian villain, if indeed he was not the prototype. Ambitious, crafty, resourceful, totally unscrupulous and unfeeling, Sejanus let nothing stand in his way in his drive for power. In short, in the words of Vicencio Squarçafigo, Sejanus "quedará para siempre por exemplo prodigioso de suma maldad y ambición." Montalbán will so portray him in *Amor, privanza y castigo*.

Unlike Sejanus, Philippa of Catania is at most a mild Machiavellian villain, although (as will be seen) Boccaccio depicts her as a ruthless intriguer and an unprincipled sycophant. She shares with Sejanus his soaring ambition and talent for duplicity, but differs from him in her capacity for affection and human warmth. This capacity — a redeeming virtue — will not be overlooked by the authors of the collaborative play, *El monstruo de la fortuna*.

Machiavelli himself says not a word about Philippa of Catania; he has little to say about Sejanus. He does not mention him by name in *The Prince*, but speaks briefly of him in the section on conspiracies in *The Discourses*. Since the passage in question deals with the conspiracy of favorites, it and a paragraph of Machiavelli's commentary are worthy of quotation:

> It would seem, then, that conspirators have all been men of standing or intimates of the prince, and, of these, those who have been moved to conspire by too many benefits are as numerous as those moved to conspire by too many injuries, as was the case with Perennis *versus* Commodus, Plautianus *versus* Severus, and Sejanus *versus* Tiberius. For to all these men their emperors had granted such wealth and so many honours and titles that there seemed to be nothing wanting to complete their power, save the imperial title; so, since with the lack of this they were unwilling to put up, they were moved to conspire against their prince, and their conspiracy in each case was attended with the results which their ingratitude merited. . . .
>
> A prince, therefore, who wants to guard against conspiracies, should fear those on whom he has conferred excessive favours more than those to whom he has done excessive injury. For the latter lack opportunity, whereas the former abound in it, and the desire is the same in

both cases; for the desire to rule is as great as, or greater than, is the desire for vengeance. Consequently princes should confer on their friends an authority of such magnitude that between it and that of the prince there remains a certain interval, and between the two a something else to be desired. Otherwise it will be a strange thing if that does not happen to them which happened to the princes we have been talking about. [1]

Unfortunately for Tiberius and Queen Joanna of Naples, they did not have the opportunity of reading Machiavelli's discourse, otherwise they would have been better prepared to deal with their ambitious favorites. Indeed, Sejanus and Philippa of Catania stand as examples of those who were too richly rewarded by their fond rulers, to the detriment of themselves and their kingdoms. Whether Montalbán had read Machiavelli or not, it seems certain that his *Amor, privanza y castigo*, believed to have been written within a year following Don Rodrigo Calderón's execution in 1621, [2] was meant to warn the recently crowned Philip IV against the dangers of conferring excessive favors on those who were privy to him. [3] However, it would be extravagant, I think, to read into *El monstruo de la fortuna*, composed c. 1630, a warning directed to Philip against his favorite, the Count-Duke Olivares, who at that time was already firmly ensconced in power.

A. JUAN PÉREZ DE MONTALBÁN, *Amor, privanza y castigo*

First printed in the *Primero tomo de las Comedias del Doctor Ivan Pérez de Montalván* (Madrid, 1635), Montalbán's play is also known by the title *El fin más desgraciado y fortunas de*

---

[1] *The Discourses of Niccolò Machiavelli*, trans. Leslie J. Walker, 2 vols. (London, 1950), I, 474-75.

[2] Because of Montalbán's statement that *Amor, privanza y castigo* was one of his earliest plays, both Dixon, p. 222, and J. H. Parker, "The Chronology of the Plays of Juan Pérez de Montalván," *PMLA*, 57 (1952), 186-210, date the play 1621 or 1622.

[3] Cauvin, p. 409, calls attention to the fact that the play contains numerous allusions to the contemporary political scene: "The allusions are evident from the opening scene. Not only is the Emperor Tiberius a replica of Philip III, but the relationship between the emperor and Seyanus closely parallels that of Philip and Lerma. References to the beginning of the reign of Philip IV are indicated in this same scene."

Seyano. Though the author claims in the closing lines to have based the play "en los ilustres escritos / de los Anales de Roma," Tacitus and other Roman historians who wrote of the reign of Tiberius served him minimally in comparison with his main source: Vicencio Squarçafigo's Spanish translation of Pierre Matthieu, *Vida de Elio Seyano, Compuesta en Francés por Pedro Matheo, Coronista del Christianíssimo Luys XIII. Rey de Francia. Traduzida en Castellano por...* (Barcelona, 1621). [4] Both Matthieu's biography and Squarçafigo's translation are notable, not so much because Sejanus is depicted as a consummate villain ("exemplo prodigioso de suma maldad"), but because the vicious Tiberius is portrayed as a benign ruler. [5] Montalbán follows suit.

Disappointing though it is to be denied the opportunity of observing two heinous monsters pitted against one another, Sejanus will not betray our expectations in his role. The sordid story of Sejanus's rise and fall, as related by Tacitus and Dio Cassius, is too well known to need retelling here, but it should be said that Montalbán (like Ben Jonson before him) became fascinated with his perversity and cast him, not only as a wicked favorite, but also as a bloody revenger of neo-Senecan stamp. [6] As a consequence, *Amor, privanza y castigo* follows the usual structure of the tragedies of *privanza* in plotting the rise and fall of the favorite, but the characters' motives and the accessories of

---

[4] The sources are discussed by Dixon, pp. 222-23, who notes that Tacitus's *Annales* served Montalbán mainly for his opening scene concerning the rebellion in Pannonia. It should be noted that there was another Spanish translation made of Matthieu's work besides Squarçafigo's: Juan Pablo Mártir Rizo, *Vida del dichoso desdichado / escrita en francés / por Pedro Matheo / Cronista del Rey Christianíssimo / y en Castellano por...* (Madrid, 1625), but it was published too late to serve as a source of Montalbán's play.

[5] Cauvin, p. 402, remarks that in her study of fifty *comedias de privanza* Sejanus is the only protagonist who is depicted as the "epitome of villainy from beginning to end." She also cites (p. 408, n. 24) Gregorio Marañón, *Tiberio, historia de un resentimiento* (Madrid, 1939), p. 252, who observes that some Roman historians, in their efforts to gratify the relatives and friends of Tiberius, exaggerated the perfidy of Sejanus in order to excuse the ruthlessness of the emperor.

[6] Ben Jonson's *Sejanus* (1603) and the anonymous *Tragedy of Tiberius* (c. 1607) are studied as revenge tragedies by Fredson Thayer Bowers, *Elizabethan Revenge Tragedy, 1587-1642* (1940; rpt. Gloucester, Mass., 1959), pp. 158-61.

the plot (most of which are found in the sources) are in the tradition of revenge tragedy. The favorite's ambition brings him initial success; his success provokes the envy of his rivals; their envy leads them to insult or injure the favorite; the latter, now turned revenger, seeks retaliation by cuckholding or murdering his offenders; the revenger is denounced by someone close to him (often his accomplice, but in this play his jilted wife) and is dealt a violent death. The whole chain of events is rife with intrigue and punctuated with omens — and to top it off, in Montalbán's play there is even a ghost to unnerve the revenger. It should be said to Montalbán's credit, however, that the intrigue does not obscure the main business of his tragedy: the fall of Sejanus as the result of the misuse of his power as Tiberius's favorite. On the other hand, Montalbán can be faulted for the obtrusiveness of the *gracioso*, Otavio, who forces his way into many situations where he has no business. But such, of course, is the prerogative of the *gracioso*, the public's favorite.

As the play begins, Seyano reports to Tiberio on his recent campaign in Pannonia, where he and the emperor's son Druso (Drusus) were sent to put down a revolt among dissident Roman soldiers. Seyano's report is a long one (more than 160 lines), but since it is so important in terms of irony, imagery, and mood, I shall quote from it extensively. The irony is underscored by his use of mythological images associated with the dire consequences of boundless ambition, images which he applies to the rebel soldiers but which will later apply to his ambitions and fall. Moreover, for greater irony, his appraisal of the revolt, rendered in terse and sententious language, bespeaks a man who, it seems, would never fall prey to destructive aspirations:

> Las legiones de Panonia
> sediciosas se atreuieron
> a pedir glorias más altas,
> y a intentar mayores premios.
> Anímanse los soldados,
> precipítanse soberuios.
> Ícaros al sol se oponen
> sin mirar vn mar en medio;
> Gigantes al cielo aspiran
> sin reparar en el riesgo, ...
> hieren, destruyen, y matan,

mas no es mucho, que en efeto
es la ambición temeraria
quando atiende a su provecho.

(Act I, fol. 153 v.) [7]

Seyano has foretold part of his own story, because he too, spurred by ambition and looking to his own profit, will commit the same acts as the rebel soldiers; he too will become another Icarus who opposes the Sun.

There follows a description of the portentous storm that blotted out sun and moon, obscuring the field of battle. (Montalbán was as fond as nineteenth-century Romantics of using wild storms to presage impending disaster — and he found a precedent in Tacitus, who describes the storms and other natural disturbances that troubled Tiberius's reign.)

Cubrióse todo de nubes,
luto antiguo de los cielos,
las nubes lloraron mares,
y escucháronse los truenos,
que desde allí parecía
que daua vozes el cielo.
Todo era horror, todo espanto,
todo confusión y estruendo,
todo tristezas, y sombras,
todo dudas, todo incendios.
Temieron los sediciosos,
y amedrentados creyeron,
que eran diuinos auisos
que amenaçauan sus cuellos.

(Act I, fol. 154 r.)

The description of the storm sets the mood of *Amor, privanza y castigo*, a mood of horror, terror, and confusion. And Seyano's own demise will be preluded by ominous natural — and supernatural — disorders.

Seyano's report concludes with his explanation as to why the rebel leaders were put to death:

---

[7] Citations are to the text in the *Primero tomo de las Comedias del Doctor Ivan Pérez de Montalván* (Alcalá, 1638).

que en semejantes sucessos
es la piedad injusticia,
es el perdón desacierto,
es la clemencia escusada,
y es el castigo discreto,
que a vezes importa más
el rigor, aunque sangriento,
que la más noble piedad,
y en fin con el viuo exemplo
los demás se sujetaron ...

(Act I, fol. 154 v.)

In a sense Seyano has finished foretelling his story, for in the end he too will be denied clemency, condemned to a violent death, and made to serve as an example to ambitious climbers.

As a reward for Seyano's services, Tiberio assures him that, "todos te han de tener/ en todo por tan mi amigo,/ que te han de igualar conmigo,/ y más si más puede ser"; and, "Tuyo es, Seyano, el Imperio" (Ibid.). But throughout this scene, Druso, envious because of the excessive honors lavished by his father on Seyano, voices his resentment in a series of asides. "Yo le quitaré los bríos," he resolves (using the same words Montalbán's Henry IV employs later to let his determination to cut Biron's wings be known).

The imagery of flight, of soaring ambition, continues. Alone with Otavio, Seyano confides to him his desire to rule the empire, to reach the empyrean:

¿No has visto vna mariposa
de vn gusanillo nacer,
y que altiua, y ambiciosa
más de lo que es quiere ser
hasta preciarse de hermosa?
Pide diuersas colores
a la madre de las flores,
vese hermosa, y no contenta,
porque más honor intenta,
y aspira a glorias mayores. ...
Vióse con ellas, boló,
cortó el ayre, el fuego vio,
y al fuego quiso aspirar,
que es de nobles intentar
cosas altas, y assí yo

nací humilde, aunque nací
con heredado valor,.. .
y para atreuerme a más
me ensueña vna mariposa.
(Act I, fol. 155 v.)

Otavio objects, warning his master: "No es buena comparación,/
que la mariposa luego/ se chamusca en su intención"; but Seyano is confident that his reason will save him: "Libraráme a
mí del fuego/ el vso de la razón" (Ibid.). Seyano's confidence
in his ability to escape the fate of others who have soared too
high recalls a passage in the Spanish translation of Pierre Matthieu, who points out that the fall of great men produces *admiración (admiratio)* but seldom serves as a lasting example for the
guidance of others because, "... cada vno se confía en su juizio,
pensando conduzirse por el mismo camino, pero con otro passo y
más seguro que los demás: ... porque cada vno cree que la mala
fortuna no se ha hecho para él." [8]

I have dwelt on the opening scenes of *Amor, privanza y castigo* because of their efficiency in setting mood, establishing dramatic irony, revealing character, and preparing for the complication and resolution of the plot. The remainder of Act I — and
the rest of the play, for that matter — can be disposed of in rather
short order. Swollen with arrogance because of newly acquired
power, Seyano mistreats his wife, enacts arbitrary laws, and lords
it over Druso and Germánico, Tiberio's nephew. Finally, Druso
can stand no more; he strikes Seyano in the face, leaving the
favorite to rage over his offended honor:

¿Tú no pusiste en mi rostro
la mano atrevida y fiera,
rayo que mi honor deshizo
a pesar de mi grandeza?
Pues prométete la muerte,
assegura tu tragedia,
ten por cierta tu desdicha,
ten tu esperança por muerta, ...
tu vida no será tuya,

---

[8] The passage comes from Mártir Rizo's translation of Pierre Matthieu,
op. cit., fols. 163 r.-v.).

porque de mi honor la deuda
por su víctima la embarga,
y en el coral de tus venas
he de lauar mis agravios...

                    (Act I, fols. 158 v.-159 r.)

From this point on, *Amor, privanza y castigo* becomes a double-edged tragedy, a tragedy of *privanza* and a tragedy of revenge. And as a Machiavellian favorite and revenger, Seyano will play his double role to the hilt.

In Act II Seyano discloses his plans for revenge to Otavio (since in a Spanish play the *gracioso* becomes a natural substitute for the revenger's accomplice, although Otavio does not like the role): Seyano will cuckhold Druso by seducing his wife, Libia; then he will have Druso killed by a slow-working poison; he will have Germánico sent to the East where he will be murdered by another accomplice; and he will persuade Tiberio to retire from Rome to Capua where he can escape the cares of government. However, two unforeseen events occur, one which threatens to thwart his plans temporarily, the other which eventually leads to his undoing (for Seyano falls in love with Libia, thereby provoking the jealousy of his wife Laura, who later denounces him).

The first event occurs before Tiberio leaves for Capua. Over-hearing Druso and Germánico complain that Seyano has usurped the emperor's authority and will not stop at treason, Tiberio becomes apprehensive of his favorite's power. His words recall those of Machiavelli in warning princes against excessive generosity:

                    ¡Ay de mí!,
        ¿qué es esto que escuché?
        Veneno en palabras fue.
        ¿Que Seyano es desleal?
        Sí, que es bastante señal,
        el quererle yo también,
        y basta auerle hecho bien,
        para que me pague mal.
        Vn gran bien, vn grande amor
        pocas vezes se agradece,
        y aun algunas acontece,
        que el hazer mal es mejor;

porque suele dar temor.
Pero aquel que liberal
haze bien a vn desleal
alienta su tiranía,
y assí en parte ser podría
más seguro el hazer mal.

(Act II, fols. 162 r.-v.)

Tiberio insists that Seyano accompany him to Capua so that he can keep an eye on him; but at the retreat Seyano saves the emperor's life at the risk of his own when, in the cave-in of the roof of a cavern (a cave-in deliberately arranged by the favorite), he shields Tiberio with his body. The grateful ruler loses all fear of Seyano's treachery:

Bien sé, amigo Seyano, que la [vida] deuo
más a tu voluntad, que a mi ventura,
pídeme quanto quieras, de nueuo
rige, gouierna, y manda.

(Act II, fol. 165 v.)

At the beginning of Act III Seyano is at the height of his good fortune. He enjoys Tiberio's confidence and rules without interference from the absent emperor. Germánico has been killed; Druso has been poisoned. In a love scene with Libia, he reveals that he plans to ask Tiberio's permission to marry her, since he has repudiated Laura. At this point Laura surprises the embracing couple, and seized by jealousy ("que soy muger y ofendida;/ que no puedo dezir más"), she goes to Capua to denounce her husband, disclosing his responsibility for the murders of Druso and Germánico. Tiberio, who has been having second thoughts about Seyano's loyalty, loses no time in ordering the arrest and trial of the tyrant. Meanwhile, Seyano is troubled by omens auguring his death (including a ghost that "kills" him); but when the end comes, he accepts his fate calmly and "philosophically." His only regret in dying is that he will be separated from Libia:

Sólo por Liuia lo siento,
que vn alma somos los dos,
que en lo demás sabe Dios
que voy a morir contento.

(Act III, fol. 172 r.)

Sertorio informs Tiberio of Seyano's noble bearing at his exe-cution (once again, reminiscent of Don Rodrigo Calderón's con-duct on the scaffold): [9]

> Ya llega al mísero trance
> sin dar de temor indicios,
> tan dueño de sus acciones,
> que va mostrando en el brío,
> que no le rinde la muerte,
> y que la combida él mismo.
>   (Act III, fol. 173 r.)

In a romantic note, Libia joins her lover in death, hurling herself down the same stairway from whence her lover's body was cast: "*Descúbrese Seyano, sangriento, y Libia como despe-ñados,*" says the stage direction. The emperor (who, historically, was not in Rome at the time of the execution) blesses their final union:

> Como viuieron acaban,
> daldes vn sepulcro mismo,
> porque los case la muerte
> pues la vida no ha podido. [10]
>   (Act III, fol. 173 v.)

Tiberio's final words make it clear why Montalbán was destined to write *Los amantes de Teruel,* also printed in the first volume of his plays.

---

[9] Both Cauvin, p. 409, and Dixon, p. 224, point out the similarity in the stoical attitude and demeanor of Sejanus and Don Rodrigo Calderón in the face of death.

[10] There is a gap of two years, covering the period of the deaths of Sejanus, his lover Livilla, and his wife Apicata, in Tacitus's manuscript (see *The Annals of Imperial Rome,* trans. Michael Grant, Penguin Classics L 60, rev. ed. [London, 1959], p. 192); but *Dio's Roman History,* trans. Ernest Cary, Loeb Classical Library, 9 vols. (London, 1924), VII, 217, states that Apicata committed suicide and Livilla was put to death — but "I have, indeed, heard that he [Tiberius] spared Livilla out of regard for her mother Antonia, and that Antonia herself of her own accord killed her daughter by starving her." Montalbán's inclusion of Libia's suicide, so that she might join her lover in death, is not noteworthy because it violates historical fact (since few Spanish dramatists let history stand in the way of their artistic aims), but because it illustrates Montalbán's artistic purpose: to provide *admiratio* and a note of lyricism and pathos to his tragedy of horror.

Amor, privanza y castigo differs from the other fallen-favorite plays in its incorporation into the conventional structure of the favorite's rise and fall many elements characteristic of neo-Senecan revenge tragedy. It also differs from the other plays in having a protagonist who is a complete villain, the embodiment of evil. Both the structure of the play and the characterization of its odious "hero" are owed, to a large degree, to the career of the historical Sejanus. Granted the difficulty of dealing with a protagonist of such evil dimensions, I think that Montalbán's play deserves to be ranked among the best examples of what El Pinciano called the *tragedia morata.* [11]

B.   PEDRO CALDERÓN DE LA BARCA, JUAN PÉREZ DE MONTALBÁN, AND FRANCISCO DE ROJAS ZORRILLA, *El monstruo de la fortuna*

Often confused with Lope de Vega's *La reina Juana de Nápoles* and its own authorship shrouded in doubt, *El monstruo de la fortuna* was first printed in *Parte veinte y quatro de comedias nuevas, y escogidas de los mejores autores de España* (Madrid, 1666) where it is attributed to *Tres Ingenios.* [12] Concerning the identity of one of the *ingenios* — the one who wrote the third act — there is little question, because the final lines of the play read,

> Y Don Francisco de Rojas,
> por el zelo de seruiros,
> pide para tres ingenios,
> con ser tres, no más que vn vitor.

And who were Rojas' collaborators? Most critics identify Calderón as the author of the first act and Montalbán as the author of the second; however, the names of Rojas' most frequent col-

---

[11] See chapter I, n. 26.

[12] For a review of the problems concerning the authorship of *El monstruo de la fortuna* see Spencer and Schevill, *The Dramatic Works of Luis Vélez de Guevara*, pp. 384-87. Part of the confusion surrounding the play is owed to the fact that the text of Lope de Vega's *La reina Juana de Nápoles*, first printed in *Parte VI* of his *comedias*, was later printed with the title of *El monstruo de la fortuna* and attributed to *Tres Ingenios* in *Parte VII* of *Comedias escogidas* (*Teatro poético en doze comedias nvevas, de los mejores ingenios de España.* Madrid, 1654).

laborators, Luis Vélez de Guevara and Antonio Coello, have also been associated with the play. It is not my purpose to examine the question of the authorship here, but I am inclined to accept Calderón, Montalbán, and Rojas as the joint authors of *El monstruo de la fortuna*. The play was first (?) performed in the Royal Palace on June 5, 1636. [13]

The ultimate source of the tragedy is Boccaccio's *De casibus virorum illustrium*, which so often served Spanish writers who chose to expatiate on the themes of fortune and *privanza*. The last biography included in Boccaccio's work (Book IX, Chapter XVI) is devoted to Philippa of Catania, the protagonist of the Spanish play, who was commonly called *la lavandera de Nápoles* because of her means of earning a livelihood before she made her way at court. Aware of the seeming anomaly of including a washerwoman among the company of illustrious men and women in his book, Boccaccio felt compelled to preface his biography of her with "An Excuse by the Author for Philippa of Catania: Why a woman of ordinary birth is admitted into this company." [14] Boccaccio then explains: "I thought I had good reason to include her; for I wish to point out that all this work, by its parts, seems to be arranged in some form: it started in happiness and will end in misery. It seems that the work began with the most noble of men, so it should end with a common and degenerate woman." [15]

Although Boccaccio claims to have been an eye-witness to some of the events involved in the story of Philippa of Catania, in point of fact his biography of her is much less vivid than his case histories of many ancients. Moreover, much of his narrative is diluted by unnecessary digressions into the genealogies of royal persons who did not figure directly in the rise and fall of the Catanese woman. But these digressions done, Boccaccio explains how Philippa, her husband Raymond of Campagno, an Ethiopian, and her children gained positions of great power in the kingdom

---

[13] N. D. Shergold and J. E. Varey, "Some Early Calderón Dates," *Bulletin of Hispanic Studies*, 38 (1961), 283-84. The date of the first performance could possibly have been February 5, 1637.

[14] Boccaccio, *The Fates of Illustrious Men*, p. 234.

[15] Ibid.

of Naples. Appointed mistress and guardian to Joanna when
the latter was still a child, Philippa and her royal charge were
bound by ties of deep mutual affection. Later, when Joanna
became queen, she was forced to marry Andrew of Hungary by
terms of her grandfather's will. The marriage was not a happy
one, either personally or politically. In particular, the Neapolitan nobility opposed Andrew's coronation. Boccaccio puts it
obliquely:

> Conspiring secretly against him, they laid plans to
> prevent his being crowned. Who they were and how
> they progressed against the boy is not our present
> business. We have enough that pertains to our purpose.
> By the stealth of the conspirators one night in the city
> of Aversa [in 1345], the boy was called from the royal
> bedroom and ended his life in a noose. [16]

Suspicion fell immediately on Philippa of Catania and members of her family, who were convicted of murder. "They were
tortured with fire and pincers, and what was left of their miserable
life ended in the flames." [17] Boccaccio then moralizes on
Philippa's demise:

> This, therefore, was the end of Philippa. Indeed it
> would have been better to maintain her poverty by labor
> in the sea than to seek a better existence in luxury by
> criminal means. When condemned to the fire she lost her
> life and all that she acquired. [18]

Although the authors of El monstruo de la fortuna probably knew Boccaccio's account of Philippa of Catania, their immediate sources were two: (1) Lope de Vega's La reina Juana
de Nápoles, first printed in 1615 but believed to have been written
between 1597 and 1603; [19] (2) Juan Pablo Mártir Rizo's Historia
de la prosperidad infeliz de Felipa Catanea (Madrid, 1625). Since
Lope's play provided Rojas and his collaborators with only a

---

[16] Ibid., p. 239.
[17] Ibid., p. 240.
[18] Ibid.
[19] Morley and Bruerton, The Chronology of Lope de Vega's "Comedias,"
p. 238.

few incidents, it will be considered first. Clearly, however, Lope's play is not a tragedy of *privanza*.

By terms of her father's will, Queen Juana of Naples is to marry Prince Andrés of Hungary, whom she heartily detests. She is in love with Prince Ludovico, who is also loved by Isabela, daughter of the Duke of Ferrara. Isabela in turn is loved by Prince Matías of Hungary, who is Ludovico's best friend and also a cousin of Prince Andrés. After Andrés's troops capture Naples, Juana agrees to marry the Hungarian in order to save the city from being pillaged. Andrés soon tires of his wife and turns his attentions to Isabela, whom he attempts to seduce. Her resistance whets his appetite, and only the timely arrival of the queen saves her from being raped.

But Andrés is a persistent fellow, and in the final act he again tries to rape Isabela. This time, when she fights him off, he orders his henchman, Count Antonio, to kill her. Andrés's other barbarities are too numerous to mention, but they include a plan to poison his wife, a plan that is disclosed to Juana. There follows a scene involving an exchange among a group of musicians, the queen, and her maid Margarita (a scene utilized by the authors of *El monstruo de la fortuna* and later praised by Menéndez Pelayo, who found little else to commend in Lope's play): [20]

CANTAN:	*Si te quisiere matar*
	Algún enemigo fiero,
	Madruga y mata primero.
MARGARITA:	¿Oyes?
REINA:	Sí.
MARGARITA:	Pues madrugar. [21]

---

[20] In his *Observaciones preliminares* to his edition of *La reina Juana de Nápoles*, in *Obras de Lope de Vega, publicadas por la Real Academia Española*, vol. VI (Madrid, 1896), p. 79, Menéndez Pelayo says of the play: "... la vulgaridad de las pasiones que en ella juegan, aunque se presenten en su mayor grado de exaltación y determinan acciones violentas, no bastan para inspirar el terror trágico, antes la misma atrocidad anula su afecto.... Pero al acercarse la conclusión cesa de dormitar el poeta, y preludia la catástrofe con escenas verdaderamente trágicas entre el Rey y la Reina. ¡Lástima que estén tan mal preparadas!"
[21] Ibid., p. 552a.

This scene is followed by a visit of King Andrés to the bed-chamber of his never-loving Juana:

ANDRÉS:	¿Qué estáis haciendo?
REINA:	Un cordón Para ahorcaros con él.
ANDRÉS:	¿Para ahorcarme?
REINA:	Para ahorcaros.
ANDRÉS:	¡Digo, qué de buena gana! . . .
REINA:	Para ahorcaros.
ANDRÉS:	¿No es bueno, Que os pienso yo dar veneno?
REINA:	¿Veneno a mí? Ya lo sé.
ANDRÉS:	Conde, ¿qué os parece de esto? Ella se burla conmigo; Yo, en burlas, veras le digo.
REINA:	Yo os he de ahorcar bien presto.
ANDRÉS:	Yo el veneno os he de dar.
REINA:	Uno será de los dos El burlado.
ANDRÉS:	Seréis vos.
MARGARITA:	¿Oyes?
REINA:	Sí.
MARGARITA:	Pues madrugar. [22]

As it turns out, the joke is on the king, for Juana is a believer in not putting off until the morrow, not even until the *madrugada,* what can be done today. With the help of her maids, she hangs Andrés before he can escape from the room. Juana then makes her husband's would-be accomplice, Count Antonio, drink the poison intended for her.

This is not the place to examine the merits, shortcomings, and neo-Senecan qualities of Lope's play, but a few observations on its general character and its influence on *El monstruo de la fortuna* are in order. *La reina Juana de Nápoles* is not concerned with the question of favoritism nor with the major themes of the fallen-favorite tragedies. Rather, it is essentially a revenge drama

---

[22] Ibid., p. 554b.

in which two parties endeavor to strike first in order to do the other in. The mutual distrust and antipathy of Andrés and Juana are a matter of historical record, but Lope, more than the historical sources, emphasizes their hatred in order to intensify the dramatic conflict. *El monstruo de la fortuna* owes to Lope's play its presentation of the embittered marital relations of the king and queen, and, more specifically, various details surrounding Andrés's murder. Though Philippa of Catania does not figure in Lope's play, her advice to Juana in the collaborative play on how to catch her husband unawares comes directly from Margarita's advice to her royal mistress: *Pues madrugar.* The wonder is that Lope, with his acute sense of dramatic intrigue and his sharp eye for picturesque characters, did not include the Catanese laundress among the conspirators who embroiled the Neapolitan court.

Much more important than Lope's play as a source of *El monstruo de la fortuna* is Juan Pablo Mártir Rizo's *Historia de la prosperidad infeliz de Felipa Catanea*, a translation from the French of Pierre Matthieu. Among the preliminaries of the Spanish translation is an *Advertimiento*, which stresses the theme of the mutability of fortune, and a letter to the king (Philip IV), which sets the moralizing tone of the biography and also provides the title of the play. The letter to the king reads as follows:

> *Señor.* El fabor encumbró a esta muger desde las ceniças a la gloria, y la arrogancia la precipitó de la gloria a las ceniças. Presento su historia a V. M. como de vn *monstruo de fortuna* [my italics] que podrá ver por curiosidad, y los demás para enseñança, por ser vna pintura que denota el naufragio de los que no amainan las velas como era justo, para disminuir la fuerça del rigor a la tempestad. [23]

Pierre Matthieu follows the major outlines of Boccaccio's biography of Philippa of Catania but dwells on her domination over Joanna and her encouragement of the queen's clandestine

---

[23] *Historia de la prosperidad infeliz, de Felipa de Catanea. Escrita en Frances por Pedro Mateo. Coronista del Rey Christianissimo. Y en Castellano, por Iuan Pablo Martyr Rizo. Año 1625.* Con licencia, En Madrid por Diego Miranda. The preliminaries are not paginated.

love affairs so that the queen would have little time or inclination to concern herself with affairs of state. Like the enemies of Don Álvaro de Luna who censured him for using his influence over John II for reasons of personal aggrandizement, Matthieu accuses the Catanese of abusing her favored position for her own ends. Not only did she appoint her own children and relatives to the highest offices of the kingdom but also, as was the case with Don Álvaro de Luna, all royal favors passed through her hands: "... no auía esperança de honor, de recompensa, de justicia, ni de fabor, de otra parte sino de sus manos." [24]

Always cicumspect with regard to royalty (after all, Matthieu was a chronicler in the employ of the King of France), Matthieu does not hesitate to blame Philippa for having originated and engineered the plot to kill King Andrew, even though he admits that Joanna may have been involved: "... puede ser que ella diesse lugar a que lo hiziesse la Catanesa, que tenía usurpada toda su autoridad sin dexarla parte alguna." [25] The circumstances of the king's murder are similar to those dramatized by Lope de Vega, except that Matthieu makes no reference to Andrew's plan to poison his wife: "... hizo la Reina vn cordón de oro y seda, Andrés le preguntó que qué hazia? y ella respondió: 'esto se haze para ahorcaros.'" [26] Then, after attempting to explain that the queen's words did not mean that she was necessarily implicated in the plot, Matthieu tells how the king met his death: "... lo cierto es, que queriendo entrar en la quadra o al salir della, alargando la cabeça, los traydores le echaron a este tiempo la cuerda a la garganta, y le ahogaron y colgaron a los hierros de la ventana." [27]

The rest of Matthieu's narrative concerning the trial and execution of the conspirators follows Boccaccio closely. And, as if the story of the *lavandera de Nápoles* did not speak for itself, Matthieu draws the moral in his conclusion:

---

[24] Ibid., fol. 33 r.
[25] Ibid., fol. 38 r.
[26] Ibid., fol. 39 r.
[27] Ibid., fol. 40 r.

> De lo que auemos referido, se puede inferir que siem-
> pre asisten los daños con la injusta prosperidad, que no ay
> maldad que no trayga su castigo y arrepentimiento, que
> quien comete vn delito no aguarde al segundo, que en
> quanto durare el Teatro del mundo la Fortuna nos re-
> presentará sus tragedias, y que tal vez da abraços a los
> que quiere ahogar entre ellos. [28]

Neither Boccaccio nor Matthieu were remiss in reminding their
readers that Philippa of Catania would have been much better
off if only she had minded her wash. In sum, the portrait that
Pierre Matthieu and his Spanish translator give of Joanna's favorite is that of an unprincipled, Machiavellian intriguer who richly
deserved her cruel fate. The authors of *El monstruo de la fortuna*
will attenuate her villainy by showing that she was capable of
warmth and generosity, but they will not excuse her Machiavellian instincts.

As to be expected of a collaborative play written by three men
of exceptional but diverse talents, *El monstruo de la fortuna*
reflects, not simply differences in style, but the lack of a unified
conception to govern its material and its characters. The first
act (which I assume to be Calderón's) is given to the exposition
of events and characters, especially to the character of Felipa Catanea. As the play begins, Prince Carlos of Salerno exhorts his
soldiers to defeat the invading army of King Andrés of Hungary,
who has come to win Juana's hand by force of arms because she
has refused to marry him as stipulated in her father's will. Juana's
refusal is owed largely to her desire to marry Carlos, who aspires
to become King of Naples. As he goes off to do battle with the
Hungarians, Carlos speaks of his ambitions. His speech not only
introduces the essential theme of ambition — ambition which will
not be daunted by the odds against its fulfillment — but it also
serves to lay the foundation for the existentialist context in which
Felipa Catanea's resolute "becoming" is set: "Anhele mi ambición osadamente;/ que aunque pese a mi estella,/ rey he de
ser de Nápoles la bella" (Act I, p. 1237). [29]

---

[28] Ibid., fol. 51 v.

[29] All citations to *El monstruo de la fortuna* are to the edition in Calderón, *Obras completas (dramas)*, ed. Luis Astrana Marín (Madrid, 1941).

Unlike the historical laundress, the Felipa of this play is un-married and childless, young and beautiful. But above all she is a woman of restless ambition, a woman who despises her lowly occupation:

> pero si me miro al alma
> por de dentro de mí mesma,
> igual me pienso a la hidalga,
> a la señora, a la reina:
> que para aquesto hizo Dios
> todas las almas eternas.
>
> (Act I, p. 1240)

But Felipa's exaltation soon gives way to anguish, for she who feels herself to be equal to queens cannot reconcile her poverty with her aspirations. In a speech of seven *décimas* (similar in form and language, if not in theme, to Segismundo's first soliloquy on liberty in *La vida es sueño*) she decries the disparity between her character and her circumstances:

> ¡Cielos!, en la confusión
> que aflige mi pensamiento,
> o dadme otro sufrimiento
> o dadme otro corazón.
> Mirad que no es proporción,
> ya que tan pobre nací,
> darme la altivez así,
> queriendo que en dura calma,
> dentro de mí viva un alma,
> sin caber dentro de mí.
>
> (Ibid.)

In successive stanzas Felipa compares man's lot with that of bird, beast, and fish, concluding that, "el hombre (¡duro pesar!), / desnudo nace a buscar / qué vestir y qué comer" (Ibid.). But if men must — and can — strive for livelihood and fame, women are doomed to menial labor. Felipa, like Semíramis in Calderón's *La hija del aire*, deplores the injustice of it:

> Con razón, no falta nada
> al hombre, hallarlo presuma
> o ya en la paz, con la pluma,
> o en la guerra, con la espada.

Mas la mujer, desdichada,
a quien ni la espada honra,
¿qué ha de vestir y comer
si el buscarlo ella ha de ser
con fatiga o con deshonra?
    Yo en mi ejercicio lo digo,
¡mísera!, pues por no dar
a mi deshonra lugar,
se le doy a mi fatiga.
Y pues mi suerte me obliga
a abatir nobles alientos,
lleven mis voces los vientos
y mis lágrimas el mar.
¡Corazón! ¿No has de lograr
tan altivos pensamientos?

(Act I, pp. 1240-41)

After this excellent revelation of her character, Felipa Catanea
is caught up in the action of the play and has little time to
explore further her restless spirit. But at the end of Act I she has
the opportunity to meet her challenge to herself; she will act
rather than bemoan her fate. Sword in hand, she rushes to the
royal palace to defend her queen against the invading Hungarians. Although Juana promises to marry Andrés in order to
avoid further destruction to her kingdom, she has found a new
favorite in the person of the intrepid laundress: "que has de ser,
mujer valiente, / en Nápoles otra yo" (p. 1245). On hearing about
Felipa's elevation, one of her former companions cannot help
making a coarse pun: "Quien lavó tantos pañales / bien ser
privada merece" (Ibid.). The theme of favoritism, quiescent
throughout the first act, is about to begin.

Whereas the first act of El monstruo de la fortuna is devoted
largely to the exposition of the character of Felipa as a woman
"with a star," the second act (which I assume to be Montalbán's)
is concerned with dramatizing her ascent — that is, with how
her star rises in the political firmament of Naples. So strong does
the queen's attachment to her new favorite become that she
tells her,

Hete cobrado
voluntad tan excesiva,

> que he de hacer que Italia aquí
> te venere como a mí.
>
> (Act II, p. 1246)

And indeed so excessive is Juana's affection (much like John II's intemperate fondness for Don Álvaro de Luna) that she proudly proclaims that, "Remedo es del sol la estrella" (p. 1253). Felipa Catanea, who once imagined that she was the equal of queens, now sees her star at its zenith. Fortune and *privanza* go hand in hand. At the queen's behest all royal favors now pass through Felipa's hands. Even Octavio, Juana's old trusted counselor who opposed Felipa's admission into the queen's service, must present a petition for a favor to the former laundress. Expecting a vengeful response, Octavio is humbled when Felipa appoints him Condestable of Naples. But Felipa wants only one thing from Octavio, not profuse promises, but gratitude — the one thing that Don Álvaro de Luna wanted from his *hechuras*: "Sólo quiero que seáis / . . . para si rueda / la fortuna, agradecido" (p. 1254). Felipa is convinced, however, that she has gained an enemy, for such is the reward for every favorite's generosity.

Meanwhile, as Felipa's fortunes prosper, Juana's marital problems intensify. She cannot abide her husband at board or abed. The basic incompatibility of the royal couple, their mutual distrust, their subterfuges, their feigned tenderness, their private fears, all are far more skillfully and humanly portrayed than in Lope de Vega's extravagant hate-fest. [30] Matters come to a head when Andrés makes a fateful slip: in his sleep he lets his plan to

---

[30] Alberto Lista, who saw a performance of the collaborative play when it was revived in 1822, was also impressed with the handling of the scenes involving the king and queen. In his review, "*El monstruo de la fortuna, Felipa Catanea*: comedia de tres ingenios," *El Censor*, 15 (1822), 103, Lista wrote in part: "Se observan en esta pieza intenciones y movimientos trágicos y algunas escenas, a las cuales sólo falta un lenguaje más sostenido y un estilo menos afectado para ser dignas de Melpómene. Tal es la escena del segundo acto entre la reyna Juana, su confidanta Felipa y el rey Andrés. La versificación de toda ella es armoniosa y noble: el odio de la reyna y las sospechas de su marido están muy bien descritas: las sentencias son graves y concisas, y el interés dramático que escita es muy grande porque se ven entre las caricias conyugales todas las pasiones funestas del corazón que dieron motivo al asesinato de Andrés, a las calamidades de una guerra estrangera, y a la condenación de Felipa."

kill Juana escape from his lips. Felipa's advice to her mistress is the same as that in Lope de Vega's play and in Pierre Matthieu's biography:

> Pues si todo está difícil
> y está tu vida en tal riesgo,
> pues que te quiere matar,
> madruga y mata primero.
>
> (Act II, p. 1257)

But there is no question here of the queen's complicity in the murder. "Pues muera Andrés," says Juana. "Muera Andrés," echoes Felipa. As the act ends, the queen pledges her favorite to secrecy.

To Rojas, as was so often the case in the plays in which he collaborated, fell the task of unwinding the plot of *El monstruo de la fortuna*. Notwithstanding Menéndez Pelayo's tribute to the Toledan dramatist ("tan apto para manejar dignamente el puñal de Melpómene"), [31] Rojas' final act is far from his best, not only because he cluttered it up with prodigal comic incursions, [32] but also because he faced a major problem in showing that Felipa Catanea's demise was determined as much by her deeds as a political activist as by her agency in the death of King Andrés. Only partially did Rojas succeed in showing that her downfall was the result of the interplay among the workings of fortune on the abstract level, Felipa's works within the politics of *privanza*, and her share in the homicide.

---

[31] Menéndez Pelayo, op. cit., p. cxxxii. It is interesting to note how much of Menéndez Pelayo's criticism of *El monstruo de la fortuna* seems to lean on Lista's earlier criticism.

[32] Rojas, of course, always used comic episodes lavishly in his plays, including the tragedies, but in *El monstruo de la fortuna* Calderón set the pattern by devoting almost half of the first act to the comic characters. Those who are fond of demonstrating the thematic connection of comic subplots with the main plot will find grist for their mill in this play because it can be shown that the servants are engaged in a *farsa de privanza* that functions as a wry commentary on the tragedy. It should be said that my observations on the play tend to give a distorted view of its structure in that I have not given due consideration to the comical elements. I have also omitted reference to an embryonic subplot involving Felipa's love for Carlos, but if it appears — momentarily — that Felipa and Juana will be pitted against each other as rivals in love, this subplot is never developed.

Alarmed because the kingdom blames her for Andrés's murder and fearful that his brother Luis will take revenge on her, Felipa confides to Octavio, her *hechura,* that she killed the king on Juana's orders and that she has written Luis to that effect. Refusing to hear any charges against his queen, Octavio renounces his benefactor. The queen herself, unaware of Felipa's accusations, continues to defend her favorite against all protests until Luis, now King of Hungary, confronts her with Felipa's letter. Angered because Felipa broke her pledge of secrecy, Juana allows her to be brought to trial. Felipa is found guilty and sentenced to die.

There follows a moving scene between the two women, whose affection still runs deep. But even though Juana admits her guilt privately, she refuses to intervene in Felipa's behalf in order to avoid the destruction of the city by the Hungarians. The favorite does not protest; she is happy to die for her sovereign:

> La vida en pago te doy
> del favor que te he debido:
> no sea yo más lo que he sido,
> si por ti soy lo que soy.
> Gozosa a la muerte voy,
> y quisiera mi pasión,
> por darte satisfacción,
> ir a tan justa crueldad
> de sólo mi voluntad
> y no de tu indignación.
>
> (Act III, p. 1266)

Felipa Catanea, once the *lavandera de Nápoles* and now the Duchess of Amalfi, is led away to the execution block. Moments later the queen (who has had a change of heart like John II in Mira de Amescua's *La adversa fortuna de don Álvaro de Luna* and Queen Elizabeth in Antonio Coello's *El Conde de Sex*) bursts in upon the scene attempting to halt the execution and proclaiming her own guilt. It is too late: "*Descúbrese la cabeza de Felipa a una parte y el cuerpo a otra.*"

El monstruo de la fortuna is both a pleasing and a disappointing play, pleasing because of its fascinating protagonist and some of its dramatic situations, disappointing because its

plot and characters drift apart and become disintegrated from
its properties as a fallen-favorite tragedy. But Felipa Catanea
herself, unlike the ruthless sycophant portrayed by Boccaccio
and Pierre Matthieu, emerges on occasion as a complex human
being caught up in her conflicting impulses of altruism and
personal ambition. A Machiavellian creature of sorts, yes — but
few favorites ever reveal so lyrically their need to rise above
themselves, their hunger to succeed.

IX

THE EARL OF ESSEX: ANTONIO COELLO,
EL CONDE DE SEX

> "L'intrigue de la tragédie n'est qu'un roman; le grand point est que ce roman puisse intéresser. On demande jusqu'à quel point il est permis de falsifier l'histoire dans un poëme? Je ne crois pas qu'on puisse changer, sans déplaire, les faits, ni même les caractères connus du public.... Mais quand les évènements qu'on traite sont ignorés d'une nation, l'auteur en est absolument le maître."
>
> (Voltaire, on Thomas Corneille's
> *Le Comte d'Essex*)

Although Antonio Coello's *El Conde de Sex* is not the last of the fallen-favorite plays (and it should be repeated that we have not been considering the plays in strict chronological order), it represents the complete disintegration of the tragedies of *privanza*. The alternative titles with which the play has sometimes been printed — *Dar la vida por su dama* and *La tragedia más lastimosa de amor* — suggest the reason: even though the subject matter and the two main characters are nominally historical, the thrust of the play has shifted from the affairs of state to an affair of the heart, from the issues of political favoritism to the demands of private passion. To be sure, a few of the old themes — fortune, envy, ingratitude — creep into the dialogue, but they are never really significant, either in contributing to the meaning of the play or in determining the course of the plot. Only the theme of ambition has any importance, and it too is subordinated to the chivalric ideal of a gentleman's willingness to sacrifice everything for the sake of his *dama*. What matters most in *El Conde de Sex* is love — love and jealousy.

Not so curiously, perhaps, Coello's play owes its little fame to factors other than its artistic quality: (1) it is said to be the earliest play written on the death of the Earl of Essex; [1] (2) Queen Elizabeth (Isabela), much to the bewilderment of Spanish critics, is portrayed so sympathetically that she could well be recognizable to Englishmen as the good Queen Bess; (3) its authorship was once ascribed to Philip IV, whose passion for the theater went beyond his fondness for actresses; (4) Lessing chose this play to generalize in his *Hamburgische Dramaturgie* on the characteristics of Golden Age drama.

No one knows where Coello got the material for his play or why he happened to dramatize events in the life of the Earl of Essex, whose forays on the Spanish coast deeply embarrassed the nation's military and naval leaders. At any rate, *El Conde de Sex* was first performed in Madrid on November 10, 1633, but it was not published until 1638. [2] It precedes by several years La Calprenède's *Le Comte d'Essex* (first played in 1637, published in 1639) and by several decades Thomas Corneille's *Le Comte d'Essex* (1678). [3] It also antedates by almost half a century the first English tragedy on the subject, John Banks' *The Unhappy Favourite; or, The Earl of Essex* (first performed in 1681 and printed in 1682). [4] There is no evidence that Coello's play influenced the later French and English tragedies (although Thomas Corneille was frequently caught with his hand in the Spanish

---

[1] Winifred Smith, "The Earl of Essex on the Stage," *PMLA*, 39 (1924), 147-73.

[2] Emilio Cotarelo y Mori, *Dramáticos españoles del siglo XVII: Don Antonio Coello y Ochoa* (Madrid, 1919), p. 25. The play was first printed in *Parte treynta y vna de las meiores comedias que hasta oy han salido. Recogidas por el Dotor Francisco Toriuio Ximenez... En Barcelona, Año 1638.*

[3] For an account of La Calprenède's tragedy and other French plays on Essex, see H. C. Lancaster, "La Calprenède Dramatist," *Modern Philology*, 18 (1920), 121-41.

[4] Ed. Thomas Blair (New York, 1939), p. 36.

cookie jar); it did, however, serve as the source of an Italian tragedy. [5]

Most Spanish critics have agreed that one of the major merits of Coello's play is the characterization of Elizabeth (Isabela), though they have been unable to suppress their surprise at the sympathetic portrayal of the heretical queen, Spain's most virulent enemy. Writing near the end of the seventeenth century, Francisco Bances Candamo expressed his bewilderment in his *Theatro de los theatros*: "Ninguna reina ha sido más torpe que Isabela de Inglaterra," but "la comedia del Conde Essex la pinta sólo con el afecto, pero tan retirado en la majestad y tan oculto en la entereza, que el Conde muere sin saber el amor de la reina." [6] And in our own century Cotarelo y Mori expressed his amazement that the "English Jezebel," a "monster of cruelty and lasciviousness," could be presented on the Spanish stage as a gentle, modest queen. [7] Perhaps both Bances Candamo and Cotarelo forgot that Cervantes, in *La española inglesa,* presented Elizabeth, not as a vice-ridden tyrant, but as a conscientious, dignified sovereign.

The fanciful notion that Philip IV was the author of *El Conde de Sex* was owed, no doubt, to the fact that several eighteenth- and nineteenth-century editions do not state the name of the

---

[5] The Italian tragedy in question is Niccolò Biancolelli's *Regina Statista d'Inghilterra ed il Conte di Esex; vita, successi e morte* (Bologna, 1668). Winifred Smith, pp. 161-73, reproduces the scenario of the tragedy.

[6] Quoted by A. Valbuena Prat, *Literatura dramática española* (Barcelona, 1930), p. 270.

[7] The vituperative terms applied to Elizabeth are not Cotarelo's but those of others whom he indirectly quotes. Cotarelo's passage on Coello's Elizabeth is worth repeating (op. cit., pp. 33-34): "Lo que más admira en este potente drama es ... el carácter de la reina Isabel. Mucho valor, mucha audacia eran, en efecto, necesarios para ofrecer al pueblo español con circunstancias nobles y simpáticas a aquella Reina tan odiada, causante principal de nuestras desdichas políticas y a quien los escritores más graves y mesurados, como el padre Rivadeneira, por ejemplo, calificaban como la Jezebel inglesa, la incestuosa hija de Ana Bolena, monstruo de crueldad y de lascivia, perseguidora inicua de católicos y otros dictados tan *suaves* como éstos. En la obra de Coello aparece dulce, sensible, honesta, digna, altiva, pero no cruel cuando ve menospreciado su amor y hasta ofendida su cualidad de Reina, y que, en lugar de gozarse en su venganza, perdona como mujer sus agravios más íntimos, los del corazón, y trata de salvar al causante de ellos."

author but attribute it to *Un ingenio de esta corte*, a mask said to have been employed by Philip to conceal his authorship of various compositions. Notwithstanding his scruples, Eugenio de Ochoa included *El Conde de Sex* under the name of Philip IV in his *Tesoro del teatro español*, vol. V (Paris, 1838); and even so experienced an editor as Mesonero Romanos was willing to concede that the king might have had a hand in its composition, even though he thought that Coello should be credited with the major part of the play. [8] It is likely, I think, that Coello had help in writing his tragedy, but to my mind we should not look to Philip IV but to one of Coello's old friends and associates to find his collaborator, either Calderón or Francisco de Rojas — or both. But trying to identify Coello's collaborator or collaborators, if indeed he had any, is a task for another day.

Criticism has singled out *El Conde de Sex* as a highly original specimen of tragedy, all the more original (so it has been held) because it was written at a time when Spanish tragedies were so few. It is termed by Mérimée and Morley as a "powerful tragedy"; [9] and Valbuena Prat concludes his analysis of the play by saying, "Con dignidad trágica, en una acción sobria, produce Coello un drama diverso de las corrientes de nuestra escena." [10] But Lessing, who left one of the most extensive analyses yet made of the play, did not find it to be a "powerful tragedy" at

---

[8] In his "Apuntes biográficos y críticos" to his collection of *Dramáticos contemporáneos de Lope de Vega*, tomo II, *BAE*, XLV, p. xxvii, Mesonero says: "Repito que ignoro el fundamento de la noticia, generalmente recibida, de ser esta comedia obra del rey don Felipe IV, como lo indican los señores Jovellanos, García Parra, Huerta, Ochoa, Ticknor y otros, fundados sólo, al parecer, en la tradición general; pero me inclino a que no sea cierto . . . ; pudiera muy bien ser que el Rey tuviese también parte en ésta (pues se sabe que Coello casi nunca trabajó solo, y aun también que fue uno de los ingenios que ayudaban a su majestad en las comedias que escribía; pero no hay, a mi ver, razón alguna para despojarle a aquel de la parte principal que debió tener en la del *Conde de Essex*." To set the record straight, it should be noted that George Ticknor, *History of Spanish Literature* (Boston, 1872), II, 397, says that the traditional attribution of the play to Philip IV is an "erroneous one."

[9] Ernest Mérimée and S. Griswold Morley, *A History of Spanish Literature* (New York, 1930), p. 385.

[10] *Historia de la literatura española*, 2nd. ed. (Barcelona, n. d.), II, 328.

all. [11] Rather, he censured it (and Spanish Golden Age drama in general) for its distortion of history, its many anachronisms, its lack of sobriety, its excess of novelistic incidents, the unnecessary complication of the intrigue at the expense of tone and mood, the obtrusive role of the *gracioso*, and the desultory mixture of the tragic and the comic. Indeed, several of Lessing's observations are informed with the same attitude that governed Voltaire's view of Thomas Corneille's *Le Comte d'Essex*.

Whereas Lessing, like so many other eighteenth-century critics, may be accused of not comprehending the spirit and esthetics of Golden Age drama, I do not think that he was far wrong in regarding *El Conde de Sex* as a sort of royal cape-and-sword drama whose principals happen to be of exalted rank and which ends with the death of the protagonist. There is nothing wrong with that sort of drama (if that is what the playwright and his audience want), but it is obvious that a play whose plot centers on the conflicts and intrigues attendant upon love and jealousy cannot at the same time focus on the existential problems of favoritism. The real merit of the play, as I see it, lies in the tension that is developed between the queen's love and jealousy, [12] tension that is rooted in her character and in her consciousness of the demands and obligations of her rank. This — the psychological penetration of character, especially of the character of the queen — is not enough to make *El Conde de Sex* a "powerful tragedy," but it lifts the play above the usual run of cape-and-sword dramas in which love and jealousy are the basic ingredients.

We need to look at only enough of the plot to see how Coello mixes love and jealousy within the loose framework of *privanza* — or, put another way, to see how the theme of *la reina enamorada* dominates the theme of *privanza*. And while looking at the plot, we should forget all the history we know about the historical Essex and Elizabeth. Returning to London in disguise from the English victory over the Spanish Armada, Essex (I hesitate to refer to him as Sex) goes to visit his sweetheart Blanca at her

---

[11] Gotthold Efraim Lessing, *Hamburgische Dramaturgie*, in *Lessings Werke*, ed. Theodor Matthias, 6 vols. (Leipzig, n. d.), III, 175-247.

[12] Smith, p. 149, also calls attention to the tension developed between the queen's love and jealousy.

villa where he thwarts an assailant's attempt to shoot a masked woman bather. The intended victim is Queen Isabela and her would-be assassin, Roberto, a Scottish sympathizer of the recently executed María Estuarda. The queen does not recognize her benefactor, to whom she gives a scarf to bind the wound he received in the struggle, nor does he recognize her. Later, Blanca, now Isabela's lady-in-waiting, reveals to Essex that she is involved in the plot to kill the queen because her father and brother were executed together with María Estuarda. Blanca asks Essex to join the conspiracy. Pretending to assent, he dictates a letter to Roberto asking him to rally his followers in London, but his intention is to capture all the conspirators. At the royal palace Isabela rewards Essex for his victory over the Armada by naming him Admiral of England. She then notices the scarf, recognizing Essex as the man who saved her life; he, in turn, suspects the queen is the woman who gave him the scarf. Although the two feel strongly attracted to one another, propriety and differences in rank prevent them from speaking openly.

In the second act Essex debates with himself as to whether he should remain faithful to Blanca, or, for ambition's sake, try to win the love of the queen:

> Loco pensamiento mío,
> Que a un imposible desvelo
> Tan reciamente me encubres
> De ambicioso o de soberbio,
> Abate, abate las alas,
> No subas tanto: busquemos
> Más proporcionada esfera
> A tan limitado vuelo.
> Blanca me quiere, y a Blanca
> Adoro yo, ya es mi dueño;
> Pues ¿cómo de amor tan noble
> Por una ambición me alejo? [13]

But ambition wins out: "Mas, oh fortuna, probemos; / Que sea más que el amor / Una hermosura y un reino" (Ibid.). These speeches (so brief in comparison with other favorites' articulation

---

[13] Citations are to Mesonero Romanos' edition, op. cit., p. 410b.

of their ambitions) represent the extent of the exploration of
Essex' ambition — ambition which is pitted against love. Then,
in the presence of the queen, Essex admits he is in love with a
woman to whom he is afraid to express his true feelings. Isabela
encourages him to speak up, but at this moment Blanca appears
wearing the scarf that the queen gave Essex. Isabela is seized
by jealousy and orders Essex to leave. To make matters worse,
Blanca tells her mistress that she surrendered her honor to Essex
on the promise of marriage, but she is now afraid that he is in
love with another woman and will break his promise. She also
implies that Isabela is jealous, eliciting the following outburst
from the outraged queen (which should be compared with Don
Gutierre's frenzied speech on jealousy in Calderón's *El médico
de su honra*).

> ¿Qué son celos?
> No son celos; es ofensa
> Que me estáis haciendo vos.
> Supongamos que yo quiera
> Al Conde en esta ocasión;
> Pues si yo al Conde quisiera,
> Y alguna atrevida loca,
> Presumida, descompuesta,
> Le quisiera, ¿qué es querer?
> Me mirara, que le viera,
> ¿Qué es verle? No sé que diga . . .
> ¿No le quitara la vida,
> La sangre no le bebiera,
> Los ojos no la sacara,
> Y el corazón, hecho piezas,
> No la abrasara? (*Ap.* Mas ¿cómo
> Hablo yo tan descompuesta?) [14]
> (Act II, 413b)

---

[14] In Calderón's *El médico de su honra* Don Gutierre addresses his wife:

> ¿Celoso? ¿Sabes tú lo que son celos?
> Que yo no sé qué son, ¡viven los cielos!;
> porque si lo supiera,
> y celos . . . llegar pudiera
> a tener . . . ¿qué son celos?
> Átomos, ilusiones y desvelos . . .
> no más que de una esclava, una criada,
> por sombra imaginada,
> con hechos inhumanos

Later, when the queen is asleep, Blanca attempts to shoot her with Essex' pistol, but he returns in time to wrest it from her at the moment it discharges. Not wanting to incriminate Blanca, Essex declares that neither she nor he fired the pistol, but of course he is unable to explain how it got in his hand. He is imprisoned in the tower.

In Act III, arrested as his master's accomplice in the attempt on the queen's life, Cosme surrenders the letter written by Essex to Roberto. Now convinced of her favorite's guilt (and still goaded by jealousy), Isabela resolves to make of him an example of her justice. She cannot refrain, however, from visiting him in the tower where she offers him a key to aid him to escape in payment for saving her life. Essex throws the key into the Thames, insisting that he will die innocently. It is his last grand gesture, a gesture that would appeal to the Spanish cult of honor and pride. Isabela orders the execution to take place immediately.

Moments later Cosme brings the queen a letter written by Essex to Blanca in which it is revealed that he has been protecting his sweetheart. Isabela hurries off to stop the execution, but (as in *La adversa fortuna de don Álvaro de Luna* and *El monstruo de la fortuna*) she arrives too late. She can only swear to avenge his death by executing Blanca.

> a pedazos sacara con mis manos
> el corazón, y luego
> envuelto en sangre, desatado en fuego,
> el corazón comiera
> a bocados, la sangre me bebiera,
> el alma le sacara,
> y el alma, ¡vive Dios!, despedazara,
> si capaz de dolor el alma fuera.
> Pero ¿cómo hablo yo desta manera?

(Quoted from my edition of *El médico de su honra*, in *Spanish Drama of the Golden Age: Twelve Plays* [New York, 1971], p. 468.) The great similarity in the violent language provoked in Isabela and Don Gutierre by the mention of *celos* may be coincidental, or it may derive from a common source (it sounds like Guillén de Castro to me). On the other hand, the similarity may be regarded as "evidence" of Calderón's collaboration in Coello's play. It should be noted, however, that *El Conde de Sex* (first performed on November 10, 1633) may antedate *El médico de su honra* (first performed on August 26, 1635). Could Calderón have borrowed the substance of Don Gutierre's speech from the youthful Coello?

As the title *Dar la vida por su dama* puts it, Essex gives his life for his lady. He is not guilty of treason; only for a moment is he guilty of trading upon the queen's affection for the sake of personal glory and ambition. And even in his final hour he remains too heroic, too firmly cast in the chivalric mold, to decry his fate and ponder the injustices of fortune. As he goes to his death, Coello's Essex has little to blame himself for; he has few regrets and no reason to warn others of his fate. He stands, not as a self-seeking favorite whose example should be avoided, but as a paradigm of the gallant courtier whose devotion to love and truth should be admired by all.

It has not been our purpose to make comparisons between the Spanish fallen-favorite tragedies and other European plays dealing with the same heroes, but it will be instructive to consider briefly the response — the very different response — of John Banks' Essex to his disgrace in *The Unhappy Favourite*. Of course, it should be kept in mind that as the "English" Essex reflects on his tragic fall, he *is* guilty of treason:

> And oh! 'tis Dooms-day now, and darkness all with me.
> Here I'll lie down — Earth will receive her son.
> Take pattern all by me, you that hunt glory,
> You that do climb the Round of high Ambition;
> Yet when y'ave reach'd, and mounted to the Top,
> Here you must come by just degrees at last,
> If not fall Headlong down at one like me —
> Here I'll abide close to my loving Center:
> For here I'm sure that I can fall no further. [15]

And as he muses upon the destiny to which his ambition and lust for glory have brought him, this abject Essex has recourse to the Lucifer-motif that earlier Spanish favorites found so fitting:

> And what has not my Guilt Condemn'd me to!
> Seated I was in Heav'n, where once that Angel,/
> That haughty Spirit Reign'd that Tempted me,
> But now thrown down, like him, to worse than Hell. [16]

---

[15] Ed. Blair, p. 24.

[16] Ibid., p. 49. The metaphor of the "envious cloud" also appears in Banks' tragedy, but here, as Lord Burleigh tells Elizabeth, it was the

Indeed *The Unhappy Favourite* is a tragedy of *privanza,* and notwithstanding its many shortcomings (it is a terribly dull play), placed side by side with *El Conde de Sex,* it serves to show how far Coello strayed from the boundaries of the genre. But it is unfair to blame Coello for not writing a conventional fallen-favorite tragedy; it would be more to the point to blame him for writing a mediocre tragedy of love if indeed that is what he meant *La tragedia más lastimosa de amor* to be.

It is also unfair, perhaps, to end a book on the tragic fall of royal favorites with the consideration of a play in which the favorite refuses to conform to the standards which we have set for him and in which the fall is more melodramatic than tragic. But *El Conde de Sex* has the value of evincing the disparate tendencies that had been gathering and intensifying in earlier tragedies of *privanza.*

---

favorite who came between the queen and the nobles: "Now we may hope to see fair Dayes again / in England, when this hov'ring Cloud is vanisht, / Which hung so long betwixt our Royal Sun / And us ..." (p. 64).

X

CONCLUSION

> "En la comedia heroica, que consta siempre de batallas o acciones grandes, labraba este suave ingenio [Montalbán] el contexto substancial de lo macizo y sólido de su invención; y luego para sazón del auditorio la adornaba de episodios líricos y trágicos. En la comedia que contiene la maraña amorosa y dulce, armaba la traza en la novela, y para adorno la vestía de episodios trágicos y heroicos. *Y en la comedia trágica que se funda en lo melancólico y fúnebre de la lástima que dispone, aunque se cargaba todo el artificio sobre el horror, la mezclaba de episodios heroicos y líricos.*"
>
> (Joseph Pellicer de Tovar, on the plays of Montalbán, 1639) [1]

Quiescent, if not moribund, for more than a century, favoritism was revived early in the reign of Philip III, who, unlike his

---

[1] Pellicer's statement concerning Montalbán's plays is contained in his "Idea de la Comedia de Castilla deducida de las obras cómicas del doctor Juan Pérez de Montalbán," in *Lágrimas panegíricas a la temprana muerte del gran poeta Juan Pérez de Montalbán* (Madrid, 1639). Sánchez Escribano and Porqueras Mayo, *Preceptiva dramática del Renacimiento y el Barroco*, pp. 352-53, have shown that Pellicer's contribution to the memorial volume dedicated to Montalbán is basically the same as his essay *Idea de la Comedia de Castilla. Preceptos del teatro de España y arte del estilo cómico*, written and presented to the Academia de Madrid in 1635 (reproduced in its entirety by Sánchez Escribano and Porqueras Mayo, pp. 263-72). Apparently, when asked to contribute to the memorial volume, Pellicer dusted off his earlier unpublished essay, and inserted the name of Montalbán in appropriate places.

father, was incapable of combining his admirable piety with active kingship. For almost two decades Philip's dominant favorite was the Duke of Lerma, under whose stewardship the affairs of the kingdom and the court went from bad to worse. Dismissed at his own request in 1618, Lerma was not around when one of his own favorites, Don Rodrigo Calderón, was beheaded three years later in the main square of Madrid. His execution not only became a *cause célèbre*; it also produced a national *crise de conscience,* joining political writers, moralists, and poets in a mutual enterprise of soul-searching and reflection. It led seventeenth-century Spaniards to view and interpret contemporary events in terms of fifteenth-century events, centering on the execution of Don Álvaro de Luna.

In the theater, early in the reign of Philip III, Damián Salucio del Poyo wrote two plays on fifteenth-century favorites, the two-part *Próspera* and *Adversa fortuna de Ruy López de Ávalos,* and *La privanza y caída de don Álvaro de Luna.* Viewed in retrospect, the two-part play, terminating with the disgrace and dismissal of its hero, seems to be a prophetic rendering of the career of the Duke of Lerma. Likewise, the second play, ending with the execution of the hero, seems to betoken the death of Don Rodrigo Calderón and the crisis that followed in its aftermath.

But much more important than the prophetic nature of Poyo's plays is the tragic vision which informs them, especially *La privanza y caída de don Álvaro de Luna,* for Poyo viewed the rise and fall of the favorite as a dramatic parable of man's earthly existence since the primal and ever-threatening Fall. Moreover, Poyo's play (which I earlier termed a *quasi*-Aristotelian tragedy) endowed the *tragedias de privanza* with the peculiar properties of plot, structure, theme, and rhetoric which later came to characterize the genre. He also dug into the sources — the chronicles and the ballads — that were to serve many later dramatists.

No tragedies of major significance on the theme of favoritism are known definitely to have been written during the long interval that separated Poyo's early fallen-favorite plays from the death of Don Rodrigo Calderón in 1621; but the political writers, perhaps more sensitive than the playwrights to the consequences

of courtly intrigue, were at work during the interim. The execution of Calderón changed all — or much — of that. The dramatists
rediscovered favoritism as a dramatic theme, as may be seen in
the fact that the great majority of the fifty *comedias de privanza*
studied by Sister Mary Austin Cauvin were written after 1621.
And all the *tragedias de privanza* considered in this book, except
the plays of Salucio del Poyo, were written (at least in the form
in which we know them) after Rodrigo Calderón's death.

Some authors reread Poyo's plays to help sharpen their
dramatizations of the tragic fall. In particular, Mira de Amescua
followed the structural principles governing the composition of
Poyo's plays, and he borrowed from them incidents of plot and
details of characterization for his masterful two-part tragedy, the
Próspera and *Adversa fortuna de don Álvaro de Luna*. And, as
we have seen, Mira's hero insists time and again that he was
chosen by heaven to serve as an "universal example." Largely a
creature of the legends and literature that grew up about him,
Mira's Don Álvaro remains one of Spain's most "metatheatrical"
personalities.

In turn, Mira de Amescua's Don Álvaro de Luna plays served
as the model for several later dramatists who ranged far beyond
Spanish history in search of favorites whose fate epitomized the
tragic fall. But no matter which favorites they chose — Spanish
or foreign, good or bad — their fate was also meant to stress the
uncertainties of human life and the final certainty, death. And
whether the plays were written shortly after Rodrigo Calderón's
execution (like Montalbán's *Amor, privanza y castigo*, c. 1621 or
1622) or many years later (like Peyrón y Queralt's *Las fortunas
trágicas del Duque de Memoransi*, c. 1640), whether they feature
Machiavellian types like Sejanus or well-meaning but errant
heroes like Montmorency, the favorites' conduct in the face of
death was modelled on Calderón's admirable bearing. Yes, even
the loathsome Sejanus, after he saw the errors of his ways, was
permitted to go nobly to his violent death. Unfortunately, however, the good death of the protagonists does not compensate,
from a literary point of view, for the mediocrity of most of the
later plays studied in our survey.

In the Preface certain questions concerning the "problem" of Golden Age tragedy were raised, and I repeat those questions now: Did — or did not — Spanish dramatists of the seventeenth century cultivate tragedy? Or, to put it more baldly, did they write any tragedies? If not, why not? If so, which are those tragedies? And, finally, are there any Golden Age tragedies that are not "problematical"? Most of these questions have been answered in the foregoing chapters, especially in chapter I, but the final question requires further examination.

Probably no Aristotelian critic, no formalist, would quarrel with the concept of tragedy within which the fallen-favorite tragedies were written, a concept which, in the words of Chaucer, involves the story "Of hym that stood in great prosperitee, / And is yfallen out of heigh degree / Into myserie, and endeth wrecchedly." But some critics might claim — and rightly so — that the adherence of the plot line of a play to an acceptable concept of tragedy does not guarantee its tragic substance, since substance is made up of more than "story," plot, or action. And those critics who are familiar with Lope de Vega's insistence, in theory and practice, on the necessity for variety in the Spanish *comedia*, might well ask: Do the authors of the *tragedias de privanza* keep their propensity for variety under control, so that variety does not destroy the integrity of their tragedies? And the answer is not wholly satisfactory (though it is not intended to be evasive or frivolous): Some do — and some do not.

Earlier I quoted a passage from Francisco de Barreda's *Invectiva a las comedias . . .*, in which he observes that the Spanish *comedia* combines qualities of all species of poetry — epic, lyric, tragic, comic, mimetic, satiric — and he concludes, "De manera que en nuestros tiempos no puede ser perfecta la comedia que no coronare toda la poesía." [2] Barreda's observation (which recalls Cervantes' vision of the potential of the novel, "Porque la escritura desatada destos libros da lugar a que el autor pueda mostrarse épico, lírico, trágico, cómico . . .") [3] is not put in the form

---

[2] See chapter I, n. 41.
[3] *Don Quijote*, Part I, chapter 47.

of a precept, but it has about it the air of an injunction directed to all those who would aspire to writing the perfect *comedia*.

What Barreda recommends is, of course, a difficult task — and an almost impossible one for the dramatist who proposed, or proposes, to write tragedy. Partly for this reason, some students of Spanish drama, under the persuasion of Barreda's argument or similar ones, maintain that it is idle to talk about Golden Age tragedy because the tragic is only one ingredient of the dramatic potpourri that the *comedia* is. But I don't think that such talk is idle. I agree with the esthetic doctrine that underlies Pellicer de Tovar's passage quoted at the beginning of the Conclusion. What determines the integrity of any dramatic genre — heroic drama, romantic comedy, or tragedy — is its "substantial context." Hence, if a dramatist proposes to write tragedy, let him adorn or mix its tragic substance with "heroic and lyric [and comic] episodes," but let him be sure that all his art and craftsmanship are weighted mainly on the tragic.

In their striving for variety, some authors of the *tragedias de privanza* often — and predictably — overreached themselves, diluting the tragic essence of their plays with a disproportionate quantity of non-tragic elements. In the main, the dilution was brought about by increasing the amorous intrigue and the comical episodes, as may be seen in Jacinto Cordero's *La adversa fortuna de Duarte Pacheco,* Mira's *El ejemplo mayor de la desdicha,* and Coello's *El Conde de Sex,* in which the tragedy is drowned, often more than temporarily, in desultory intrigue. Such intrusions (because indeed they are intrusions) may create variety, but at the same time they may disturb the tragic atmosphere beyond recovery.

Another problem may be raised with regard to some of the *tragedias de privanza,* but I doubt that many contemporary readers will take the problem very seriously: It may be objected that several of the plays violate the historicity of their arguments by disregarding or altering historical facts and by introducing new fictions. We cannot go into the much debated question of the historical and the factual versus the fictional and the probable in tragedy, [4] but suffice it to say that the students of Golden Age drama have long accepted the fact that Spanish dramatists were lax in adhering strictly to historical sources, and that fact has ceased to concern them. As Voltaire said — disapprovingly — of the non-historicity of Thomas Corneille's *Le Comte d'Essex* (quoted at the beginning of chapter IX), "... quand les évène-ments qu'on traite sont ignorés d'une nation, l'auteur en est absolument le maître" — and so be it, say most students of Spanish drama. And I suspect that most seventeenth-century theatergoers, if they ever thought about the matter, would say the same. But if there are any present-day critics left who, like many Renaissance and post-Renaissance theorists, insist that the quality of tragedy depends on its "truth of argument" — if they derive their chief pleasure from historically verifiable details in tragedy — they will find most *tragedias de privanza* to be largely false.

But it is my conviction that the best fallen-favorite plays are tragedies of considerable merit — and, in one or two cases, tragedies of exceptional merit. Not only do the better plays succeed in accomodating a variety of elements to the tragic mode, they also succeed in communicating a sense of history measured in terms of the human experience of those who were destined to suffer the tragic fall.

In the minds of many, the greatest tragedy that can befall one reared in the Judaeo-Christian tradition is to lose faith in God. No favorite in the Spanish plays loses his faith; rather, several of them renew their faith in their final moments. In that they are blessed. But probably the second greatest tragedy that can befall a human being is to lose faith in himself and in his fellow men. That is the tragedy several favorites come to know — as summed up in Don Álvaro de Luna's plaintive warning,

> Alerta, humanos, alerta,
> no confiéis en el hombre.

---

[4] The question is examined by G. Giovannini, "Historical Realism and the Tragic Emotions in Renaissance Criticism," *Philological Quarterly*, 32 (1953), 304-20, and by Joseph Allen Bryant, Jr., "The Significance of Ben Jonson's First Requirement for Tragedy: 'Truth of Argument,'" *Studies in Philology*, 49 (1952), 195-213.

ABBREVIATIONS USED IN THE BIBLIOGRAPHY

Acad. *Obras de Lope de Vega, publicadas por la Real Academia Española.* Edited by Marcelino Menéndez Pelayo. 15 vols. Madrid, 1890-1913.

Acad. N. *Obras de Lope de Vega, publicadas por la Real Academia Española (nueva edición).* 13 vols. Madrid, 1916-1930.

BAE *Biblioteca de Autores Españoles.*

NBAE *Nueva Biblioteca de Autores Españoles.*

PMLA *Publications of the Modern Language Association of America.*

BIBLIOGRAPHY

Andrea, Peter Frank de. "El 'Ars Guberandi' de Quevedo," *Cuadernos Americanos,* 24 (Nov.-Dic., 1945), 161-85.

Aníbal, Claude E. Ed. *El arpa de David,* by Mira de Amescua. Columbus, Ohio, 1925.

――――. "Observations on *La Estrella de Sevilla,*" *Hispanic Review,* 2 (1934), 1-38.

Alfonso X. *Las siete partidas del rey Don Alfonso el Sabio . . .* Nueva edición. 5 vols. Paris, 1847.

Aristotle. *On the Art of Poetry.* Translated by S. H. Butcher. New York, 1948.

Avalle-Arce, Juan Bautista. *El cronista Pedro de Escavias. Una vida del siglo XV.* University of North Carolina Studies in the Romance Languages and Literatures, No. 127. Chapel Hill, 1972. (Contains the heretofore unpublished chapter 146 of Escavias' *Reportorio de príncipes* covering the reign of John II of Castile.)

Bacon, George W. "The Life and Dramatic Works of Doctor Juan Pérez de Montalbán (1602-1638)," *Revue Hispanique,* 26 (1912), 1-474.

Banks, John. *The Unhappy Favourite; or, The Earl of Essex.* Edited by Thomas M. H. Blair. New York, 1939.

Barreda, Francisco de. *Invectiva a las comedias que prohibió Trajano y apología por las nuestras* [Madrid, 1622], in Federico Sánchez Escribano y Alberto Porqueras Mayo, *Preceptiva dramática española del Renacimiento y el Barroco.* 2nd ed. Madrid, 1971. Pp. 216-26.

Bell, Aubrey F. G. *Portuguese Portraits.* Oxford, 1917.

Bentley, Eric. *The Life of the Drama.* New York, 1964.

Bergamín, José. *Mangas y capirotes (España en su laberinto teatral del XVII).* Madrid, 1933.

Biancolelli, Niccolò. *Regina Statista d'Inghilterra ed il Conte di Esex; vita, successi e morte.* Bologna, 1668.

Blanco-González, Bernardo. *Del cortesano al discreto. Examen de una "decadencia."* Madrid, 1962.

Bleznick, Donald W. "Spanish Reaction to Machiavelli in the Sixteenth and Seventeenth Centuries," *Journal of the History of Ideas,* 19 (1958), 542-50.

Boccaccio, Giovanni. *De casibus virorum illustrium.* Paris, 1520; rpt. Gainesville, Florida, 1962.

――――. *The Fates of Illustrious Men.* Translated and abridged by Louis B. Hall. New York, 1965.

Boughner, Daniel C. "Sejanus and Machiavelli", *Studies in English Literature 1500-1900*, I, No. 2 (1961), 81-100.

Bowers, Fredson Thayer. *Elizabethan Revenge Tragedy, 1587-1642*. Princeton, 1940; rpt. Gloucester, Mass., 1959.

Bradner, Leicester. "The Theme of *Privanza* in Spanish and English Drama 1590-1625," in *Homenaje a William L. Fichter. Estudios sobre el teatro antiguo hispánico y otros ensayos*. Madrid, 1971. Pp. 97-106.

Bryant, Joseph Allen, Jr. "The Significance of Ben Jonson's First Requirement for Tragedy: 'Truth of Argument,'" *Studies in Philology*, 49 (1952), 195-213.

Buero Vallejo, Antonio. *La señal que se espera*, in *Colección Teatro*, No. 21. Madrid, 1953.

————. "La tragedia," in *El teatro. Enciclopedia del arte escénico*. Edited by Guillermo Díaz-Plaja. Barcelona, 1958. Pp. 61-87.

Buckhardt, Jacob. *The Civilization of the Renaissance in Italy*. New York, 1954.

Burke, Kenneth. *A Grammar of Motives*. New York, 1945.

Calderón de la Barca, Pedro. *La hija del aire*, in *Obras completas*, Tomo I, *Dramas*. Edited by A. Valbuena Briones. Madrid, 1966.

————. *El médico de su honra*, in *Spanish Drama of the Golden Age: Twelve Plays*. Edited by Raymond R. MacCurdy. New York, 1971.

————. *Verdadera quinta parte de comedias del célebre poeta español don ...* Edited by Juan de Vera Tassis. Madrid, 1682.

————, Juan Pérez de Montalván, and Francisco de Rojas. *El monstruo de la fortuna. La lavandera de Nápoles, Felipa Catanea*, in D. Pedro Calderón de la Barca, *Obras completas (Dramas)*. Edited by Luis Astrana Marín. Segunda edición revisada. Madrid, 1941.

Camões, Luiz de. *Os Lusíadas*, in *A Chave des Lusíadas*. Edited by José Agostinho. 7th edition. Porto, n. d.

Cascales, Francisco. *Tablas poéticas*. Madrid, 1617; rpt. Madrid, 1779.

Castillejo, Cristóbal. *Diálogo y discurso de la vida de corte*, in *Poétas líricos de los siglos XVI y XVII*. Edited by Adolfo de Castro. BAE, XXXII. Madrid, 1950. Pp. 214-32.

Castro, Joseph Julián. *Más vale tarde que nunca*. Valencia, 1763.

Castro y Bellvís, Guillén de. *Las mocedades del Cid*, in *Spanish Drama of the Golden Age: Twelve Plays*. Edited by Raymond R. MacCurdy. New York, 1971.

Cauvin, O. P., Sister Mary Austin. "The *comedia de privanza* in the Seventeenth Century." Unpublished Ph. D. dissertation, University of Pennsylvania, 1957.

Céspedes y Meneses, Gonzalo de. *Primera parte de la Historia de D. Felippe el IIII. Rey de las Españas*. Lisboa, 1631.

Chapman, George. *The Conspiracy and Tragedy of Charles Duke of Byron*, in *The Plays of George Chapman*. Edited by Thomas M. Parrott. New York, 1961.

Chaucer, Geoffrey. *The Canterbury Tales*. Edited by J. M. Manly. New York, 1930.

Chaytor, H. J. *Dramatic Theory in Spain: Extracts from Literature before and during the Golden Age*. Cambridge, 1925.

Cordero, Jacinto. *La entrada del rey*. Lisboa, 1630.

Cordero, Jacinto. *La Gran Comedia de la Segunda Parte de la Adversa Fortuna de Duarte Pacheco* ..., in *Seis comedias famosas*. Lisboa, 1630.

———. *La primera parte de Duarte Pacheco*. N. p., n. d.

Corneille, Thomas. *Chefs-d'Œuvres de* ..., *avec les Remarques de Voltaire*. Paris, 1815.

Cotarelo y Mori, Emilio. *El Conde de Villamediana, estudio biográfico-crítico, con varias poesías inéditas del mismo*. Madrid, 1886.

——— *Dramáticos españoles del siglo XVII: Don Antonio Coello y Ochoa*. Madrid, 1919.

———. *Mira de Amescua y su teatro: Estudio biográfico y crítico*. Madrid, 1931.

Cox, Roger L. "Tragedy and the Gospel Narratives," *The Yale Review* (Summer 1968), 545-70.

Crónica de don Álvaro de Luna. Edited by Juan de Mata Carriazo. Madrid, 1940.

Crónica del rey Juan II, in *Crónicas de los reyes de Castilla*. BAE, LXVIII. Madrid, 1923. Pp. 277-695.

Diekstra, F. N. M., editor. *A Dialogue between Reason and Adversity, a Late Middle English Version of Petrarch's "De Remediis."* Assen, 1968.

Dio's Roman History. Translated by Earnest Cary. Vol. 7. Loeb Classical Library. London, 1924.

Dixon, Victor F. "The Life and Works of Juan Pérez de Montalbán, with Special Reference to His Plays." Unpublished Ph. D. dissertation, University of Chambridge, 1959.

———. Review of Lope de Vega, *El Duque de Viseo*. Edited by Elizabeth Auvert Eason. *Bulletin of Hispanic Studies*, 48 (1971), 354-55.

Elliot, J. H. *Imperial Spain, 1469-1716*. New York, 1966.

Emerson, Ralph Waldo. "Alphonso of Castile," in *Poems*. Rev. ed. Boston, 1888.

Enríquez Gómez, Antonio. *El siglo pitagórico, y vida de don Gregorio Guadaña*. 2nd. ed. Rouen, 1682.

Felipe IV [apocryphal]. *La tragedia más lastimosa, el Conde de Sex*, in *Tesoro del teatro español*. Edited by Eugenio de Ochoa. Paris, 1838.

Fergusson, Francis. *The Idea of a Theater*. Princeton, 1949; rpt. New York, 1953.

Fernández de la Mora, Gonzalo. "Maquiavelo visto por los tratadistas españoles de la contrarreforma," *Arbor*, 13 (1949), 417-49.

Fernández Navarrete, Pedro. *Carta de Lelio Peregrino a Estanislao Borbio, privado del rey de Polonia* (printed together with the *Conservación de monarquías* ...), 4th ed. Madrid, 1792.

———. *Conservación de monarquías y discursos políticos sobre la gran consulta que el consejo hizo al señor rey don Felipe Tercero*. 1st ed. Madrid, 1621 [?]; 4th ed. Madrid, 1792.

Foster, David W. *The Marqués de Santillana*. New York, 1971.

Gallardo, Bartolomé José. *Ensayo de una biblioteca española de libros raros y curiosos*. 4 vols. Madrid, 1863-89.

García Peres, Domingo. *Catálogo razonado biográfico y bibliográfico de los autores portugueses que escribieron en castellano*. Madrid, 1890.

García Soriano, Justo. "Damián Salucio del Poyo," *Boletín de la Real Academia española*, 13 (1926), 269-82, 474-506.

Geckle, George L. "Fortune in Marston's *The Malcontent*," *PMLA*, 82 (1971), 202-09.

Gicovate, Bernard. "Observations on the Dramatic Art of Tirso de Molina," *Hispania*, 43 (1960), 328-37.

Gillet, J. E. "A Note on the Tragic *Admiratio*," *Modern Language Review*, 13 (1918), 233-38.

Giovannini, G. "Historical Realism and the Tragic Emotions in Renaissance Criticism," *Philological Quarterly*, 32 (1953), 304-20.

Golden, Bruce. "Elizabethan Revenge and Spanish Honor: Analogues of Action in the Popular Drama of the Renaissance." Unpublished Ph. D. dissertation, Columbia University, 1969.

González de Salas, Jusepe Antonio. *Nveva idea de la tragedia antigva, o ilvstración última al libro singvlar "De Poética."* De *Aristóteles Stagirita*. 2 vols. 1st ed. Madrid, 1633; rpt. Madrid, 1778.

Graf. A. *Miti, leggende e superstizione del Medio Evo*. 2 vols. Torino, 1892-1893.

Green, Otis H. *Spain and the Western Tradition*. 4 vols. Madison, 1963-68.

Guevara, Antonio de. *Aviso de privados o despertador de cortesanos*. Paris, n. d.

————. *Aviso de privados y doctrina de cortesanos*, in *Prosa escogida de Fray Antonio de Guevara, predicador y cronista de Carlos I.* Edited by Martín de Riquer. Barcelona, 1943.

Homenaje a William L. Fichter. Estudios sobre el teatro antiguo hispánico y otros ensayos. Edited by A. David Kossoff and José Amor y Vázquez. Madrid, 1971.

Horozco y Covarrubias, Juan. *Emblemas morales*. Segovia, 1589.

Jones, C. A. "Tragedy in the Spanish Golden Age," in *The Drama of the Renaissance. Essays for Leicester Bradner*. Providence, Rhode Island, 1970. Pp. 100-07.

Jonson, Ben. *Sejanus*. Edited by Jonas A. Barish. New Haven and London, 1965.

Juderías, Julián. *Don Francisco de Quevedo y Villegas. La época, el hombre, las doctrinas*. Madrid, 1922.

Keniston, Hayward. *Francisco de los Cobos. Secretary of the Emperor Charles V*. Pittsburgh, 1960.

Kennedy, Ruth Lee. "*La prudencia en la mujer* and the Ambient That Brought It Forth," *PMLA*, 63 (1948), 1131-90.

La Barrera y Leirado, Cayetano Alberto de. *Catálogo bibliográfico y biográfico del teatro antiguo español desde sus orígenes hasta mediados del siglo XVIII*. Madrid, 1860.

Lancaster, Henry C. *A History of French Dramatic Literature*. Part I, Vol. 2. Baltimore, 1929.

————. "La Calprenède Dramatist," *Modern Philology*, 18 (1920), 121-41.

Latassa y Ortín, Félix de. *Biblioteca antigua y nueva de escritores aragoneses, de Latassa; aumentadas y refundidas en forma de diccionario bibliográfico-biográfico por don Miguel Gómez Uriel* ... 3 vols. Zaragoza, 1884-86.

Laynez, Fray José. *El privado christiano, deducido de las vidas de Joseph y Daniel* ... Madrid, 1641.

Leech, Clifford. *Shakespeare's Tragedies and Other Studies in Seventeenth-Century Drama*. London, 1950.

Lessing, Gotthold Efraim. *Hamburgische Dramaturgie*, in *Lessings Werke*. Edited by Theodor Matthias. Vol. III. Leipzig, n. d.

Lida, Raimundo. "*Cómo ha de ser el privado*: de la comedia a su *Política de Dios*," in *Letras hispánicas*. México-Buenos Aires, 1958. Pp. 149-56, 332-33.

Lista, Alberto. "*El monstruo de la fortuna, Felipa Catanea*: comedia de tres ingenios," *El Censor*, 15 (1822), 103.

López Pinciano, Alonso. *Philosophía antigua poética*. Edited by Alfredo Carballo Picazo. 3 vols. Madrid, 1953.

López de Zárate, Francisco. *Obras varias de . . . Dedicadas a diferentes personas . . .* Alcalá, 1651.

McClelland, I. L. *Tirso de Molina: Studies in Dramatic Realism*. Liverpool, 1948.

McCrary, William C. "The Classical Background of Spanish Dramatic Theory of the Sixteenth and Seventeenth Centuries." Unpublished Ph. D. dissertation, University of Wisconsin, 1958.

McCready, Warren T. *Bibliografía temática de estudios sobre el teatro español antiguo*. Toronto, 1966.

MacCurdy, Raymond R. *Francisco de Rojas Zorrilla and the Tragedy*. University of New Mexico Publications in Language and Literature, No. 13. 1st ed., 1958; rpt. Albuquerque, 1966.

———. Ed. *El burlador de Sevilla* and *La prudencia en la mujer*, by Tirso de Molina. Laurel Language Library. New York, 1965.

———. "Lope de Vega y la pretendida inhabilidad española para la tragedia: resumen crítico," in *Homenaje a William L. Fichter. Estudios sobre el teatro antiguo hispánico y otros ensayos*. Madrid, 1971. Pp. 525-35.

———. "The 'Problem' of Spanish Golden Age Tragedy: A Review and Reconsideration," *South Atlantic Bulletin*, 38 (1973), 3-15.

———. *Spanish Drama of the Golden Age: Twelve Plays*. New York, 1971.

———. "Tragic 'Hamartia' in *La próspera y Adversa fortuna de don Álvaro de Luna*," *Hispania*, 47 (1964), 82-90.

Machiavelli, Niccolò. *The Discourses of . . .* Translated and edited by Leslie J. Walker. 2 vols. London, 1950.

———. *The Prince. A Bilingual Edition*. Translated and edited by Mark Musa. New York, 1964.

Maestre Pedro. *Libro del consejo e de los consejeros*. Edited by Agapito Rey. *Biblioteca del Hispanista*, Vol. V. Zaragoza, 1962.

Manrique, Jorge. *Coplas por la muerte de su padre*, in *Antología general de la literatura española*. Edited by Ángel y Amelia del Río. Vol. I. New York, 1960.

Marañón, Gregorio. *Tiberio, historia de un resentimiento*. Madrid, 1939.

———. *Antonio Pérez, el hombre, el drama, la época*. Séptima edición. Madrid, 1963.

Maravall, José A. *La teoría española del estado en el siglo XVII*. Madrid, 1944.

Mariana, Padre Juan de. *Historia general de España*. 2 vols. BAE, XXX and XXXI. Madrid, 1923.

Marín, Diego. *La intriga secundaria en el teatro de Lope de Vega*. Colección Studium, No. 22. México, 1958.

Martínez de la Rosa, Francisco. *Apéndice sobre la tragedia*, in *Obras literarias* (volumes unnumbered). Paris, 1827. Pp. 101-314.

Martins, Heitor. "Jacinto Cordeiro e *La Estrella de Sevilla*," in *Actas do V Colóquio Internacional de Estudos Luso-Brasileiros*, Vol. IV. Coimbra, 1966.

Mártir Rizo, Juan Pablo. *Historia de la prosperidad infeliz, de Felipa Catanea. Escrita en Francés por Pedro Mateo, Coronista del Rey Christianíssimo. Y en Castellano, por . . .* Madrid, 1625.

———. *Historia trágica de la vida del Duque de Birón*. Barcelona, 1629.

———. *Norte de Príncipes y Vida de Rómulo*. Edited by José A. Maravall. Madrid, 1945.

———. *Vida del dichoso desdichado escrita en francés por Pedro Matheo Cronista del Rey Christianíssimo y en Castellano por . . .* Madrid, 1625.

Mena, Juan de. *El laberinto de fortuna o Las trescientas*. Edited by José Manuel Blecua. *Clásicos Castellanos*, Vol. 11. Madrid, 1943.

Menéndez Pelayo, Marcelino. *Orígenes de la novela*, Vol. II. Santander, 1948.

Menéndez Pidal, Ramón. "Del honor en el teatro español," in *De Cervantes y Lope de Vega*. Buenos Aires, 1940. Pp. 153-84.

———. "Lope de Vega, el arte nuevo y la nueva biografía," *Revista de Filología Española*, 22 (1935), 337-98.

———. *Poesía árabe y poesía europea*. Buenos Aires, 1943.

Mérimée, Ernest, and S. Griswold Morley. *A History of Spanish Literature*. New York, 1930.

Mesonero Romanos, Ramón de. "Apuntes biográficos y críticos," in *Dramáticos contemporáneos de Lope de Vega*, II. BAE, XLV. Madrid, 1951.

Miller, Arthur. "Tragedy and the Common Man," in *Tragedy: Vision and Form*. Edited by Robert W. Corrigan. San Francisco, 1965. Pp. 148-51.

Mira de Amescua, Antonio. *Adversa fortuna de don Álvaro de Luna*. Edited by Luigi de Filippo. Firenze, 1960.

———. *El arpa de David*. Edited by Claude E. Anibal. Columbus, Ohio, 1925.

———. *Comedia famosa de Ruy López de Ávalos (Primera parte de don Álvaro de Luna)*. Edited by Nellie E. Sánchez-Arce. México, 1965.

———. *El ejemplo mayor de la desdicha*, in *Teatro*, II. Edited by Ángel Valbuena Prat. *Clásicos Castellanos*, Vol. 82. Madrid, 1947.

———. *El esclavo del demonio*, in *Diez comedias del Siglo de Oro*. Edited by Hymen Alpern and José Martel. New York, 1939.

———. *Próspera fortuna de don Álvaro de Luna y adversa de Ruy López de Ávalos* and *Adversa fortuna de don Álvaro de Luna*, in *Comedias de Tirso de Molina*, Tomo I. Edited by Emilio Cotarelo y Mori. NBAE, IV. Madrid, 1906.

———. (probable author). *La próspera fortuna de don Bernardo de Cabrera* and *La adversa fortuna de don Bernardo de Cabrera*, in *Doce comedias de Lope de Vega Carpio. Parte veinte y nueve. . . .* Huesca, 1634. Also printed in *Acad. N.*, III. Madrid, 1917.

———. *La segunda de don Álvaro* [*Adversa fortuna de don Álvaro de Luna*]. Edited by Nellie E. Sánchez-Arce. México, 1960.

Moir, Duncan. "The Classical Tradition in Spanish Dramatic Theory and Practice in the Seventeenth Century," in *Classical Drama and Its In-*

fluence. Essays Presented to H. D. F. Kitto. Edited by M. J. Anderson. London, 1965. Pp. 193-228.

Molina, Tirso de. *Los cigarrales de Toledo.* Edited by V. Said Armesto. Madrid, 1913.

―――. *Comedias.* Edited by Emilio Cotarelo y Mori. 2 vols. *NBAE,* IV an l V. Madrid, 1906-07.

―――. *Doña Beatriz de Silva,* in *Obras dramáticas completas,* II. Ed. Doña Blanca de los Ríos. Madrid, 1952.

―――. *Segunda parte de las comedias del Maestro Tirso de Molina.* Madrid, 1635.

Montiano, Agustín. *Discurso sobre las tragedias españolas.* 2 vols. Madrid, 1750.

Morales, paje de don Álvaro de Luna. MS (without place or date), Biblioteca Nazionale, Naples.

Morby, Edwin S. Ed. *La Dorotea,* by Lope de Vega. Berkeley, 1958.

―――. "The *Hercules* of Francisco López de Zárate," *Hispanic Review,* 30 (1962), 116-32.

―――. "Some Observations on 'tragedia' and 'tragicomedia' in Lope," *Hispanic Review,* 11 (1943), 185-209.

Morley, S. Griswold, and Courtney Bruerton. *The Chronology of Lope de Vega's "Comedias."* New York, 1940.

Muller, H. J. *The Spirit of Tragedy.* New York, 1956.

Nerval, Gérard de. *Œuvres,* Vol. I. Edited by Albert Béguin and Jean Richer. Paris, 1952.

Ortega y Robles, Jerónimo. *El despertador que avisa a un príncipe católico . . .* Madrid, 1647.

Ossorio, Ángel. *Los hombres de toga en el proceso de D. Rodrigo Calderón.* Madrid, n. d.

El paje de don Álvaro. MS (without place or date), Palatinate Library, Parma.

Palencia, Alonso de. *Crónica de Enrique IV.* Translated by A. Paz y Melia. 4 vols. Madrid, 1904-08.

Parker, Alexander A. "Towards a Definition of Calderonian Tragedy," *Bulletin of Hispanic Studies,* 39 (1962), 222-37.

Parker, J. H. "The Chronology of the Plays of Juan Pérez de Montalván," *PMLA,* 57 (1952), 186-210.

Paso, Alfonso. "La tragicomedia," *ABC* (Madrid), 30 May 1961 (unpaginated).

Patch, Howard R. *The Goddess Fortuna in Medieval Literature.* Cambridge, Mass., 1927.

Paz y Melia, A. *El cronista Alonso de Palencia.* Madrid, 1914.

Pellicer de Tovar, Joseph. "Idea de la comedia de Castilla, deducida de las obras cómicas del Doctor Juan Pérez de Montalbán," in *Lágrimas panegíricas a la temprana muerte del gran poeta y teólogo insigne Doctor Juan Pérez de Montalbán . . .* Madrid, 1639.

―――. *Idea de la comedia de Castilla. Preceptos del teatro de España y arte del estilo moderno cómico . . .* (MS, 1635), in Federico Sánchez Escribano y Alberto Porqueras Mayo, *Preceptiva dramática española del Renacimiento y el Barroco.* 2nd ed. Madrid, 1971. Pp. 263-72.

Pérez, Antonio. *Norte de príncipes, virreyes, presidentes, consejeros, y gobernadores, y advertencias politicas sobre lo publico y particular de una monarquia importantisimas a los tales: fundadas en materia y razon de estado y govierno....* Nota preliminar de Martín de Riquer. Madrid, 1969.

Pérez Gómez, Antonio. "Un romance de don Álvaro de Luna," *Romance Philology,* 5, Nos. 2 and 3 (Nov. 1951-Feb. 1952), 202-05.

Pérez de Guzmán, Fernán. *Generaciones y semblanzas.* Edited by J. Domínguez Bordona. *Clásicos Castellanos,* Vol. 61. Madrid, 1941.

Pérez de Montalbán, Juan. *Amor, privanza y castigo,* in *Primero tomo de las Comedias del Doctor Ivan Pérez de Montalván...* Alcalá, 1638.

―――. *El Mariscal de Birón,* in *Primero tomo de las Comedias del Doctor Ivan Pérez de Montalván...* Alcalá, 1638.

Petrarca, Francesco. *Francisci Petrarchae poetae oratorisque clarissimi de remediis utruiusque fortunae...* Lugduni, 1582 (?).

Peyrón y Queralt, Martín. *Las fortunas trágicas del Duque de Memoransi,* in *Parte cuarenta y cuatro de Comedias de diferentes autores.* Zaragoza, 1652.

Procopius of Caesarea. *Anécdota. Arcana historia...* Translated by Nicolaus Alemmanus (from Greek to Latin). Lugduni, 1623.

Pujals, Esteban. "Shakespeare y Lope de Vega," *Revista de Literatura,* 1 (1952), 25-45.

Quevedo, Francisco de. *Cómo ha de ser el privado,* in *Teatro inédito de... Quevedo.* Edited by Miguel Artigas. Madrid, 1927.

―――. *Obra poética.* Edited by José Manuel Blecua. 3 vols. Madrid, 1971.

―――. *Política de Dios. Govierno de Christo.* Edited by James O. Crosby. Madrid, 1966.

Ramírez de Prado, Lorenzo. *Consejo y consejero de príncipes.* Edited by Juan Beneyto. Madrid, 1958.

Reichenberger, Arnold G. "Calderón's *El príncipe constante,* a Tragedy?" in *Critical Essays on the Theatre of Calderón.* Edited by Bruce W. Wardropper. New York, 1965. Pp. 161-63.

―――. "La comedia clásica española y el hombre del siglo XX," *Filología Moderna,* 4 (1961), 21-43.

―――. "The Marqués de Santillana and the Classical Tradition," *Iberoromania,* 1 (1969), 5-34.

―――. "The Uniqueness of the *Comedia,*" *Hispanic Review,* 27 (1959), 303-16.

Rennert, H. A. "Notes on the Chronology of the Spanish Drama," *Modern Language Review,* 2 (1906-07), 331-41; 3 (1907-08), 43-55.

―――. *The Spanish Stage in the Time of Lope de Vega.* New York, 1909.

―――, and Américo Castro. *Vida de Lope de Vega (1562-1635).* Madrid, 1919.

Restori, Antonio. "La collezione CCIV. 28033 della Biblioteca Palatina-Parmese," *Studi di Filologia Romanza,* 6 (1893), 1-156.

Richer, Jean. *Nerval, expérience et création.* 2nd ed. Paris, 1970.

Riley, Edward C. "Aspectos del concepto 'admiratio' en la teoría literaria del siglo de oro," in *Studia Philologica: Homenaje ofrecido a Dámaso Alonso...,* III. Madrid, 1963. Pp. 173-83.

―――. "The Dramatic Theories of Don Jusepe González de Salas," *Hispanic Review,* 19 (1951), 183-203.

Rivadeneira, Padre Pedro de. *Tratado de la religión y virtudes que debe tener el príncipe cristiano para gobernar y conservar sus estados, contra lo que Nicolás Maquiavelo y los políticos de este tiempo enseñan,* in *Obras escogidas . . . , BAE, LX.* Madrid, 1927. Pp. 449-587.

Rizzo y Ramírez, Juan. *Juicio crítico y significación política de don Álvaro de Luna.* Madrid, 1865.

Rodríguez-Moñino, Antonio. Ed. *El cancionero manuscrito de Pedro del Pozo (1547).* Madrid, 1950.

Romancero de don Álvaro de Luna (1540-1800). Edited by Antonio Pérez Gómez. Valencia, 1953.

Romancero de don Rodrigo Calderón (1621-1800). Edited by Antonio Pérez Gómez. Valencia, 1955.

Romancero general o colección de romances castellanos, II. Edited by Agustín Durán. *BAE, XVI.* Madrid, 1945.

Rosales, Luis. *El sentimiento del desengaño en la poesía barroca.* Madrid, 1966.

Rubio, P. Fernando. "El tema de la fortuna en la literatura castellana del siglo xv," in *Prosistas castellanos del siglo XV,* Vol. II. *BAE, CLXXI.* Madrid, 1964.

Rubió y Lluch, Antonio. *El sentido del honor en el teatro de Calderón.* Barcelona, 1882.

Sáinz de Robles, Federico Carlos. *Ensayo de un diccionario de la literatura.* 2 vols. Madrid, 1949.

Salomon, Noël. "Sur les répresentations théâtrales dans les 'pueblos' des Madrid et Tolède [1589-1640]," *Bulletin Hispanique,* 62 (1960), 398-427.

Salucio del Poyo, Damián. *La privanza y caída de don Álvaro de Luna,* in *Parte tercera de las comedias de Lope de Vega, y otros avtores.* Valencia, 1614.

Salustrio (for Salucio) del Poyo, Damián. *La próspera fortuna de Ruy López de Ávalos* and *La adversa fortuna de Ruy López de Ávalos,* in *Dramáticos contemporáneos a Lope de Vega.* Edited by Ramón de Mesonero Romanos. *BAE, XLV.* Madrid, 1951.

Sánchez Escribano, F. "Cuatro contribuciones españolas a la preceptiva dramática mundial," *Bulletin of the Comediantes,* 13 (Spring, 1961), 1-2.

———, and Alberto Porqueras Mayo. *Preceptiva dramática española del Renacimiento y el Barroco.* Segunda edición muy ampliada. Madrid, 1971.

Santa María, Fray Juan de. *Tratado de república y politicia christiana. Para reyes y príncipes y para los que en el gobierno tienen sus veces.* Valencia, 1619.

Santillana, Marqués de. *Comedieta de Ponza,* in *Epistolario español.* Edited by Eugenio de Ochoa. *BAE, LXII.* Madrid, 1917.

———. *Doctrinal de privados,* in *Cancionero castellano del siglo XV.* Edited by R. Foulché-Delbosc. *NBAE, XIX.*

———. *Páginas escogidas.* Edited by Fernando Gutiérrez. Barcelona, 1939.

Schack, A. F. von. *Historia de la literatura y del arte dramático en España.* Translated by Eduardo de Mier. 5 vols. Madrid, 1885-87.

Schwartz, Kessel. "Buero Vallejo and the Concept of Tragedy," *Hispania,* 51 (1968), 817-24.

Sender, Ramón. "Valle-Inclán y la dificultad de la tragedia," *Cuadernos Americanos,* 11, No. 5 (1952), 241-54.

Sepúlveda, Lorenzo de. *Romances nuevamente sacados de historias antiguas de la crónica de España.* Anvers, 1566.

Sewall, Richard B. *The Vision of Tragedy*. 1st ed., 1959; rpt. New Haven, 1962.

Shakespeare, William. *The Complete Works of Shakespeare*. Edited by Hardin Craig. Glenview, Illinois, 1961.

——. *The Tragedy of Richard the Second*, in *Shakespeare: Twenty-three Plays and the Sonnets*. Edited by Thomas Marc Parrott. Rev. ed. New York, 1953.

Shergold, N. D., and J. E. Varey. "Some Early Calderón Dates," *Bulletin of Hispanic Studies*, 38 (1961), 274-86.

Sloman, Albert E. "*El médico de su honra*," in *The Dramatic Craftsmanship of Calderón*. Oxford, 1958. Pp. 18-58.

Smith, Winifred. "The Earl of Essex on the Stage," *PMLA*, 39 (1924), 147-73.

——. "The Maréchal de Biron on the Stage," *Modern Philology*, 20 (1922-23), 301-08.

Somers, Melvina. "Quevedo's Ideology in *Cómo ha de ser el privado*," *Hispania*, 39 (1956), 261-68.

Spencer, F. E., and R. Schevill, *The Dramatic Works of Luis Vélez de Guevara*. Berkeley, 1937.

Spingarn, J. E. *A History of Literary Criticism in the Renaissance*. 2nd ed. New York, 1930.

Squarçafigo, Vicencio. *Vida de Elio Seyano. Compuesto en Francés por Pedro Matheo, Coronista del Christianíssimo Luys XIII. Rey de Francia. Traduzida en Castellano por* ... Barcelona, 1621.

Stuart, Daniel Clive. "Honor in the Spanish Drama," *Romanic Review*, I (1910), 247-58, 357-66.

Suetonius Tranquillus, Gaius. *The Lives of the Twelve Caesars*. New York, 1937.

Tacitus, Cornelius. *Annals of Imperial Rome*. Translated by Michael Grant. Penguin Classics L 60. Rev. ed. London, 1959.

Thomas Aquinas, Saint. *De regimine principum ad regem Cypri* ... Taurini, 1945.

——. *On Kingship, to the King of Cyprus*. Translated by Gerald B. Phelan. Toronto, 1967.

Ticknor, George. *History of Spanish Literature*. 3 vols. 4th ed. Boston, 1872.

Tres Ingenios. *El monstruo de la fortuna*, in *Comedias escogidas (Teatro poético en doze comedias nuevas, de los mejores ingenios de España. Séptima parte)*. Madrid, 1654.

Turia, Ricardo de (pseudonym of Pedro Juan de Rejaule y Toledo?). *Apologético de las comedias españolas*, in *Poetas dramáticos valencianos*, I. Edited by Eduardo Juliá Martínez. Madrid, 1929. Pp. 622-27.

Unamuno, Miguel de. *Del sentimiento trágico de la vida en los hombres y en los pueblos*. Buenos Aires, 1937.

——. "El individualismo español," in *El concepto contemporáneo de España, antología de ensayos [1895-1931]*. Edited by Ángel del Río and M. J. Benardete. Buenos Aires, 1946. Pp. 96-106.

Valbuena Prat, Ángel. *Historia de la literatura española*. 2 vols. 2nd ed. Barcelona, n. d.

——. *Historia del teatro español*. Barcelona, 1956.

——. *Literatura dramática española*. Barcelona, 1930.

248　　　　THE TRAGIC FALL

Valera, Mosén Diego de. *Crónica abreviada de España* (chapter 124, included as a supplement in his *Memorial de diversas hazañas*). Edited by Juan de Mata Carriazo. Madrid, 1941.

Valiente, Francisco Tomás. *Los validos en la monarquía española del siglo XVII.* Madrid, 1963.

Vega, Lope de. *Las almenas de Toledo,* in *Acad.,* VIII. Madrid, 1898.

———. *Arte nuevo de hacer comedias en este tiempo.* Edited by Alfred Morel-Fatio, in *Bulletin Hispanique,* 3 (1901), 365-405.

———. *El castigo sin venganza.* Edited by A. Van Dam. Groningen, 1928.

———. *Doce comedias de ... Parte veinte y nueve.* Huesca, 1634.

———. *El Duque de Viseo.* Edited by Francisco Ruiz Ramón. Madrid, 1966.

———. *La hermosa Ester,* in *Obras de ... BAE,* CLIX. Madrid, 1963.

——— (apocryphal?). *El milagro por los celos y don Álvaro de Luna,* in *Acad.,* X. Madrid, 1899.

———. *Obras de Lope de Vega, publicadas por la Real Academia Española.* Edited by Marcelino Menéndez Pelayo. 15 vols. Madrid, 1890-1913. (Abbreviated *Acad.* throughout the Bibliography.)

———. *Obras de Lope de Vega, publicadas por la Real Academia Española (nueva edición).* Edited by Emilio Cotarelo y Mori *et al.* 13 vols. Madrid, 1916-30. (Abbreviated *Acad. N.* throughout the Bibliography.)

———. *La reina Juana de Nápoles,* in *Acad.,* VI. Madrid, 1896.

Velázquez, Baltasar Mateo. *El filósofo del aldea, y sus conversaciones familiares, y exemplares, por casos, y sucessos casuales, y prodigiosos ...* Zaragoza, n. d.

Vélez de Guevara, Luis. *El espejo del mundo,* in *Tercera parte de las comedias de Lope de Vega, y otros autores.* Madrid, 1613.

———. *El privado perseguido,* in *El mejor de los meiores Libro* [sic] *que han salido de comedias nuevas.* Alcalá, 1651.

———, and Francisco de Rojas Zorrilla. "An Annotated Critical Edition of *También tiene el sol menguante,* by ... Edited by James S. Rambo. Unpublished Ph. D. dissertation, University of New Mexico, 1972.

Villamediana, el Conde de. "A la muerte de don Rodrigo Calderón," in *Poetas líricos de los siglos XVI y XVII.* Edited by Adolfo de Castro. *BAE,* XLII. Madrid, 1951.

Voltaire (François-Marie Arouet). *La Henriade,* in *Œuvres complètes de Voltaire,* Vol. 8. Paris, 1877.

Vossler, Karl. *Lope de Vega y su tiempo.* Translated by Ramón de la Serna. Madrid, 1933.

Wardropper, Bruce W. "Poetry and Drama in Calderón's *El médico de su honra," Romanic Review,* 49 (1958), 3-11.

———. "The Unconscious Mind in Calderón's *El pintor de su deshonra," Hispanic Review,* 18 (1950), 285-301.

Watson, A. Irvine. "*El pintor de su deshonra* and the Neo-Aristotelian Theory of Tragedy," in *Critical Essays on the Theatre of Calderón.* Edited by Bruce W. Wardropper. New York, 1965. Pp. 203-23.

Whitney, James Lyman. *Catalogue of the Spanish Library and of the Portuguese Books Bequeathed by George Ticknor to the Boston Public Library ...* Boston, 1879.

Williamsen, Vern G. "The Dramatic Function of 'Cuentecillos' in Some Plays by Mira de Amescua," *Hispania,* 54 (1971), 62-67.

Wilson, Edward M. "La discreción de don Lope de Almeida," *Clavileño*,
Año II, No. 9 (1951), 1-10.

———. "Gerald Brenan's Calderón," *Bulletin of the Comediantes*, 4 (Spring,
1952), 6-8.

Wilson, Margaret. *"La próspera fortuna de don Álvaro de Luna*: An Outstanding Work by Mira de Amescua," *Bulletin of Hispanic Studies*, 33
(1956), 25-36.

———. *Spanish Drama of the Golden Age*. Oxford, 1969.

INDEX

admiratio, 30-31 and n. 31, 75 n. 11, 89 n. 31, 205 n. 10
La adversa fortuna de don Álvaro de Luna. See Mira de Amescua, Antonio
La adversa fortuna de don Bernardo de Cabrera. See Mira de Amescua, Antonio
La adversa fortuna del Caballero del Espíritu Santo. See Grajal, Juan de
La adversa fortuna de Duarte Pacheco. See Cordero, Jacinto
La adversa fortuna de Ruy López de Avalos. See Salucio del Poyo, Damián
Aliaga, Fray Luis de, 39
Andrea, Peter Frank de, 58 n. 16
Aníbal, Claude E., 11, 12, 73 and n. 9, 171 n. 14
Alfonso X, 48-49
Aristotle: theory of the marvelous, 31; neo Aristotelianism, 31-32; mentioned, 26, 27, 72 and nn. 7, 8; 76, 111-112, 142
Artigas, Miguel, 56 n. 13
Augustine, Saint, 50, 51, 55, 59

ballads: as sources of the Don Álvaro de Luna plays, 107-09; mentioned, 46 and n. 15, 92 and note, 118 and n. 35, 138-39, 142, 144 and n. 63, 152 and n. 68
Bances Candamo, Francisco, 222
Banks, John 221, 228-29
Barreda, Francisco de, 35, 233-34
Barrientos, Fray Lope, 47 n. 16
Belisarius: as hero of Mira de Amescua's *El ejemplo mayor de la desdicha,* 158-66 *passim;* mentioned, 74, 78, 168 and n. 12, 171, 175, 176
Bell, Aubrey, 167, n. 10
Bentley, Eric, 28 n. 26
Bergamín, José, 23-24
Biancolelli, Niccolò, 222 n. 5
Bidermann, Jakob, 160 n. 1
Biron, Duke of: as hero of Pérez de Montalbán's *El Mariscal de Birón,* 178-88 *passim;* mentioned, 37, 77, 195
Bleznick, Donald W., 63 n. 23, 64 n. 27
Boccaccio, Giovanni: influence of his *De casibus virorum illustrium,* 37, 53, 67, 69 and n. 1; 77, 207-08 and nn. 14-18; mentioned, 99
Boethius, 47 n. 16
Bowers, Fredson Thayer, 198 n. 6
Bradner, Leicester, 68 n. 35
Bruerton, Courtney, 83 n. 24, 208 n. 19
Buero Vallejo, Antonio, 28 n. 26
Burckhardt, Jacob, 23 n. 13
Burke, Kenneth, 142
Byron, George Gordon, Lord, 48

Calderón, Rodrigo: trial and execution of, 38-47 *passim;* mentioned, 13, 37, 89, 178, 180, 189, 197, 205 and n. 9, 231, 232
Calderón de la Barca, Pedro: as collaborative author of *El monstruo de la fortuna,* 89 n. 31, 206-07 *passim;* mentioned, 30-34 *pas-*

NORTH CAROLINA STUDIES IN THE
ROMANCE LANGUAGES AND LITERATURES

I.S.B.N. Prefix 0-8078-

Recent Titles

When ordering please cite the *ISBN Prefix* plus the last four digits for each title.

Send orders to: University of North Carolina Press
                  Chapel Hill
                  North Carolina 27514
                  U. S. A.